D1609845

ALL THE WIDE BORDER

Also by Mike Parker

Map Addict
The Wild Rover
On the Red Hill
The Greasy Poll
Neighbours From Hell?
Real Powys
Mapping the Roads
Coast to Coast

www.mikeparker.org.uk

ALL THE WIDE BORDER

WALES, ENGLAND AND THE PLACES BETWEEN

MIKE PARKER

Harper
North

HarperNorth
Windmill Green
24 Mount Street
Manchester M2 3NX

A division of
HarperCollins*Publishers*
1 London Bridge Street
London SE1 9GF

www.harpercollins.co.uk

HarperCollins*Publishers*
Macken House
39/40 Mayor Street Upper
Dublin 1
D01 C9W8

First published by HarperNorth in 2023

1 3 5 7 9 10 8 6 4 2

Copyright © Mike Parker 2023

Mike Parker asserts the moral right to
be identified as the author of this work

A catalogue record for this book
is available from the British Library

HB ISBN: 978-0-00-849918-1

Printed and bound in Great Britain by
CPI Group (UK) Ltd, Croydon

With love to Sue, Alison, Helen and Phil
– we've straddled some borders between us

Gwen has put out her blackberry wine; it sets the men to singing reckless words from 'Men of Harlech', despite his mutters and angry looks.

One of them jumps up from his place shouting:

'I drink to Wales!'

Gabriel roars:

'And I to England!' and stands facing the other across the table. Megan and Margiad clap their hands; Mary looks serious.

'There'll be trouble in a minute, the men are hot as coals,' she whispers.

Gwen purses up her lips.

'I give the Border,' she says, very quiet.

Margiad Evans: *Country Dance* (1932)

CONTENTS

PART THREE – WYE / GWY

Each chapter begins at a specific border crossing,
its location found on what3words.com.
This is shown at the beginning of each chapter,
starting with ///

PROLOGUE
Thursday 8 September 1966

Daytime television was a distant dream in black-and-white Britain, but on a grey midweek morning in 1966 there was something special: a ninety-minute live outside broadcast of the Queen opening the new Severn Bridge. Viewers watched her arrive at Aust, on the English bank of the river, shake a lot of hands and give a little speech, before climbing into her official car and being driven across the bridge to do it all again, to a rather smaller crowd, at the Newhouse roundabout, on the Welsh side. The second ceremony, according to a spokesman for the royal household, was 'almost as important' as the first.

In an instant, the bridge became visual shorthand for the border, for the coming together of two old neighbours, an outstretched hand-shake high above the silver tides. Thirty years later, a second bridge was added, longer and even more graceful than the first, and together their elegant functionalism became the icon not just of a line on the map, but of a tangled ancient relationship too. No TV producer could resist their gimcrack symbolism, the soaring shots and swollen soundtracks.

You can't blame them, for finding the essence of this furtive border is a notoriously fraught occupation. Crossing the divide, there's almost always some disjunction to be found or felt, but peer too closely, or light it too brightly, and it might just evaporate. The March, the middle land, is a will-o'-the-wisp. Hillforts and castle mounds growl from the green;

church bells toll in lonely sunset skies; lanes twist and creak through the woods to take you where you least expected. Even the names on the map refuse to choose a side, written in a mash of two languages that have coupled in a hayrick and spawned a beautiful bastard third.

To Mary Webb, this is 'the country that lies between the dimpled lands of England and the gaunt purple steeps of Wales – half in faery and half out of it', and in its very mutability lie so many of its truths. When travelling from England into Wales, it is invariably so that the greens swell deeper, the contours sharper and the crags sulkier, but in ways that are somehow both imperceptible *and* sudden. No less a stereotype, crossing into Wales often seems to provoke a downpour, as if the two countries are governed from different heavens. And perhaps they are: for all the egalitarian pose of the Severn Bridge, you need not go far either side of it to be reminded that these are neighbours of radically, almost comically, mismatched weight and wealth.

The border has been just as capricious temporally too. In its 2,000-year history, the lines have been drawn and redrawn, have surged and shrunk in and out of focus, like rocks in a fogbound estuary – the Severn probably, this southern end, or perhaps the Dee, its northern. A straight line between them is little over 100 miles long, but the England–Wales border takes a leisurely 160 miles to make the same journey. Like a wayward contour, it wriggles across moors and mountain, skips along rivers and burrows deep through forests and vales. More prosaically, it also runs down the middle of urban streets, divides industrial estates and golf courses, and splits suburbs and stations from their own town centres.

Today, after more than twenty years of political devolution, the border seems suddenly sharper than ever. In 2014, David Cameron came as Prime Minister to address the Welsh Conservative Party Conference, and in an attempt to score points about the handling of the health service by the Labour administration in Cardiff, declared that 'Offa's Dyke is now the line between life and death'. Six years later, during the coronavirus outbreak, his gaudy soundbite echoed in ironic reverse, when the Welsh government's far more cautious approach bore early dividends. In a poll during the first wave of the pandemic, seven out of ten Welsh voters said that they preferred to take their orders from Cardiff over London, and that Wales 'felt safer' than England. Numbers for outright independence soared too.

Even if enthusiasm for that remains a minority sport, growing devolution will surely mean greater legislative divergence. Until now, all this had seemed small-scale, benign, *amusing*. If it made the news, it was likely to be as the 'and finally …' bit at the end. At the Deva Stadium for instance, home of Chester FC, you enter in England to watch the match in Wales. The border runs along the back of the main stand, and when the smoking ban was introduced by the Welsh Senedd three months before Westminster followed suit, Tannoy announcements had to remind the crowd that it was the new Welsh law they should obey. Visiting supporters bellow at the Chester fans, to the tune of 'Go West', 'You're Welsh, and you know you are!' It is not a compliment.

The first modern legal incarnation of the border, the dry Welsh Sunday, is now only a nostalgic hangover. Legend has it that the Lion Hotel in Llanymynech, split between Shropshire and Montgomeryshire, had to close one bar on Sundays, while the other did a roaring trade, but as so often hereabouts, legend is lying, for the whole place was shut on the Sabbath. True enough though that many a first building after the 'Welcome to England' sign was a pub, and that they made Sunday whoopee for decades, as charabancs, bicycles and ramshackle Austins sped their way there and, hours later, wobbled their way home. True too that in the Llanymynech Lion, as a regular once put it to me, 'I sup my pint in Wales, and piss it out in England.'

Go back further, much further, and the line is live. Defining it, then defending it, took a hugely disproportionate chunk of Roman military might during their occupation of Britain. The frontier is home to Britain's first Norman stone castle (Chepstow, 1067), its last medieval castle (Raglan, 1435), and dozens of fortresses in time and place between, from tell-tale bumps in far-off fields to melodramatic ruins that have gathered whole towns around their stone skirts. Though far out on its western edge, this is Europe's most heavily castellated strip.

In the shadows between the Romans and the Normans is the most stubborn and intriguing of all border evidence: Offa's Dyke, the eighth-century earthwork separating Mercia, the kingdom of middle England, from Wales. Coming across it, especially unexpectedly, is like meeting God herself. How can something be so old, yet so distinct; so weathered but still such a precise demarcation of two tribes? Often coterminous with the modern border, the dyke was not, we are told, built with any significant military purpose in mind. It was just a reminder, a line in the sand, an early leylandii hedge (itself a plant of the border, first hybridised at Leighton Hall, near Welshpool). Offa's Dyke wasn't razor wire or an electric fence, but it certainly wasn't a gate on the latch either.

What it most reminds me of is a country house ha-ha, a ditch that acts as a highly effective dividing line, but that remains unseen on the ground until you are practically in it. That fits too the cultural truth of the England–Wales border, invisible to many, deep as a Pacific trench to those who cannot keep out of it. On both sides of the line, numbers of the latter are growing, but especially – inevitably – to the west. Offa's Dyke looms far larger on the emotional horizon of the Welsh than it does the English, for although it acts as a reminder that this land border is sufficiently ancient to be almost inviolate, it has also, as Emyr Humphreys wrote in his cultural history *The Taliesin Tradition*, served to promulgate a siege mentality in Wales. Impregnable fortress to some on that side, neatly delineated *al fresco* playpen to many on the other: either way, it is perhaps less than helpful.

Even the dyke's own physicality is a quiet reminder that this is no meeting of equals. Its Mercian builders placed the raised bank on their side, affording lofty vantage into enemy territory, and on the far side dug a deep ditch, making it harder for Welsh border raiders to return their booty home. Like a stone dropped into a well, this is the echo down the centuries. Today, Wales's population is around one-twentieth of England's, yet it is home to half of their combined poorest districts. An economy based so heavily on blasting coal, slate and minerals from the ground has left it bruised, blistered and in chronically poor health. Meanwhile, the wealth of the plush parts of England has grown giddily, and the gap widens daily. Every recession, every crisis stretches the balance sheet only further, and yet … and yet, beyond the numbers, by any token that cannot be counted or quantified, Wales holds fistfuls of trump cards, and knows it.

We know it too, those of us from the English side of the line who have been so readily seduced by our next-door neighbour. We fell for the rugged beauty and dark-eyed charm, the hint of something wilder and earthier beneath the starch of Sunday best. Many cross in the other direction too, of course. Aside from the necessities of economy or opportunity, nowhere in Wales can offer the freedom of the great English cities, their intoxicating blasts of anonymity irresistible to anyone strangled by too-tight apron strings.

Criss-crossing the border too are centuries of rumour and legend, hearsay and hubris, dark shadows and shafts of heathen light; also countless paths, hundreds of streams, nine railways and 202 public roads. None come trumpeted so loudly as the Severn bridges, which carry the motorist on to what, fifty-six years later, is still the only motorway in Wales. Most crossings are quiet B-roads and mud-puddled lanes, where only a change in the tarmac lets you know that you have gone over to the other side.

The main road between Shrewsbury and Welshpool is firmly mid-rank, busy and slow through dusty villages and often clogged with caravans, but it is the border crossing that I make far more than any other, and love with a fierce, weird pride. In all its mongrel clutter, it's me. Thirty years on the English side, and nearly twenty-five on the Welsh, as I cross the line in either direction I feel it pluck inside me like a piano string, its plaintive vibrato persisting long after the signs have receded. Heading east, I'm poised for the first view over the wide plains of my Midland upbringing, and thinking of beer and spices and warm red brick. Heading west, I sink into the stony embrace of the hills and let my thoughts decouple, and drift home.

My favourite border crossing has to be done on foot. It is the sweetest of clichés, where the nub of both nations appears to have burst free, and poured down like lava to crystallise on opposite banks of the River Wye. Park up – and pay – in England, the trim Gloucestershire village of Redbrook to be precise, under the imperial gaze of Victorian villas called Applegate, Mandalay and Bona Vista, and then follow the path down to the river's edge and over the water to wild Wales.

It's not for everyone: the walkway is pinned to the side of a rusty viaduct, out of use for so long that if a new-born baby had been on the final train to cross it, she'd now be drawing her pension. Chunks of missing metalwork catch the eye and hasten the step over to the far side, to Penallt, Monmouthshire and the Boat Inn, its chimney puffing out a cartoon *croeso*. Above the slate roof, woods heave with foreboding, though a terraced beer garden has been hacked from the depths and landscaped, all mosses and ferns, picket fences and tinkling waterfalls. Birds chitter, dogs smile. In five minutes flat, courtesy of a rickety *via ferrata* and apparent time tunnel, you have passed from the world of Mary Poppins into that of Bilbo Baggins.

Here the gap is paper thin, like the line between the worlds at Halloween. At other times, in other places, it is wide, outlandish, a whole principality of betwixt and between. So too the people drawn into it: the fey, the gay, the Hay-terati (Arthur Miller, on being invited to the festival: *Hay-on-Wye? Is that some kind of a sandwich?* Yes. Yes, it is). Here in the fold of the map lie Housman, Machen and Kilvert; Father Ignatius and Brother Cadfael; Jan Morris and April Ashley; Eric Gill and Raymond Williams; Dymock poets, daughters of Glyndŵr; the battlefield ghosts of Edward Thomas and Wilfred Owen. In the March, it is almost always dawn or dusk.

* * *

On that far morning in September 1966, as the royal Bentley purred across the new bridge, a flotilla of boats in the estuary below sounded their horns in celebration. Among them was the *Severn Princess*, the car ferry that plied the channel under skipper Enoch Williams. The television commentators praised his generosity in saluting the very thing that was putting him out of business, but his joy was genuine, and not just for the cameras, nor even the Queen. He'd received a fat lump sum pay-off, but more to the point, he'd run a daily service across the fearsome estuary since the General Strike forty years earlier, and was more than ready to bow out.

Drivers were even happier. The ferry, which could squeeze only seventeen cars onto its tiny deck, cost nine shillings and sixpence per crossing, and often necessitated hours of waiting, either for the tide, the second largest in the world, or because it was busy. With a toll of 2s./6d., the bridge was irresistible, and by the third day of its new life there was a 5-mile queue of traffic at the toll booths coming from England, and an 8-mile queue from Wales. The future had arrived. Four months earlier, Enoch Williams had ferried Bob Dylan and his entourage across the water, between gigs in Bristol and Cardiff. The iconic photo of a gaunt Dylan waiting on the slipway at Aust, with a near-complete bridge looming out of the mist behind him, said it plain: the times, they were a-changin'.

Though not fast enough. The filthy truth of that came only six weeks after the flags and fanfare of the bridge's opening, when a slithering mountain of coal slurry buried a primary school, and over a hundred of its pupils, at Aberfan. Wales slipped quickly back into its habitual place in the British family photo, eyes downcast, in Bible-black mourning. The 1960s were beginning to swing, but not down here, not now, for the clock had stopped, at 9.13 on a shrouded autumn morning.

On a tidal wave of bewildered grief, Tom Jones's 'Green, Green Grass of Home', an American country hit recast by his baritone boom into an anthem of lost Welsh horizons, surged up the charts, hitting the top and staying there for the rest of the year. It was there on the midwinter night I was born, and has haunted me ever since. For those of us living on a frontier, any frontier, it is our siren song, a warning not to fall for the old lie that on the other side of the line the grass will surely be green, greener.

Less than 30 miles from the gleaming optimism of the Severn Bridge, the old order ripped open a wound that seeps still now. The bridge was no meeting of equals. When the Palace described its Welsh opening ceremony as 'almost as important' as the main one, the word 'almost' was stretched to breaking point; to an impossible width that no bridge will ever quite span.

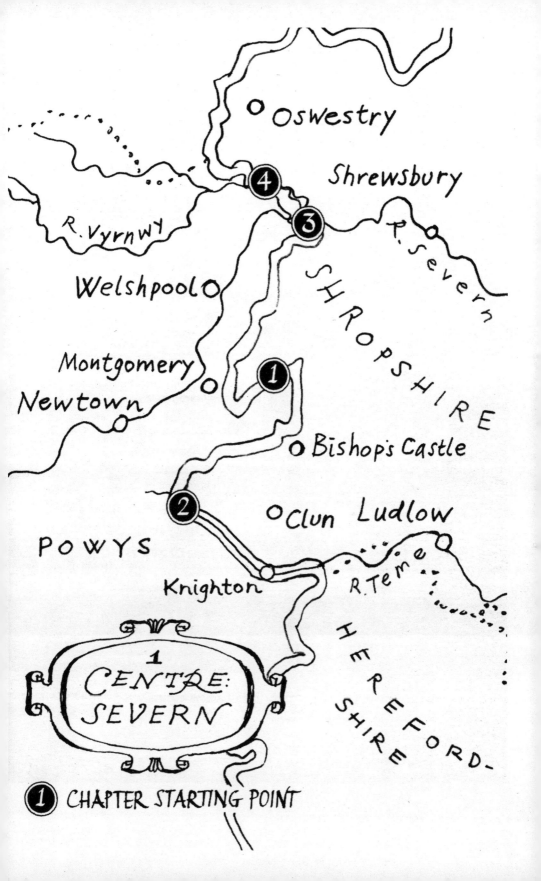

O Oswestry

Shrewsbury

R. Vyrnwy

R. Severn

SHROPSHIRE

Welshpool O

Montgomery

Newtown

O

① Bishop's Castle

② Clun Ludlow

POWYS

Knighton R. Teme

HEREFORD-SHIRE

1
CENTRE:
SEVERN

① CHAPTER STARTING POINT

1.

JIGSAW

/// method.revealing.bond

There's no sign. Well, there's a battered brown one pointing towards the stone circle, and underneath that, another warning that this is a Home Watch area, but nothing to mark that on this sharp corner you skid from one country into another. It goes unsaid and unsigned, as it often does around here. Best to check the bins at people's front gates, and see which council logo is blazed across them. Powys or Shropshire? Wales or England? Neither – or both? All options are open.

In these pitted hills, the border wriggles like a toddler, forever escaping your grasp and scampering off where least expected. Even the roads and rivers conspire to confuse. Here the lane goes west into England, and east into Wales. A couple of miles south, the A489 dances across the border and back again, four times in eight miles. The main road to Shrewsbury, a few fields away, hugs the line even more closely, criss-crossing and straddling it in an increasingly intimate *pas de deux*. Two nearby sections of the frontier run along the Camlad, the only cross-border river, among dozens, that rises in England and disgorges in Wales. Everything here prefers to go against the flow.

In Britain's jigsaw puzzle of histories and identities, this is the tab that locks together its key pieces. Draw a square on the map, with the Welsh town of Montgomery top left, and its English sibling Bishop's Castle bottom right. The 50 square miles between them is split pretty equally between two interlocking tabs, a peninsula of each country, distinct and intact, hooked deep into the other. The tongue of England nudged into Wales is a soft patchwork of farms and fields, wide horizons washed by rainbows; curled around it to the east, the *presque-île* of Wales a hard plug of ancient rock folded in on itself, impossibly green and shrouded in secrets. For so long, we've been used to the pieces slotting together with a satisfying snap, yet suddenly they seem as loose as old teeth, rubbing up against each other and causing friction, wear, pain. Perhaps it was always so, but we chose not to notice.

Commanding this border crossing is Corndon Hill, the very last crag of the Welsh, and on its summit I watch two ravens act out the last twenty centuries. One sweeps in from the east, one from the west; they collide in a caterwaul of jet-black feathers, plunging, screeching, beaks wide and eyes beady. Then, out of nowhere, a sudden ceasefire; they soar and swoop on the thermals, the very picture of cloak-and-dagger togetherness. For a happy half-hour, the pattern repeats itself, fight then flight, over and over, in what looks to be a very well-choreographed show.

So mesmeric is the dance that I fail to notice the cloudburst inching towards us from the Welsh mountains. A curtain of grey is sweeping imperiously down the Vale of Kerry, and will hit within minutes. The only possible shelters on this bald summit are the rocky cairns dotted far and wide; I take a gamble on one a few hundred yards away, and luckily, it's a good call. Facing away from the oncoming rain, there's a large monolith with a slight overhang, into which the dog and I can tuck ourselves, eat snacks and watch the world gauze over and blank out. Everything vanishes, all borders dissolve, and in our stone womb, we are cosy and dry.

Soon, the rain thins to drizzle and then mist. With a magician's timing, that too is parted and there, facing me with a fierce new clarity across the valley, across the border, are the Stiperstones, that sky-clad ridge of serrated granite outcrops. According to D. H. Lawrence in his novella *St Mawr*, this is 'where the spirit of aboriginal England still lingers'. Other shapes swim through the haze. To the north, a hill far less lofty, but one I cannot keep my eyes from all the same. I never can. Bromlow Callow is a cartoon of a peak, a round green hump capped by a toupee of trees. Gazing regally over its surroundings, it is special, and knows it. From my viewpoint on Corndon, the Callow is the full-stop to a long ridge that snakes along the plain between us. The ridge is Stapeley Hill, a very shapely hill, spattered with megalithic remains and braided between two nations.

In this rough-arsed Eden, many have also seen the snake, and eaten of its apple. Eighteenth-century antiquarian William Stukeley declared that Stapeley Hill was the shape of a dragon, a sentiment echoed and elaborated upon by the author of *Salopia Antiqua* (1841), the Reverend Charles Henry Hartshorne. Looking at the three stone circles along its 2-mile ridge, he identified the Whetstones below me on the flank of Corndon as the serpent's head, the Hoarstones down on the marsh at the other end as its tail, and the main one between – Mitchell's Fold, the middle fold – as the body. To the excitable priest, that the stones were of religious intent 'will not admit of a doubt'; more, that the 'curvature of the avenue of approach to the great temple is precisely similar' to that of the famous avenue at Avebury.

Hartshorne noted that 'owing to the soft and boggy nature of the soil' the Whetstones were leaning, and ponders their name. Comprised of basalt, useless as a whetting stone, he conjectures that it is instead a corruption of the Brythonic (Welsh) term *gwaed-faen*, blood-stone, and was thus a likely place of sacrifice. Shortly after his ideas were published, the circle itself was sacrificed when the common land around the base of Corndon Hill was enclosed, the stones broken up and used for boundary walling. They're still there today; as I began my ascent of the hill ignorant of any of this, I was drawn to them, green with age and lined up under a ragged hawthorn. On the hill's summit half an hour later, I could see the sad debris of the smashed stone circle far below, but for all that, the power of the place is undimmed.

Mitchell's Fold, the belly of the beast, is testament to that. Although it has also suffered depletion over the centuries, it still astounds. The fifteen surviving stones sit in a perfect circle, but it is the setting that truly transcends. On a high saddle of moorland, with a girdle of buxom hills held firmly at bay, the sensation of being on a mighty threshold is thrilling: hovering between earth and sky, then and now, this world and the next. In such contexts, that this is also the cusp of two countries feels prosaic, almost mundane. Yet that too is so much more than the mere stroke of a cartographer's pen. Here, in the inter-locking jigsaw tabs, on the hinge between England and Wales, the line is etched not just across the topsoil, but through the bedrock far beneath, the skies above and all the senses within.

The border is as much shaped by immutable geology as it is by human geography. When the contours start tightening, where the rocks get harder and older, when the soils thin out, there England will end and Wales begin. And here, though the map looks muddied, this truth is as clear as anywhere. From the east, from an English perspec-tive, Corndon Hill is just one of many, the last of a series of shapely great whalebacks that pleat the south Shropshire plains: Stiperstones, Clee, the Long Mynd, Wenlock Edge, the Wrekin. From the west, through Welsh eyes, it has a far more singular and strategic position, guarding an uncharacteristically soft underbelly of the country, the gentle scoop of the Vale of Kerry. Bone-hard Corndon, quarried over millennia for stone axes and veins of lead, is Wales's heavily fortified front door.

On sentry duty, flanking it either side, are the secondary peaks of Lan Fawr and Roundton. Like Corndon they are volcanic outcrops, pocked with mines, cairns, pits and holes that seep the sweet icy air of aeons ago. Roundton is perfection: from its stone skullcap, views seem infinite across both place and time, and it takes no leap to be back in its Iron Age hillfort, one of hundreds studded along the fringe of England and Wales. This was a major tribal faultline long before the arrival of the Romans.

In pursuit of the border, its stories and shadows, this is the place to start, where the two countries are interlocked, and we need to reach for the arcane to understand the actuality. Here, legends sit closer to the surface, myth helps us see. Stone circles and hillforts, dragons, dykes and devils, recumbent landscape figures and lingering cults: all vie for attention and help to refocus our sense of self, and view of the world beyond. Britain's last 'sin-eater' is buried here, as is one of our greatest metaphysical poets; this is a home too for modern neo-pagans, from fluffy hippies to a neo-fascist sect that has been based here for generations. For all the solidity of this area's geology, its mines, quarries and igneous outcrops, it is a place of opaque nationality, antique religion and blurry watersheds. Me too, on all counts.

* * *

If there is one moment, over all others, that sparked into life the England–Wales border, it is the battle in 51 CE, somewhere in the Marches, when the Romans finally defeated the British chieftain Caratacus. The occupying forces had landed on the Kent coast in the spring of 43 CE, and rapidly harried their way across England. As ever, the flat and fertile south and east of the island had succumbed relatively easily, while the stubborn north and west held out. After defeat in various battles in the south, Caratacus had fled west, far west, into the perennial rebel hills of Wales. The Romans continued to consolidate their gains. By 47 CE they were constructing the Fosse Way, a 200-mile line that shoots straight from Devon to Lincoln, built at breakneck speed as both military highway and unambiguous delineation of the territory thus far conquered.

From there, they could skirmish into enemy territory, sometimes being held temporarily back but more often successful in advancing ever further, into the Midlands, the north and south-west of England. In exile in Wales, Caratacus – known there as Caradog – had established himself as compatriot of the tribal leaders, and with them had hatched plans to lure the Roman legions as far as possible onto their turf. After so many Roman victories in the easy lowlands, the best hope for the combined Welsh tribes was to use their intimate knowledge of the terrain, its harsh mountains and unexpected bogs, to their best advantage. Upon the outcome of this stand would hang the future of Britain; as Caratacus put it to his troops on the eve of battle, it would 'win back their freedom or enslave them forever'. Roman historian Tacitus sets the scene in his *Annals*: 'Inferior in military strength, but deriving an advantage from the deceptiveness of the country, he [Caratacus] at once shifted the war by a stratagem into the territory of the Ordovices [north and central Wales], where … he resolved on a final struggle. He selected a position for the engagement in which advance and retreat alike would be difficult for our men and comparatively easy for his own, and then on some lofty hills, wherever their sides could be approached by a gentle slope, he piled up stones to serve as a rampart. A river too of varying depth was in his front, and his armed bands were drawn up before his defences.'

He describes the view faced by the Roman commander, Ostorius: 'The river too in his face, the rampart they had added to it, the frowning hilltops, the stern resistance and masses of fighting men everywhere apparent, daunted him. But his soldiers insisted on battle, exclaiming that valour could overcome all things.'

So it proved, for once the Romans had broken through the ramparts, their victory was swift. Caratacus's wife and children were taken prisoner, though he escaped and sought refuge in Brigantia, the province of the north of England. Afraid of possible reprisals, the queen of the Brigantes turned him in and he was sent as a prisoner to Rome.

This one event pivoted our history and forged our identities, yet we have no real idea where it happened. That there are two rival Shropshire hillforts called Caer Caradog, and a third in Herefordshire, is only the beginning of the problem. Tacitus's text has been combed exhaustively for evidence, but his *Annals* were written more than fifty years after the event, and are inevitably spiked by winners' bravado and the exaggerations that grow with each retelling.

Even if every word is true, it's still an intractable treasure hunt. Theories are plentiful, but clues sparse. We have sharp slopes, 'frowning hilltops' and ramparts, the British troops towering over the Romans above a river wide and deep enough to have been a defensive asset. The lack of a substantial river should discount both Shropshire Caer Caradogs, and many other favourite candidates, including the British Camp in the Malvern Hills. Though the Herefordshire Caradoc has the river, for it sits above a loop of the Wye, its gentle promontory is easily surmountable, and it is many miles south of the Ordovici territory in which Tacitus explicitly locates the battle.

The enthusiastic Victorian reverend, Charles Hartshorne, who we left salivating at the recumbent serpent of Stapeley Hill, has much to say on the question in his *Salopia Antiqua*. He rubbishes the theory of William Camden, the Elizabethan father of British antiquarianism, that the Caer Caradog near Clun is the true site, acidly reminding his readers that Camden never himself visited and had lifted his information wholesale from Welsh scholar Humphrey Llwd. This was necessary, Hartshorne slyly reminds us, because Camden was afraid of going anywhere near Wales, having been hounded out of Denbighshire as a suspected spy.

Other suggestions for the battle site have included Coxall Knoll, a hillfort split between Shropshire and Hereford; Caer Ddunod, far north in the Clocaenog Forest; Dolforwyn, near Newtown, where Prince Llywelyn was to build his castle; Blodwel Rocks, the great plug of limestone that towers over the border village of Llanymynech; and the triple peak of the Breidden Hills near Welshpool. That feels likelier. Sat slap on the national border, the Breiddens burst out of the plains and are visible for scores of miles in all directions. Most pertinent to Tacitus's account is that they sit immediately above the River Severn, as does the Reverend Hartshorne's preferred battlefield candidate 20 miles further upstream, deeper into Wales: Cefn Carnedd, near Caersŵs.

Exploring these sites is a superlative way to see the borderland from unexpected angles. Having done them all, through heat, hail and farm dogs, I am firmly with Hartshorne. The Breiddens are the romantic option, but their very prominence makes them highly unlikely, for there is nowhere to hide. Cefn Carnedd is the one: a mighty hillfort, a giant of a location slumbering almost unnoticed in the bracken and gorse. Poke it awake, though, and out spill the secrets. Far below, the young Severn slides by in a lazy S-bend, poised like a snake and flanked by massive Montgomeryshire oaks and ashes. From the valley, you sweat up the steep slope to the fort, and are in its outer ditches before you've even seen them. Sit, breathe, inhale the green breeze, and Tacitus's description, almost 2,000 years old, comes roaring to life.

From the fort's lip, look far up the valley of the Severn, Britain's longest river, towards Newtown and Welshpool, towards England. There came the Roman legions, lulled by the familiarity of the river and its vale, yet lured deep into enemy territory by those who knew how to exploit its every contour. Cefn Carnedd was less than a day's march from their riverside camp at Montgomery, but suddenly, almost imperceptibly, the gentle hills had swollen into mountains. Caratacus and the tribal leaders of Wales knew that this was their best, their *only*, hope.

Stand there now, and the battle still echoes. The sensation of being on a tight and very specific cusp is as sharp as ever. Turn towards the east, and the decibel level is noticeably higher, as traffic and trains thrum incessantly up the valley. Compare the contrails, hear the planes: even the skies are more congested and noisier over there. Look west, towards the purple ramparts of Cadair Idris, and all is hunkered and hushed. It is a countryside in which to melt away.

Prior to Caratacus's last stand, there was a patchwork of tribal divisions across the island, their boundaries perpetually shifting. This battle scored one far deeper than the others; there was now a clear line running from the Dee estuary to the Severn, and obvious distinctions between the lands either side of it. The line was destined only to harden. In cutting off the land to the west, denying the tribes there any useful supply and defensive links with the South West and North, the Roman commanders succeeded in penning in the hill people, inadvertently creating Wales, and by default 'not-Wales', or England. The frontier was fractious from the get-go. Maintaining it demanded disproportionate military might, so that two of the three main legionary bases of early Roman Britain were located on it, in the north at Deva (Chester) and the south at Isca (Caerleon). So too the legionary fortresses; of the first seven, three were at Viroconium (Wroxeter), Glevum (Gloucester) and Burrium (Usk).

Templates were cast, and echoes still sound. The Roman imperial tactic of divide and conquer became the prototype for the emerging

English state, while for the Welsh it established a pattern of perpetual retrenchment. Even the figure of Caratacus himself has been appropriated to fit accordingly. To exponents of English exceptionalism, Caratacus was a founding hero, already a Christian missionary and putative martyr when he was taken prisoner to Rome. Though that transpired to be a huge overdose of wishful thinking (and more specifically a misreading of the word 'chieftain' for 'Christian'), the notion has proved enduringly stubborn, and to many, particularly Victorians and Edwardians, utterly irresistible. The conceit of Caratacus in chains, up against it but then winning over the Roman emperor and Senate with only wisdom and quiet humility, has lacquered England's most cherished self-image for centuries.

For the Welsh, the same scene is replayed for its punchline, when Caradog, their version of Caratacus, is spared his life and gets to see the wealth and splendour of the imperial capital. A historian after Tacitus records his reaction: 'Why do you, with all these great possessions, still covet our poor huts?' It is a maxim tattooed across many a Welsh heart, and has cemented Caradog in the affections of his (briefly) adopted land. True to form in the nation that can spin a yarn out of the ether, he appears in the Old Welsh genealogies of the tenth century, the *Mabinogi* and other medieval mythologies, and stars in Iolo Morgannwg's lavish eighteenth-century imaginarium. As for any perpetually embattled nationality, there's no narrative more narcotic than that of heroic failure.

To a culture hooked more on expansion and power, the takeaway from Roman rule is very different. In the English mindscape, or at least in the fading version that schooled me in the 1970s, the Romans have always exercised an inordinately powerful pull. Their arrival at more or less the same time as Christ helped that: BCE was prehistory, the before times, a far-off world of animal skins and mud huts. The Romans brought speed, sophistication, cities and imperial swagger, and when they went, Britannia collapsed once more into savagery. Not until 1066 and the arrival of the Normans was the clock restarted. The inference is clear: a well-run empire – *ours* for example, now that you mention it – is a thing of beauty, a streamlined engine running

slick and purposeful. Brutality may be necessary, but only the barest modicum, and all for the greater good of course. The refrain was drummed in at every turn and from every angle.

Back on the jigsaw tab between Montgomery and Bishop's Castle, I'm walking Offa's Dyke, recalling my dad's idea of this border and what lay beyond. His take had been forged at Solihull School in the decade after the Second World War, and remained unchanged ever since. Some history teacher had taught him that the Welsh always hid in the moors and mountains of their godforsaken landscape, buried themselves deep in the mud and indiscriminately ambushed anyone who passed. The schoolmaster must have acted out the attack, because Dad always did too, squatting down and peering out from an imaginary bog, only the exaggerated blinking of his eyes giving him away. His re-enactment came caked in the chalk dust of a minor Midlands public school at the turn of the 1950s, a curdled muscle-memory of happier, simpler times. It always made him roar with laughter.

To my dad, that was the Welsh way, and not only in warfare. He suspected ambush at every turn, and smelt it in the air whenever he visited. Shortly after I first moved to Wales, he came to stay, and in a rush of goodwill on the journey there was enticed off the main road by a farmer's sign promising the sweetest mountain lamb for sale. I cannot recall what exactly he came away with, or whether it lived up to its billing, but twenty years on I can remember that it cost £44, because I heard him say so on at least a dozen occasions, in tones of outraged incredulity that soon coagulated into one of his most cherished anecdotes. He padded it out with a description of the filthy farmyard and rusting tractors, and acted out a shifty-looking farmer, who bore an uncanny resemblance to his ancient Celt lurking in the bog. Dad's giddy altruism was never repeated; from then, he took to stocking up from Lidl before they set out. After many more years than it deserved, that story was eventually deposed in his repertoire by the observation, made unfailingly every time he visited, that the roads in Wales were so much better than those in England. Occasionally, the dark shadow behind that thought would surface too: that this could only possibly be so because the English were subsidising every last inch of silky Welsh tarmac.

A 150-mile-long watchtower, Offa's Dyke is an ancient embodiment of the same superiority. Yet even within the context of its age, this barely stands up. To the English, these were the Dark Ages, between-the-empires, the centuries of barbarity that barely get a paragraph in the school history books; to the Welsh, it was an Age of Saints, of missionaries and monasteries, coastal trade and pan-Celticism.

The Romans drew the line in the soil; Offa baked it into place. Construction of the dyke sealed the border, not just on the ground but in the collective psyche on both sides. Yet as I walk the stretch that forms the western edge of the jigsaw tab near Montgomery, one of the clearest and straightest extant sections of the entire dyke, it seems to dissolve beneath my feet. The linear earthwork is plain enough, its bank crowned by gargantuan oaks, the ditch puddled with nettles. Officially, the picture is dark and defensive, but it takes only the slightest refocus of the eye and a million greens begin to billow softly, bluebells and purple orchids plump up the edges, and this strip across the fields might be nothing more menacing than a farm boundary, or perhaps the relic of a much-loved branch line closed in the sixties.

From the windswept summit of Corndon Hill, the disjunction is even more acute. Ordnance Survey in hand, I look down the wide bowl of the Vale of Kerry and try to match up the features. On paper, Offa's Dyke looks to be by far the most significant landmark for miles around. Like a knife wound slashed through the gentle patchwork of fields, it is scored deeply, three times over, on the map: the spiky hachures of the earthwork itself, overlaid with the symbolic barbed wire of the modern political border, and then the lurid dots and dashes of the Offa's Dyke National Trail footpath that runs along it. Using binoculars, I squint hard to see the reality, and can barely make anything out, for the line of the dyke is faint, sporadic, uncertain. On the OS, it marches across the landscape like a booted centurion; on the ground, it sighs and shifts like a ghost.

At the foot of this section of the dyke is the Blue Bell hotel. That's a ghost now too. I'd passed by dozens of times over the decades, and had occasionally stopped to see if it was open. It never was, and though desperate to see inside, part of me was quietly relieved. The place intrigued but perturbed me, with its Rotary Club sign on the pebbledash porch, its ersatz mullioned windows, antique petrol pumps, and above all, literally above all, a frayed Union Jack hanging limp in the borderland drizzle. You'd only just passed the 'Welcome to England' sign, and in less than a mile would be heading back into Wales again. To my younger, spikier self, the flagrant Britishness – even the petrol pumps were painted red, white and blue – seemed deliberately provocative, and if not quite that, then at least reeking of long-dead uncles, their cheap whisky, stale tobacco and sour opinions.

I only finally made it through the door at lunchtime on Christmas Day a couple of years ago. My sister and her partner had recently moved nearby, and made the Blue Bell their local of choice. They understood its erratic opening hours, forgave its lack of draught beer, and loved the unpredictable gaggle of regulars drawn into a parlour unchanged since the sixties. Perched behind the bar, queen of her wipe-down sanctum of Formica and leatherette, was landlady Helen Jones. She stood us all – farmers, locals, incomers, first-timers alike – a Christmas drink, and the conversation flowed just as freely too.

Helen's father had bought the Blue Bell in 1926, transforming a rustic pub at a dusty crossroads into a swanky roadhouse to catch the motorists heading from the Midlands to the Welsh mountains and coast. It *oozed* aspiration. At almost any hour, you could get a bed for the night, a fishing permit, a pot of tea, a pint of Watney's, a port and lemon, a plate of ham and eggs or a gallon of four star. The function rooms bustled with wedding breakfasts and funeral teas, agricultural auctions and election hustings. Helen was born there in the mid-1930s, and remained there all her long life.

By a matter of metres, the Blue Bell is in Shropshire, in the old civil parish of Brompton, the very last bulge at the far end of the English tab poked deep into Welsh turf. Though technically not an exclave, all four roads that radiate out from the pub head into Wales. The old Sundays were the heyday of the Blue Bell of course, when all the surrounding countryside was dry, but here the pumps flowed merrily, the bars were full, the air thick with smoke and merriment.

Though defunct now for nearly thirty years, the Sunday Closing (Wales) Act of 1881 still casts a long shadow. It was the first piece of parliamentary legislation to treat Wales as a distinct and discrete entity, setting a precedent that has progressed directly to devolution. It also secured in the British imagination a very particular perception of Wales. Historian John Davies wrote that 'above all, [it] connected Welshness with negativity': the bromide sluice of pulpit prohibition of course, but also hints of sanctimony and the slitheriness of those dedicated to circumventing the rules, who revelled in the power of their nod and a wink.

From 1961, local votes were held across Wales every seven years to decide if the policy should continue; 'rallying the prim and self-denying for their last stand in defence of the traditional gaunt Welsh Sabbath', wrote Gwyn Thomas. In the first referendum, only five of the thirteen traditional counties opted to go 'wet', but they included

Glamorgan and Monmouthshire, between them accounting for almost two-thirds of the Welsh population. Seven years later, three more counties – Montgomeryshire included, surrounding the Blue Bell on all sides – opted for Sunday drinking, leaving only five of the most westerly counties 'dry'. These were also the most Cymraeg, and the teetotal Sunday became enmeshed in a cultural and linguistic identity that it perhaps neither merited nor much needed. It cemented a popular image of Wales – Welsh-speaking Wales especially – as the land of Thou Shalt Not, and unquestionably punctured the appeal of change in the first devolution referendum in 1979. The fear of a priggish theocracy, Welsh governance as a perpetual chapel Sunday, was plenty enough to move many waverers from a maybe to a reluctant no.

There was no ignoring a border of booze, though, especially in the years between the first referendum in 1961 and the last in 1996, the era when Britain's appetite for beer and fags was at its most insatiable. The contrast was all the more exaggerated for it: on the one side, dour Wales, purse-lipped in disapproval even as it sipped hypocritically on a warm stout; on the other, Olde England, bursting with beef and ale and roaring red-faced in backroom snugs. Pubs just on the English side of the border, the Blue Bell included, fully played up to the cliché, and it paid them back handsomely.

Now, country pubs are family food barns, a quarter of twenty-somethings don't do alcohol at all, and real drinkers stay at home with their supermarket take-outs. Though there is a legacy of fewer pubs on the Welsh side of the line than the English, any real border difference is long gone. So too the Blue Bell. Helen died in the summer of 2020, and it won't reopen. The doors are bolted, the Rotary plaque has been jemmied off the front, and even the pub signs, erected only fifteen years ago, are fading. *THE BLUE BELL HOTEL*, they declare, *Proprietor Helen Jones, Freedom for Brompton*. Freedom for Brompton? Ah yes, this very last parish of Shropshire, little more than a cross-roads, a scatter of farms and the pub, was itself done away with in 1987, absorbed into – or taken over by, depending on your view-point – its more substantial neighbour, Chirbury. There's no unit of land too lowly, no identity too tiny, to let a tinkering with its borders pass unlamented.

About 5 miles east is Brompton's inverted twin, the last Welsh parish poking deep into England. Dutifully true to national cliché, Hyssington has no pub, its tidy village green overlooked instead by a small, prim Methodist tabernacle. With the same sense of inevitability that has seen off the Blue Bell, it too has closed recently, and is doubtless destined to become The Old Chapel, dream home for downsizers, joining the Old Post Office opposite, the Old School next door, and down the lane, the Old Barn and Efail Hen ('the old forge' in slightly clunky Welsh). One by one, the communal spaces go private.

From the green, a sunken lane, dark with age, rises towards the original nucleus of Hyssington, a quarter of a mile away. Here, folded into the fronds, are the church, castle and an old drovers' inn on what was once a busy thoroughfare. Like almost all of the churches around here, St Etheldreda's is a stolid Victorian rebuild of a medieval original, and though the building rarely raises the pulse, the setting is symphonic. Some 900 feet up, the single stone cell sits at an angle on a rounded rectangular dais of grass and graves, ancient yews and gargantuan oaks, with views one way down into the Vale of Kerry, and the other, up impossibly green fields that gradually leach into the rusty scree of Corndon Hill. There's cloud obscuring its summit, but I know that up there the ravens are still circling.

Looming over the churchyard is the motte and bailey of Hyssington's Norman castle, one of so many in the area. As for the Romans, the Saxons and the Mercians before them, this was a western edgeland for the Normans too. Following their invasion of 1066, William the Conqueror established earldoms to control the demarcation line at the three border towns of Chester, Shrewsbury and Hereford, on the Dee, the Severn and the Wye respectively. For all invaders before and since, from those routing Caratacus to those towing jet skis, the principal route of incursion into the heart of Wales was along the broad valley of the Severn.

The first Earl of Shrewsbury was Roger de Montgomery, a toponymic surname from the Calvados region of Normandy. His name was given to the most important of the new castles built along the frontier, where Offa's Dyke meets the River Severn. It was already in service, and named Montgomery, by the time of the Domesday survey of the 1080s. In the early thirteenth century, the castle was rebuilt on a stronger defensive site a mile away, and the name passed to the town that grew up around it and then the shire that stretched all the way to a tidal port on the far west coast.

Such was the magnitude of the Normans in the school-book British story. As with the Romans, we wilt in the blaze of their imperial potency. Their combined influence on our landscape, both topographic and figurative, is so entrenched, from the location and layout of our towns and the routes between them to the stories that were spun about them on the way, that we routinely overstate their case. Easily eclipsed were the legacies of cultures marginalised by accident or design, those more colonised than colonising, or those that lean more on an oral than a written tradition.

Hyssington seems unexpectedly sure of its nationality. It is, like all good Welsh villages, loomed over by its mountain: Corndon, its watchman and totem. Though the church of St Etheldreda is named after a Saxon saint, its graveyard is full of Hamers, Gwythers and Thomases, old Montgomeryshire families whose tendrils go deep and spread far into the west. The Old School has recently changed hands, and been recast as Yr Hen Ysgol. And there's a distinctly Welsh countenance to the people I meet: proper country faces, open but shielded, then suddenly cracked apart by an unselfconscious grin, a shaft of sunlight bursting through grey clouds.

There are those same faces again, a few years leaner and greener, on the film of the 2014 celebration of Hyssington's most enduring legend: the Raging Bull of Bagbury. The story goes that once upon a time, the squire at Bagbury Farm, the last in Wales and just one field away from the border, was a notorious blackguard. Upon his death, brought about with help from a local witch, the spell rebounded and the squire was reborn as a raging demon bull, striking even greater terror into the community than had his antecedent. In desperation, the bull was lured into St Etheldreda's church, and 'read down', surrounded by a dozen priests reading the gospel aloud. This had the effect of shrinking the furious bull, but when nightfall came and they could no longer see to read, the creature swelled once again, and grew even larger than before. By morning, when they could resume reading, it filled the church, cracking the walls and dislodging masonry. By the end of the second day, however, the reading down had reduced the bull to a miniature, whereupon it was hastily crammed into a boot, a silver snuff box say some, and buried under the church step. Should he be disturbed, he may yet grow out of control once again.

Hyssington residents commemorated the legend with a procession from Bagbury to the church, through the middle of the village. At the front of the parade was a massive wicker bull, horns prinked for action and with hot scarlet dahlias for eyes. In his wake, the villagers processed, rattling tambourines and hitting drums, bells and sticks. In Hebden Bridge or Haverfordwest, such activity would have been the preserve of jolly incomers in daft hats and jerkins, but not in Hyssington. The vicar blessed proceedings and everyone pitched in. After a village feast in the graveyard – a beef roast, inevitably – and a concert in the church, the wicker bull was left to guard the grounds, under the ancient yews and gazing up at Corndon.

Troublesome ghosts and bulls are a regular shtick of borderland legend; evidence, say folklorists, of local ox cults, as well as a nod to the long significance of cattle in these lush lands. There's something else in the Hyssington story, though, a symbolism that hangs in the air, one that I can taste ripening fast right now. The idea of something of great potential power being literally belittled, shrunk to impotence by the continuous declamation of conservative orthodoxy, then locked away and entombed, seems just too tidy on the threshold of the final/first church in Wales. What force lies deep, biding its time, perhaps beginning to stir? Might something solid and strong and with roaring red eyes come bellowing back to life?

2.

EXILE

/// fulfilled.scarecrow.flask

Summer vanished a few miles ago, when I climbed the hairpins into autumn and up into the Clun Forest. The temperature plunged, the air grew damp and trails of mist swirled through the trees. It invariably seems to be shrouded in fog up here, not that I come this way that often. This is a road I regularly drive, but it's wooded, potholed and slow, with sudden narrow stretches and unexpected bends, so that by the time I reach civilisation my knuckles are white from gripping the wheel. It's such a lonely road too, through haunted, heartbroken countryside. It can crush you or make your spirit soar, depending on its mood, and yours. A few times, I've done it alone at night, been thoroughly spooked and sworn that I won't make the same mistake again. I do, of course, and love it.

This is my first trip to England in well over half a year, the longest I've ever stayed away from my native country. Since the first lockdown in March 2020, the Wales–England border has taken on new significance, as the two sides followed different rules and timetables to address the pandemic. For months, crossing the border, for any reason other than the absolutely essential, was *verboten*. Definitions of 'essential' proved to be highly elastic, particularly for the perennially entitled. Some English owners of Welsh holiday homes snuck over the border in the dead of night, others down country lanes and back roads like this one. A few people were caught trying to send their luggage separately by taxi or hire van.

There was no mistaking the supercharged sense of prerogative on display. In the first few weeks of the pandemic, a well-known rock star fled – *with Covid* – to his country pile in Powys, bringing family and friends from London with him, to an area then free of infection yet already desperately stretched for hospital provision. In the middle of a village near us, some second-homers snuck in at four in the morning, only to be given their marching orders the next day by a consortium of villagers. Tempers flared, old grudges were buffed to a shine and scabby wounds prised wide open. Still they bleed.

Today, as it's my first trip to England since all this kicked off, I'm committing only the lightest of border raids: a visit to Castell Bryn Amlwg, 'the castle on the prominent hill', 1,300 feet up in the Clun Forest. Founded in the twelfth century by the Normans, it is only yards into Shropshire, at the westernmost point of the entire frontier, where a scoop of England lunges deepest into Wales. Take a map, and you'll see that the border between Shropshire and Powys looks like the sideways profile of an old witch from a fairy tale. The S-shape of the jigsaw tab between Bishop's Castle and Montgomery is her hooked nose and mean mouth. To the north, the bulge around Oswestry is her prominent brow, and to the south, the Clun Forest her protruding chin, with Bryn Amlwg the hard, hairy wart at its tip. The crone is staring west, and is none too thrilled at what she sees.

Though it meanders through some of the least populated areas of southern Britain, this section of the border is an electric fence: live and potentially lethal when plugged in, but once the switch is flicked, inert and almost invisible. Right now, with everyone so twitchy in the pandemic, the gauge on the dial is rising, and there's every chance of a shock. This is a border whose significance ebbs and flows, that swims in and out of focus down the centuries, and there's no more apposite symbol of that than Castell Bryn Amlwg. Like Frankenstein's monster, it only flickered into life when power surged along the line and it once again became a key garrison, of either side. Between times, it slipped back into torpor, a forgotten corner of a far-away field.

You could easily miss it, as I have on every occasion that I've passed, dozens of times over decades. It sits low on the brow of a slope, a series of green ripples and mounds like a massive landform sculpture. Yet as I walk nearer, pulling up the hill from the stream that forms the border, it swells into view with startling clarity, and assumes a status and a size that I would never have guessed at. By the time I'm in it, I'm overwhelmed. Though no buildings remain, there's a thumping functionalism here, a hardness even in the wiry grass folds and wind-bitten hawthorns, and it's clear that this was never a place for the courtly life. Bryn Amlwg, high in the hills and with its outer walls nearly nine feet thick, was brute force.

At this border crossing, lawlessness hangs like cordite on the breeze, and seeps into everything. A century ago, there was much more of the castle to see: as well as fragments of the walls, there remained the base of a Norman keep and a later double gatehouse. It all disappeared in the 1950s. Contractors working for a Shrewsbury seed merchant, who'd bought two local farms and wanted to pave the track between them, plundered every last stone. A passer-by reported it to the police, but by the time the case came to the magistrates at Clun Town Hall too much time had elapsed for a successful prosecution.

Even the course of the border was a victim of crime. In 1691, a pedlar died – murdered, it's said – a couple of miles further north on the Kerry Ridgeway, an ancient droving track that has long been the divide between England and Wales. His death caused a dust-up between the parishes on each side of the line, for neither wanted the responsibility and expense of his burial. Eventually, goes the story, the authorities of Bettws-y-Crwyn accepted his corpse, buried him in the churchyard and placed a stone where they said that he died, some distance north of the track. Almost two centuries later when the land was being enclosed, the position of the stone was used to fix the border, giving Bettws – and the local landowner MP – some extra acres at the expense of the parish of Kerry. There's still a small hiccup in the line of the border there today.

Bettws-y-Crwyn in England *versus* Kerry in Wales; the sense of identity here is as mashed as the names. After dipping my toe into

England at Bryn Amlwg, I return a few months later and plunge into the land beyond, the Clun Forest proper. Though there are many patches of woodland, broadleaf and the dark slabs of the Forestry Commission alike, the word 'forest' refers here to its ancient status as an upland hunting ground. Despite frequent excursions along the roads and rivers around its edges, the forest is somewhere I've barely explored before, and it thrills me.

Much to my surprise, it also makes me cry. I followed the lanes up to Bettws-y-Crwyn church, one of the highest in Shropshire, sat looking down over its diffuse parish of farms, woods and fields of thin pickings. My expectations were of a single-cell barn, thickset and windswept, tucked into the corner of a gloomy cemetery. Instead, there's a grand, green avenue leading to the gate, flowers flooding the graveyard and a sense of such occasion that by the time I try the door, and find that after so many months of lockdown it creaks open and I'm embraced by the dark wood interior and musty scent of centuries, the relief punches me in the gut and tears start to fall, hot and grateful. I knew that I'd missed ambling around country churches, a favourite pastime since childhood, but not that I needed it like I needed to breathe. The tears were a long-overdue admission of that, but they were also the uncorking of a sadness that had been brewing throughout the pandemic, and had pooled into the dark corners of my psyche where I hardly dare look.

That this all came tumbling out in St Mary's, Bettws-y-Crwyn, was not just about this moment in history. It was also a response to a very specific geography, one that rouses me without fail every time: the historic districts of Wales that are now administratively in England. The Normans established the concept of the Marches, a wide and distinct buffer zone between England and Wales, an official land of neither-here-nor-there, where each country shaded into its neighbour. Four and a half centuries later, in order to bring all of Wales into the English county system, the border that we know today was defined in the Acts of Union (officially, the Laws in Wales Acts) of 1536 and 1542. Inevitably, chunks of territory on both sides ended up on the 'wrong' side of the line.

Bettws-y-Crwyn is a prime example: Welsh in name and temperament, well to the west of Offa's Dyke, yet surgically excised from its motherland by turf wars, treaties and the slow hiss of time. In the churchyard, happily ablaze with fox-and-cubs and buttercups, I meet a couple laying flowers on a grave; his grandmother's, it turns out. He grew up nearby and now lives in Kerry village, over the border, though as far as he's concerned it's *all* Welsh. Half a millennium has barely scratched the surface.

I love these displaced nuggets of old Wales: here in the moody uplands of the Clun Forest; the villages and valleys around Oswestry at the other end of Shropshire; the broad-skied and bovine Archenfield and Ewyas districts of Herefordshire; or the weird old Monmouthshire exclave of Welsh Bicknor on the banks of the Wye, opposite the Forest of Dean. Although very different, they all have a common feel, a bite. There's an appealing element of limbo, of having a foot in both camps, which I suppose matches my own.

It's not a predilection that works the other way round, though, in those places that are more spiritually English but have been marooned in Wales. The most obvious example is the Maelor, that medieval relic that pokes into Shropshire and Cheshire, trying to snuggle in between them; 'Flintshire (Detached)' as it was so beguilingly labelled on the maps of my childhood. Near Chester are a couple of others: the north bank of the Dee estuary, and the city's own suburb of Saltney. Though I find their estrangement and odd atmosphere fascinating, it's an anthropological interest rather than an emotional pull, and I'm not much minded to linger. There's a faint chippiness in the air, a kind of weary resignation that they're seen – and perhaps see themselves – as poor neighbours. They are also by definition lowland places, so easily overrun by roads and railways, pylons, industrial parks and spreading suburbs that promise proximity to the M6, HS2, Chester, Crewe, Manchester or Birmingham, but never Wrexham, Bangor or Rhyl (and who the hell ever mentions *Cardiff*?).

To someone of my perspective, a romantic who for all his protestations of adopted Welshness will never expunge nor excuse his Middle England origins, there is a clear antithesis here that says much about the dynamics of power and history: the remnants of Wales-in-England combine the best of both, and the bits of England-in-Wales the worst. Here in the forest, and in the other Welshries on the wrong side of the border, there is an untarnished light and lyricism to the Welsh identity; it has not been clipped by the tedium of administrative reality, nor weighed down by too heavy a history. It is Wales with its claws removed, pet Wales, all poets and pedigrees in oh-so-green hills, with no hint of surly pebbledash or angry graffiti in a difficult tongue. It is a nation in exile, a condition at which Wales habitually excels. Far too much, sometimes.

* * *

Heading down into town from the dark heights of its forest, Clun appears as quite the metropolis. This comes as a surprise. I've long loved the one-horse wonder of the place, its sleepiness and the sensation that you'll only ever find it at the end of a raggedy rainbow. The railway never came here and the roads are dreadful: witness the tiny fifteenth-century packhorse bridge, over which the A488 – and a constant throb of lorries and vans – has to tiptoe. At the town's May Day festival, the green man and the ice king scrap it out for prominence on the bridge, a contest always won of course by the spirit of summer. Lest things should get too capriciously pagan, everyone then goes to the meadows below the castle to race plastic ducks.

Clun is the Oniton of Forster's *Howards End*, where 'a little river whispered, full of messages from the west'; the Garde Doloreuse of Walter Scott's *The Betrothed*, 'a place strong by nature, and well fortified by art'; it is Francis Brett Young's Chapel Green, recalled for 'the quietude and sweetness of the air, the general atmosphere of ease and irresponsibility'.

Most of all, by a full country mile, it is *that* poem by A. E. Housman.

You cannot lift a teacake in the Clun valley without being politely assaulted by *A Shropshire Lad*. In the famous fiftieth poem of the sequence, the scene is set by some doggerel that Housman found in a guide book ('Clunton and Clunbury / Clungunford and Clun / Are the quietest places / Under the sun'), before he takes up the mantra and dances away with it, like a maiden aunt after a festive sherry:

In valleys of springs and rivers,
By Ony and Teme and Clun,
The country for easy livers,
The quietest under the sun.

Unsurprisingly, it has become the *de facto* motto of every local business, society or publication, chiselled into the common consciousness with a sclerosis that belies its airy origins. The words are in danger of being sucked dry of meaning – and worse, sucked dry of place too. We know that it's Clun, because we are repeatedly told so, but beyond that, we appear to have landed in generic countryside, the version that has no real identity of its own save for whatever is stamped on it.

This is not to blame Housman. He could never have foreseen that his modest little volume of verse, self-published in 1896 and with a run of just 500 copies, was destined to become a leviathan, never out of print in three different centuries. *A Shropshire Lad* has shape-shifted for every era in turn, into musical incarnations from classical airs to rap numbers, its poems quoted on *Inspector Morse*, *The Twilight Zone* and *The Simpsons*, and in novels by Alice Munro, Kingsley Amis, Dorothy L. Sayers and Chimamanda Ngozi Adichie.

In Adichie's *Half of a Yellow Sun*, for the Igbo people of south-eastern Nigeria, the short-lived republic of Biafra is their 'blue remembered hills … that cannot come again', and in that tale of the brutal 1960s uprising we see the force that lit the fuse of *A Shropshire Lad* and has kept it burning ever since. It is war. Housman's verse, aching with loss and longing, has proven to be its evergreen antidote. The book sold in its hundreds for the first few years, but then came the second Boer War, and sales began to climb. A decade later, the Great War broke out. Tucked in the kitbags and breast pockets of tens of thousands of British troops was something to remind them of just what they were fighting for: a copy of *A Shropshire Lad*, bristling with bucolic adolescence, stout country towns and muscular comrades. Some copies, it is said, stopped bullets.

The evocation of an England just slipping out of reach has long been our national narcotic, and Housman became its inadvertent pusher. Yet for all his posthumous domination of the Clun valley, there is no record of him ever having come here. He grew up in industrial north Worcestershire ('I had a sentimental feeling for Shropshire, because its hills were our western horizon,' he wrote), and as an adult lived in dusty self-denial in London and Oxford academe. Many of the poems in *A Shropshire Lad* had been written before he set foot in the county, and when he finally came, in order to 'gain local colour' of the places he was committing to verse, his perambulations brought him only as far as Ludlow, Bridgnorth and Wenlock, in its south-eastern corner. His was a Shropshire of the mind.

Yet still we flock to Clunton and Clunbury, Clungunford and Clun, armed with our Housman, using it like an *i-Spy* book to tick off its locations. We like the mix: topography so clear you can pinpoint it on an Ordnance Survey, together with a powerful sense of myth, that we are in a fold of time and space that can hold any dream we care to conjure. It's a combination that will probably one day have its own symbol on the map, and when it does, it will be dotted in greater concentration along the England–Wales border than anywhere else.

For years, I have been looking at Clun through the wrong end of the binoculars, miniaturising it, reducing it to the size of a stanza. Time in the Forest entirely changes the view. After the emotional purgative of Bettws-y-Crwyn, a steep hike along Offa's Dyke and an afternoon in a farm kitchen with Miriam, whose family have been here for generations, I descend into town – 'people call it a village, but it's always been a town to us,' she tells me – and the binoculars have flipped. I see the grain of centuries in deep-set brick, and every bead of civic swagger. The castle no longer looks like a watercolour sketch, but a dark tyrant keeping watch down the passes, and outstaring the great stone barn of the parish church, its twin fortress across the valley. I swear that the church has doubled in size since I last saw it.

In its graveyard, I follow threads of names and wonder how many are Miriam's relatives; her mother, she told me, had sixty-five first cousins in and around the town. As I look down at one grave that's swathed in fresh flowers, a man walking his dog shouts across, 'That's Dummy Lock!' I must have looked confused. 'Have you not heard of him?' I hadn't, but I soon do. William Lock was born in Churchstoke and died in Knighton, both just over the border in Wales, but he was Clun to his core. Deaf, dumb and toothless, with a love of bright clothes and the strength of an ox, he worked as an itinerant on local farms, liked to wrestle horses on the Stiperstones and terrified – but enthralled – generations of Clun children with his indecipherable shouting and stick-waving. Though the only person who could control him was the landlord of the Buffalo Inn, and that only by threatening to bar him when he acted up, the entire town kept an eye on him, and he on them.

Hundreds packed into the churchyard for his funeral in November 2000, including the local Morris men, who finished their dance around his coffin by vigorously shaking their sticks at it, in just the way that he used to do to startled tourists. Around him lie dozens of his relatives, a huge Romani gypsy clan. Many have a fiddle carved on their headstones, including one who was found dead by the road on a freezing night, still clutching his instrument.

On a quiet evening, as bats swoop through the gloom, that church-yard must get awfully raucous. By the exquisite poetry of posthumous proximity, across the path from Bill Lock is the playwright John Osborne, someone who also loved to harangue passers-by, albeit from a stage or page and usually for a very good price. He'd wanted to live in the borderlands of Wales since his earliest successes, but a full-blooded commitment to London theatre life – the first nights and fisticuffs, vintage champagne on tap, the Garrick, the groupies, the lot – kept him in the capital's avaricious orbit.

Osborne's yearning for the borderland, the acute *hiraeth*, was homage to his father, whose early death forged an anguish in him that no amount of awards, money or wives could ever quite assuage. His dad had come from Monmouthshire, and to John, his Welsh family was of totemic significance. 'Their value system was quite different,' he wrote in 1957, the year after the breakthrough triumph of *Look Back in Anger*. 'What impressed me most when I was a small boy …

was the calm that surrounded them. Not only were their voices soft, but they actually *listened* to what you were saying.' In the play, he distilled their qualities into the character of Cliff Lewis.

The move west finally happened in 1986, when Osborne was fifty-seven and on his fifth (and final) wife. They drove to Shropshire and bought The Hurst, a tumbledown Georgian pile a mile from Clun, without even bothering to commission a survey. Though their time there was relatively happy, the job of country squire one that the original Angry Young Man seemed destined to fulfil, it was plagued by ill health and money worries. In 1994, in the last few months of his life, he wrote to fellow playwright David Hare, 'I look out on the blue, remembered hills and they are saying to me, "Oh bugger off!"' He duly – and terminally – did so at 10.10pm that Christmas Eve. True to form, it's hard to imagine a logistically more awkward time to die.

In his eulogy at Osborne's memorial service the following year, Hare said that 'It is impossible to speak of John without using the word "England".' This is true; throughout his career, Osborne straddled both the visionary idealism and the flyblown, dyspeptic reality of Englishness, but it was a take that was always sharpened by his sense of Welshness. It gave him piquancy, the necessary salt for the over-boiled, post-war stodge that was his muse and torment. For the full stereo effect, Jimmy Porter needed his Cliff.

In Clun, he found the physical manifestation of this same force. He hankered not for Wales proper, the land of his father, but its edge, a leather strop on which he could hone his sense of England, scrape it up and down, sharpen it to a gleam. It suited him well to be in both countries, and neither. There are parts of the border where the divide is relatively clear, even in convoluted sections like that of the previous chapter, where the line heads in all four compass points in rapid succession. Here's England, and just there, Wales. At some points along the way, though, the border sags and sighs, stops for a breather and lets out its belt. Clun and its Forest is one such corner, a siren place that calls quietly to those who also inhabit some kind of between-scape of their own, be it familial, political, cultural – or sexual.

And there's a lot of *that* about. I first sniffed it on the Clun breeze decades ago, without quite having a name for it. I still don't. It was the smell of old oak and fresh sweat, a heady, horny fug of pheromones and promise, and I was far from the only one who caught it. A long line of sexual outlaws, from the brazen to the irredeemably broken, has beaten a path this way. Osborne was both: a serial bridegroom and bully, soppy misogynist and solipsistic man-child, with a pissed-up hatred of 'pouffs' (that word! that *spelling*!) that kept him looking, and looking, and looking again. Though the *Evening Standard* headline a month after his death – JOHN OSBORNE'S SECRET GAY LOVE – proved to be opportunistic embroidery, it wasn't tugged out of thin air. When a predatory Noel Coward asked a young Osborne over dinner, 'How queer are you?', he replied, 'Oh, about twenty per cent.'

An hour's walk from The Hurst is the house that begat the greatest bisexual borderland tale of all: Bruce Chatwin's *On the Black Hill* ('Twins – one queer, the other not', he wrote in his notebook). For two months in early 1979, Chatwin lodged in a cottage at Cwm Hall, writing every morning from seven o'clock, and after lunch, heading out on his bicycle on a tour of farms, pubs, antique shops and village libraries, picking up anecdotes and ideas for his embryonic saga. Though the story is placed on the Herefordshire/Breconshire border south of Hay, much of its atmosphere is that of the Clun valley. There are Black Hills in both. The blackest of all though was the backdrop to Chatwin's own life at the time: a marriage disintegrating as he delved deeper, and darker, into his suppressed gay side.

Of all the district's lawless traits, its allure for the illegal libido lingers perhaps the longest. Convention would have it that life was far tougher for Clun's earlier gay cheerleaders, A. E. Housman (born 1859) and E. M. Forster (1879) than it was for Bruce Chatwin (1940), but that is to make the flawed assumption that progress is a smooth, straight line. Though Chatwin was still a young man when homosexuality was finally decriminalised in 1967, the upsurge in its prohibition after the comparative *laissez-faire* of the war scorched his adolescence. Between 1951 and 1954 especially, under the vindictive eye of the new Conservative Home Secretary, David Maxwell Fyfe, prosecutions for gay offences soared, as did press and public vitriol. Paranoia spread like cancer, and under its dark cloaks so too did pederasty. In 1954, Chatwin was at Marlborough College; caught up in the fever, the headmaster initiated a crackdown, interrogating scores of boys, one at a time, about their sex lives. 'It was a dreadful time which left a good many emotional scars,' remembered Peter Ryde, a fellow Marlburian. Three years later, when Chatwin was still there, a Classics master blew his and his dog's brains out on the school playing field, after being caught in a boy's bed.

Sex and sentiment intertwine through the Clun valley like a thin morning mist. 'And, at night,' wrote Helen, the fifth Mrs Osborne, 'when the last owl is silent, there is sometimes such a deep peace that I don't quite know what it means.' She lies now by her husband's side in Clun churchyard, having outlived him by ten years. Her grave states that she was a *JOURNALIST, WIFE AND FRIEND*; his *PLAYWRIGHT, ACTOR AND FRIEND*. Despite having had so many goes at it, being a husband did not make the cut.

There I might have left it, mid E. M. Forster's 'ghosts that sigh among the alders' of Clun churchyard, were it not for a sudden discovery. Buried just behind and slap between the Osbornes is someone intimately woven into my own life. The grave of the artist Brigid Wright seems to act as a triangular counterpoint to John and Helen, hewn from the same black slate and carved with the same bold clarity. Born in 1939, the same year as Helen, Brigid died in 2000, midway between them. Her artwork, a semblance of which is seen on her headstone, filled our house 40 miles west, for she was a dear friend of Reg and George, the old couple who left Rhiw Goch to my partner and me. When I wrote about them in *On the Red Hill*, I noted Brigid had page after page to herself in their address book, for she could never settle in one place. She peers diffidently out in a few of George's photographs from the 1980s, usually accompanied by her two grinning teenage children, both about my age. One of them, I see with a lurch, was buried alongside her the best part of a decade ago.

The ghosts continue to sigh, and the sound is so very familiar. Growing up in Kidderminster, 40 miles in the other direction, I remember the local theatre making much of the fact that John Osborne had been in rep there when he began to write *Look Back in Anger*. Although the 'large Midlands town' in which it is set is principally Derby, the infinitesimal tedium of a Kiddy Sunday is there for those who know it. An emotional umbilicus stretches into these hills from that part of north Worcestershire, the county's industrial end as it scuffs into the sooty coat-tails of Birmingham and the Black Country. A. E. Housman hailed from neighbouring Bromsgrove, as did poet Geoffrey Hill, whose 1971 *Mercian Hymns* invoke Offa as

'overlord of the M5: architect of the historic rampart and ditch ... guardian of the Welsh Bridge and the Iron Bridge'.

'Before I knew anything about the psychology of Housman,' wrote Hill, 'I knew what his "Shropshire" meant to him on an intuitive level, because the Shropshire Hills were the western horizon of the village landscape of my childhood.' Me too, and – to my surprise – Bruce Chatwin. For all his Marlborough College and Sotheby's plum, he was the son of aspirational Brummies, and grew up in and around the south-west of the city, facing, *worshipping* – as did we all – the sunsets of our borderland.

Another of our locale, the author Francis Brett Young, carved a substantial career out of the link. Between the first and second world wars, when prose was at its most purple, he churned out two dozen novels, many set in a lightly fictionalised west Midlands landscape. Tilting precociously at the crown of Thomas Hardy, they were packaged as the Mercian Novels, though they had none of the dexterity or emotional depth of Hardy, and even if they had, few readers were as keen to lose themselves in a parallel Dudley or Stourbridge as they were Dorchester or Salisbury. Young was also bewitched by the borderland, and many of his novels included characters and plots that headed west from the grime in order to find 'some lost paradise':

He wanted to make a clean start in a new country. As the mists ascended, showing May Hill and Malvern, Abberley, Clee

43

and all the nearer hills of Wales, he knew that they promised freedom.

The Black Diamond (1921)

As they crossed the Severn above Bewdley, Dick underwent an odd metamorphosis. The passage of that boundary washed away from his mind all the preoccupations of the last months. He expanded and bloomed in this land west of the Severn.

Mr and Mrs Pennington (1931)

The green foothills of the Malverns rolling away into Herefordshire, and beyond them all the tumbled hills of the Marches of Gwent and Radnor. 'The March of Wales', Mr Lucton thought. The phrase was an incantation. Repeating the words for the mere relish of their sound, he was exalted and drunk with them. 'The March of Wales ... of course that's where I'm going.'

Mr Lucton's Freedom (1940)

In title, theme and timing, it was the latter novel that sang the age-old song the loudest. Published in the first year of war, and set in the last summer of peace, it was both a final hurrah for the satyric nationalism of the 1930s, the Merrie England re-enactments of Arthur Mee, H. V. Morton, Petre Mais and so many of their ink-stained ilk, and a rallying cry to stiffen sinews in the struggle ahead. Mr Lucton found his Freedom in somewhere called Chapel Green, which looked a lot like Clun. At every turn of the tale, Young evokes *A Shropshire Lad*; in the US, the book's title was *The Happy Highway*, one of Housman's best-known lines. It was an act of love and homage of course, but also, remembering the original's skyrocket sales in the Great War, a calculated attempt at getting lightning to strike twice in the same place.

In a way it did, but not as intended. *Mr Lucton's Freedom* sold very modestly, though the borderland did still produce the surprise publishing hit of the Second World War. The sixty-year-old diaries of the late Francis Kilvert, a young mid-Victorian cleric in Radnorshire and Herefordshire, were published in three volumes between 1938 and 1940. Their vivid bucolic was balm for a jittery nation, a super-saturated evocation of an era just slipping out of sight – always our favourite view. And there was no more reliable locale in which to place that than on the cusp of England and Wales. Once again, the borderland sprang to mop the national brow in its hour of need.

When war or disease is raging; when you hail from a place of perpetual, bewildering change; when your inner landscape is fractured in the most intractable of ways – then this land, this between-world, promises a lost paradise bespoke to your aching needs. The illusion of timelessness, in every era and for every purpose, is itself utterly timeless.

It is an illusion though. Housman gave voice to Clun, without ever coming here. Forster breathed sweet life into its contours, but excused both himself and his characters as only a fleeting presence. Chatwin flattered and flirted with everyone to get what he wanted, before fleeing with not so much as a backwards glance. Francis Brett Young found that his lost paradise soon curdled in the tedious heat of reality, so moved on to the next one: apartheid South Africa. With grim inevitability, that quickly soured too: 'the rising tide of colour is lapping our feet', he wrote in a 1948 letter, 'and the return of the Nationalist Government has made the coloureds truculent'.

Stand in the churchyard, just across from Dummy Locke and Brigid Wright, and there above the sighing trees you might just catch the strains of *The Lark Ascending* billowing up the valley. John Osborne is up and at it once again. In his final years, Osborne's godson Ben Walden was one of the few visitors who stayed over at The Hurst. He tells of long, drunken nights when they would 'talk and talk and talk and drink lots of champagne and *collapse*'. Even at four in the morning, Osborne liked to crank up the Vaughan Williams, Elgar or Purcell to its loudest, throw open the doors and bellow his love at the surrounding hills.

To find the centre of his identity, he had had to migrate to its outer edge. In the area's blurry lines, he found precision, a perfect fit, and though so many aspects of his life and character leave me frozen, I get that completely. I sense his heartbeat in my veins, and it quickens me. Osborne felt both spiritually Welsh and viscerally English, felt them at the very same time, yet had no truck with any artificial fusion of the two for nefarious political gain: 'nor am I a citizen of the UK', declared his alter ego Jimmy Porter in the character's 1992 reprisal in *Déjàvu*, his last play, 'that sounds like belonging to the Co-op – under-washed, under-endowed, unappealing … *un-English*'.

So many pilgrims to Clun, literary and otherwise, have looked at this landscape, these people and these places through the wrong end of the binoculars, have quite literally belittled them. Did Osborne, living here for his final decade, manage to turn them round and look properly at the town and valley? To some extent, though his view was always from the hauteur of a grand Georgian mansion. The clarity of his vision failed completely though when he looked in the mirror. His disdain for conformity was coupled with a bellicose certainty that he had always struck out alone, with no fear or favour, and damned the consequences. 'Does he have a name, or is he a *group*?' sneered one of his characters, in the unmistakable voice of its creator. Groupthink was his sworn enemy, and he was drenched in self-satisfaction at having not played that game.

Yet he *was* part of a group, one of the most powerful of its age. For decades, he was centre stage in a gilded circle of Englishmen, self-declared iconoclasts all, who lorded it over Britain's cultural landscape. They went to each other's first nights and launches, drank themselves under the table, fell over, fell out and made up, swapped wives and mistresses, walked out on their children, sacked their agents and crashed their Bentleys, and all in the full glare of the papers. They wrote often mediocre books, plays, songs, films and features about themselves and each other, mutually reviewed them in the qualities and were invited to discuss them earnestly – and endlessly – in smoky TV studios. And for the privilege of this, for being cocksure and loud, they earned a fortune.

When the tide began to turn on this pampered existence, they felt bewildered, abandoned, the victims of treachery that they came to see everywhere, and so lashed out with ever-increasing ferocity. Osborne became more of a symbol of England than he could ever have realised. Had he lived longer, it's not hard to imagine what might have filled his elegantly splenetic column in *The Spectator*: visceral hatred of Tony Blair, intemperate rants about the smoking ban, a drunken cheerleading for Brexit, perhaps even the full Farage.

Sitting outside a Clun café, enjoying a very fine home-made turmeric cake, I watch dippers skim the river by the medieval bridge. In The Square up the hill the butcher has gone and the Buffalo Inn is long closed and crumbling. This is the small town's nucleus now, by the packhorse bridge on which the green man symbolically slays the ice king every May Day, where people tuck into their Tupperware lunches by the car park packed with seniors lacing up their walking boots on the bumper of shiny electric cars. Everywhere I look, it's grey hair and white faces; almost always only white faces. I look again, and realise that it's my own reflection in the café window.

Time to head back into the hills, into the Forest, and with the literary companion we most needed all along. No one has caught Shropshire

and this yarn of borderland better than Mary Webb, the sylph who died in 1927, aged only forty-six, without ever having tasted much success. Six months after her death, a reference to her as 'a neglected genius' in a literary dinner speech by Prime Minister Stanley Baldwin ignited interest in her novels, which began to sell in some number as the new decade dawned. Ironically, her reputation was further enhanced by the sharp snark of Stella Gibbons's *Cold Comfort Farm* (1932), the wildly successful pastiche of the 'loam and lovechild' genre, of which Webb was seen as a prime exponent. The 1950 Powell and Pressburger film of her book *Gone to Earth*, starring a phosphorescent Jennifer Jones, brought her work to new generations.

Shropshire to her marrow, Mary Webb looked intently at this landscape through both ends of the binoculars, and all at the same time. She is there in the folds of the hills and the scratch of damp earth, on a sudden sunrise and a dusk breeze, dug in unobserved, watching, listening. Her descriptions of both place and people come illuminated from deep within, and none more lucid than her novel set in the Clun Forest, *Seven for a Secret* (1922). It's a voluptuous tale, centred on a remote and ancient coaching inn, the Mermaid's Rest, whose 'neighbouring fields always seemed to be tentatively asking each other's protection against the wild that lay, vast, purple, and silent, on every side'.

The inn – known also as 'the Naked Maiden', after its sign – is bought almost on a whim by Ralph Elmer, a swashbuckling stockman with a mysterious entourage. Only a couple of years after Webb's death, some strange parallel version of the story happened for real, when the Anchor Inn, high up in the Clun Forest, was bought by C. N. de Courcy Parry, for decades the author of the 'Dalesman' column in *Horse & Hound* magazine. He and a companion were hunting the wide open runs of the Forest on a baking hot day, and called at the Anchor for refreshment. 'If you want a drink,' said the landlord, 'you must buy the house', and slammed the door on them. Undeterred, de Courcy Parry pushed a cheque for £700 under the door 'and the house was ours', he wrote in his memoir. 'Two pints at £350 apiece – and well worth it, too.'

EXILE

We're back with the smell of lawlessness, sharp and coppery, raw as
a razor. Perched old and alone a couple of fields from the remains of
Castell Bryn Amlwg, the Anchor is the penultimate building in
England, where it leaches furthest into Wales. It has always set its own
rules. 'Seven Day Licence' it used to boast on the sign, in the days of
the dry Welsh Sunday; 'those who had walked and cycled up from
Newtown were very thirsty indeed', wrote de Courcy Parry. Having
sold the pub in the Second World War, he bought it back at the beginning of the 1960s, before it was transformed in the following decade
into an unlikely, but legendary, nightclub.

'It was a brilliant place for a fight or a fuck. Sometimes both,' a
friend told me. He and his gang used to wedge themselves into his
mum's Mini and grind their way up the hairpins from the Severn
valley far below. Another pal used to putt-putt his way there on an old
Vespa, praying that it wouldn't conk out in the dark and lonely forest.
He's a music obsessive, and the Anchor was the only place for 100
miles where he could see obscure punk bands fresh off the *John Peel
Show*. On other nights, the jerry-built 'dance hall' at the back was
home to middle-of-the-road favourites (Frank Ifield and Max Boyce
were regulars) or stars of the country and western scene. You didn't
need a flagon of ale to conjure up the spirit of the Wild West at the
Anchor. On the far, high edge not just of Wales and England, but of
different constabularies too, the police hardly ever bothered coming.
Security, such as it was, consisted of a couple of local farm lads as
famously hopeless bouncers.

Things became more fraught with the free festivals. Through the
1980s, the annual Cantlin Stone gathering took place under the conifer plantations a mile away, straddling the Kerry Ridgeway and the
border. One of an annual cycle of festivals for the growing number of
urban dropouts who'd taken to the road, its homegrown hippy vibe
attracted sometimes hundreds, a fair few locals included. A week of
different faces, some wacky baccy and good sport was a welcome addi-
tion to the year's calendar.

In June 1985, the scene changed for good, when 1,300 police
busted a convoy heading for the Stonehenge free festival, the biggest

of the lot. Deploying the same tactics that they'd recently used on miners in the year-long strike, the police weighed in, smashing up and burning vehicles, most of them lived in, and indiscriminately battering festival-goers, including pregnant women. Sixteen were hospitalised. On that night's *News at Ten*, ITN reporter Kim Sabido described it as 'some of the most brutal police treatment I've ever witnessed in my career as a journalist'. His was a lone voice at the time. Margaret Thatcher, and the press that worshipped her, had a new 'enemy within' – and the demonisation was total.

It filtered even into this hitherto happily lawless fold of the map. By 1991, landowners had dug trenches across the remote forestry tracks that led to the Cantlin Stone festival site, preventing access. Hundreds of festival-goers turned south to Llanbister common instead and partied there for days, fuelled by a far more audible combination of Ecstasy and techno rather than the joints and guitars of Cantlin's early years. The following summer, weeks after the vast free festival at Castlemorton, near Malvern – an unplanned event that had sent the media rabid – Llanbister common was sprayed with manure to put off anyone returning there. Draconian legislation soon followed.

Six or seven years later, as the new millennium loomed, I was camped in my van to the north of Powys, and stuck with only one listening option, BBC Radio Shropshire, which to this day appears to have a signal strong enough to penetrate mountains. There were rumours that an 'illegal rave' was being planned that weekend some-where in the county, and although it never actually happened, it was the headline news and topic of every phone-in for all three days that I was there. One councillor gleefully took to the airwaves to promise that he would be delighted personally to aim a water cannon at anyone caught rollicking within the county boundaries ('let's see 'em try and dance when they're soaked to the bone!' he cackled). Newsreaders and daytime DJs competed with each other to sound the most affronted. The unspecified (and perhaps largely fabricated) threat was seen off. Telford could sleep easy.

I never made it inside the Anchor, and it looks to be too late now. It was not for want of trying. At least half a dozen times over the years,

I stopped to see if it was serving, and it never was (it 'opens when it feels like it', said the *Daily Telegraph* in 2004, observing that if you did make it inside, 'it was not uncommon to find a hundred farmers in there after market at Knighton or Newtown, their conversation and bodies lowing and rubbing against you like the cattle they loved'). Once, a vanful of us returning from a free party somewhere in the Welsh hills pulled in, hopeful of a field for the night in which to camp and a few cold beers to calm the comedown skitters. Our driver was the most jittery of us all, so when the pub door remained resolutely locked, it was with terrible collective dread that we all climbed back into his van and slalomed off down the road towards the next option. That came some tortuous miles further on, in a village down in the Teme valley, just on the Welsh side this time.

The pub was open but the landlady looked us up and down very, very hard as we hopped from foot to foot, trying to shape-shift from bombed-out ravers to respectable tourists. A man sat by the bar forced her hand somewhat by saying, 'I've got a field you can camp in for the night,' so there was little she could do but warn us in block capitals that she would tolerate no funny business nor illegal substances, and then graciously allow us to empty our wallets into her till. And still, every time I looked up, she was glaring icily at us, waiting to pounce. 'Excuse me!' she shouted at one point across the bar. 'Are you mixing that lager and cider? Is that a snakebite?' Mumbled denials all round, and another game of pool.

Almost twenty-five years later, after quietly weeping in Bettws-y-Crwyn church, I decide to find that pub again. Normally, my recall of place is pin-sharp, so I realise how very blurry things must have been at the end of that long, lost weekend, for I can narrow it down only to a string of villages on the back road to Knighton. I've not been in any pub for well over a year, but they're tentatively reopening after the third lockdown. Some of them, that is. Many will never return.

As soon as I walk into the right pub, mask on, dipped in sanitiser, I am walloped by *déjà vu*. I look down into the bar that we filled with beery, smoky laughter and it all comes roaring back. From tentative beginnings, it turned into a riotously fun night, a party that sparked out of nowhere to engulf plenty of the pub's regulars and even defrost the landlady. 'Did that bar used to have a pool table?' I ask the barmaid through a plexiglass screen. She shrugs. 'Can you write your number down please for track and trace?' she replies, pushing a clipboard under the plastic. Her smile is tiny and tense. A couple of men, masks half-mast, sit silent on stools at the bar. Although it's summer, the place is chilly, and I sit alone in the lower bar, nursing a coke and a pounding nostalgia, for lost youth, lost friends and lost pubs too.

3.

FLOOD

/// decompose.alongside.pumps

From across the river, I watch the last cow in England, unperturbed, chewing a cud as green as baize. Her comrades are lying down – both they and the sky say that rain is on the way – but she has shambled down to the water's edge, where the Vyrnwy slides into the Severn. From the safety of the third bank, a heron eyes us both cautiously.

Down the centre of the slow, brown Vyrnwy comes the border. At this T-junction, the line takes a sharp left and for just a single, solitary mile runs along the middle of the River Severn, Afon Hafren. It then scampers south along a tiny tributary, before breaking its cover and striding across fields and hills.

Rivers make for easy demarcation lines. About half of the 160 miles of the England–Wales border runs along waterways, from the Dee in the north to the Severn in the south, via the Ceiriog, Cynllaith and Camlad, Tanat and Teme, the Wye and the Wych Brook, the Arrow, Lugg and languid Monnow. Though the border post on a bridge is a potent romantic symbol – a lonely sentry box in the morning mist, Cold War *ostalgie* forever frozen – there are downsides. Splitting domains this way ends up dividing otherwise natural brethren, pitching citizens of essentially the same city, plain or valley against each other. It teaches us that the river is a divide, when the opposite is true: it is the unifying factor in any topography, the tendrils of its watershed reaching up into the hills and gathering its flock with gentle insistence.

Neither does a river necessarily make for a tidy line. Follow the Vyrnwy the dozen or so miles upstream to Llanymynech, and there are numerous odd loops of land on the 'wrong' bank: Welsh fields orphaned in England, and vice versa. In the 500 years since the Acts of Union, the river course has changed, sometimes significantly, but the border has not. Toggle between a large-scale map and the satellite images, and you'll see the administrative divide running along oxbow lakes, some reduced to strips of trees, or fading even further into reeds and nettles, or lurking in shadows across fields, a spirit border visible only from above. It is the same with many other frontier rivers, most egregiously the Teme. For 15 miles around Knighton it is nominally the national border, but the shallow waters, sidling their way through soft pastureland, have shifted so much that they coincide for less than half of that.

Every drop of water on the border flows ultimately into one of three catchment basins, or watersheds: the Dee in the north, the Severn here in the middle, and in the south, the Wye. Each has a distinct identity that dictates the flavour of everything: agriculture to architecture and attitude, the cadences of a local accent to the intricacies of its microclimate. We overlay them with territorial claims and protestations of identity, cover them with tarmac and brick, but ultimately it means so little next to the geology or the watersheds. The rock and the water will out; will swat us aside if necessary.

In his book, *The Map that Changed the World*, Simon Winchester told the momentous tale of William Smith's 1815 geological map of England, Wales and southern Scotland, the first time our – or anyone else's – bedrock had been so thoroughly charted. Smith was born into a world in which Bibles included October 4004 BCE as the empirical date of creation; to challenge that by talking about fossils, deep time or evolution amounted to sedition. Even if its truths seem self-evident to us now, his map, so hard won, was red-hot revolutionary. On it we see such familiar cultural and political patterns emerging from the layers: the diagonal slash from The Wash to the Severn estuary that has always divided England's wealth and power; the well-drained chalk downs, ripe for arable and a big farm economy; the limestone and sandstone pasturelands whose grand churches and ruined abbeys sang of a medieval heyday; the moors, heaths and wolds that kept traditions of common land alive when everything else was being eaten by enclosure. Starkest are Smith's coalfields, coloured forebodingly black on his map but still little exploited in 1815. Overlay his geological map with one of modern income, health or voting habits, and the correlations could not be clearer.

Smith's map, and the many subsequent geological charts that have fine-tuned his initial discovery, are comfortably familiar to us now, as is their underlying concept that bedrock is destiny. We know the shapes of our skeleton, but not so well the veins and arteries that pump around it. In 2016, Hungarian geographer Robert Szucs published online dazzling images of different countries, continents and states comprised only of their rivers. Each river basin was distinct and vividly coloured, each component waterway given a width commensurate with its depth and flow, so the mother river is a jugular, its tributaries billowing out into a great frill of capillaries. The maps went viral and quickly leapt into the real world as a poster business. The lure was simple: we saw for the first time our most intimate geographies interpreted in a thrilling new way.

Available on Szucs's website are both England-only and Wales-only versions of his river maps. Neither looks right. Any England-only map appears odd at the best of times, like a severed torso, though that is perhaps because for so long we've conflated England with Britain that there's never been much call to map it as a solo entity. The shape of Wales as a distinct polity is much more readily assimilated, though not so well in this rivers version. In a fetching shade of pink, we see the beginning of the Wye in mid Wales, and its end in Monmouthshire, but with nothing in between, as if it has been swallowed by a gargantuan sink hole. Likewise, the mighty Severn, after gathering its many feeder rivers into its arms, appears to vanish over a cliff. Smaller cross-border tributaries hang in mid-air, entirely disconnected from the wider system. In this at least, the only map to make sense, geographically, culturally *and* aesthetically, is one of the whole island.

The three border watershed rivers all rise in Wales – the Severn and the Wye on the same mountain – and flow into England. With the sole exception of the Camlad that we met earlier, this is the case with every cross-border river. It is true too of so much else: minerals, metals, slate, coal, goods, people, wealth, drinking water, power, electricity and gas have all long flowed downhill, west to east, Wales to England. Here, where the cow, the heron and I all meet on opposite banks, there is a graphic symbol of that: the only bridge that crosses the Severn where it carries the border.

For something so momentous, it's pretty rickety, a massive Meccano piece straddling the mud-brown swirls. Ferns and grasses sprout through its gaps and tumble over rusty rivets; in another place, in a different context, it could be an installation or an expensive 'living wall' to brighten a commuter's morning. Here though, on the shit-spattered pastures between the villages of Crewgreen (Wales) and Melverley (England), it's a relic and perpetual worry.

A tarmac lane now crosses the bridge, though it was built for trains. This was a branch of the Potteries, Shrewsbury and North Wales Railway, or the 'Potts line' as it became affectionately known (affectionately *and* grandly ambitious: it reached neither the Potteries nor north Wales). The 1947 Bailey bridge we see today was the third to carry the railway to the Breidden hill quarries; the first timber bridge was declared dangerous in 1880, which closed the line for three decades; a further thirty years on, the winter floods of the Severn destroyed its successor. When the line finally hit the buffers in 1959, parts of the track bed, the bridge included, were repurposed as a road.

The Potts was one of so many dead-end branch lines that limped across the border, sputtering to a halt at termini on the edge of tiny towns – Presteigne, Kerry, Llanfyllin, Llangynog, New Radnor, Glyn Ceiriog, Bishop's Castle – or at quarries and mines in the hills. None has survived; indeed, most were already long gone by the time Beeching started to sharpen his axe. Each little railway was a fiercely autonomous operation, conceived in a very Victorian kerfuffle of splendiferous prospectuses and wildly optimistic projections, slathered with parochial pride and bigwiggery. Each degenerated into tinpot inconsequence, teetering bankruptcy and patched-up rolling stock that puffed up and down the line a few times daily, at the speed of a moth. Ivor the Engine coupled with the Titfield Thunderbolt, and spawned a dozen spidery offspring up and down the backwaters of the border.

These railways were an encore of the streams as they trickled out of the Welsh hills, snuck across the border and washed down into the plains of England. Everything has gone that way, not just goods and people, but also our very sense of self. This has been the case for so long that we assume it to be the natural order of things, rather than centuries of political priority. 'It is as though the British Isles are tilted permanently to one corner – the southeast corner, bottom right, where London stands seething upon the Thames,' wrote Jan Morris in a 1980s essay about driving across Europe from her home in north-west Wales. 'Everything slithers and tumbles down there, all the talent, all the money …'

* * *

Even though it looks much like any other slick brown river, swirling its way towards a distant sea, I'd recognise the Severn anywhere. I've known it all my life, grew up alongside it, went to school on its bank and now live just beyond its source. Finding it here is a treat, like meeting a dear old friend, and we fall into a comfortable side-by-side along the bank for the single mile where the river and the border coincide. As I pitch along, over broken stiles and under billowing skies, I try and work it out: just what *is* that familiarity? This stretch of the Severn at Melverley is somewhere I've never been before, but I know it instinctively. I know the river's ice-cool balance of poise and power, feel the deep tug of its placid smile, yet understand full well that it can – and it will – be goaded when needs be to rise and overwhelm these meadows.

The Severn floods so prodigiously that it has become an article of faith, even a totem of identity: 'Some are of the opinion', wrote Daniel Defoe in 1726, 'that the very water of the Severn, like that of the Nile, impregnates the valleys, and when it overflows, leaves a virtue behind it, particularly to itself; and this they say is confirm'd, because all the country is so fruitful.' The wide scoop of the floodplain runs in a fertile swathe across four counties, and affords its people – us, *me* – a quiet sense of kinship. At any point on the long loop from Pumlumon to Gloucester, in Upton or Newtown, Wroxeter or Worcester, we recognise, we belong.

If there is a danger of this tipping into ugly sentiments of superiority, or worse, then the Severn's glorious ordinariness is the best corrective. Walking these few fields, first on the English bank and then the Welsh, confirms it. The ramshackle bridge sets the scene for a palpably Severnside vista: cattle and buttercups, a few solitary fellas fishing, a caravan park and a shiny cluster of brand-new glamping pods, but also raw scars of quarrying, crumbling sandstone retaining walls, a boarded-up pub, blocked paths, mysterious aerials, scratty wire fences and abandoned farm machinery. The Thames this is not, and thank the goblins of the west for that. There's no Hampton Court, Greenwich, Westminster or Windsor along the Severn; the big houses, such as they are, keep a wary distance from the water's edge and are largely owned by parvenu Brummies. Henley-on-Thames would never hang out with Stourport-on-Severn. Oxford would give Shrewsbury five minutes before remembering an urgent Zoom call with Harvard and Dubai.

When I decided to move to Wales in the first spring of the new millennium, it was to Llanidloes, the first town on the Severn, that I initially went house-hunting. It seemed like a safe place to land, where the river rushes in off the forested hills and chatters through town like a crocodile of kids on a school outing. I thought that it might be the place to marry my old and new lives, hold them in some sort of sustainable balance, and that the river would be the chord to bind them. Could it be the best of both? There were the stern grey chapels and half-timbered crucks of picture-book Wales, but also the solid Severnside cottages of slate and blood-red brick, the kind that I had known all my life. I went to look, and though I had a fine time in the town's many pubs, met plenty of simpatico souls, and checked out a few of the places available to rent, something wasn't quite clicking. Only when a man said to me in the pub – and with some considerable pride – that he'd lived in 'Lanny', as he called it, for more than ten years and still didn't know any Welsh people, did the penny drop. For too many, this was an exclave of Englishness, like the walled towns of Edward I in the Middle Ages. I wanted Cymru, not a simulacrum. I supped up, left town and headed over the mountains.

Walking both banks at Melverley, that memory re-surfaces, and it takes a moment to work out why. I'm trying to focus on the border, tease out its shadows, but here, there seem to be none. The river is the only feature that counts, and for all the comfortable familiarity of its shapes and colours, even its faintly meaty smell, I cannot ignore its historic power as a conduit into Wales, a route of invasion, from the Romans to the dreamers. This is the identity that trumps all others.

On its website, a nearby B&B on the Powys side of the river tells us that 'there is much to see and do in Shropshire', and locates itself in the county; the only hint that it might actually be elsewhere comes in admitting that they have to adhere to Welsh government Covid regulations. Their stated style is 'cottagecore', an Instagram-fuelled décor of turbocharged rusticity, for people who wish they could live forever in their childhood doll's house. All swirls, curls and bunting, flowers and flounces, it recycles the nearby aesthetic of Laura Ashley, but amplifies it so artlessly as to makes her look practically minimalist. Less than half a mile down the road is another pot-pourri of chintz and gingham, a café that calls itself a 'Vintage Tea Room and Pie Parlour', offering sugar-mountains of cake with, ironically, mock ration books as labels.

This pic 'n' mix of histories – Victorian, Edwardian, Thirties, wartime – is a style that has engulfed white England over the last twenty years, and nowhere more than in its post-industrial regions. It's a look that's rife the whole length of the Severn, a good match for its warehouses and lock cottages, a deathbed chime of long-gone metal-bashing, and homage perhaps to memories of school trips to Ironbridge. While the girls glug Prosecco in cottagecore grottoes, their menfolk are having beards tweaked and 'taches trimmed at the

WOTHERING & HEPPLEWHITE GENTLEMAN'S GROOMING EMPORIUM (Est. 2017). We seem so much happier living in a museum.

The trouble really comes when we try. I know the Severn intimately, love it fiercely and feel it flowing through every vein, but something lurking beneath its inscrutable surface alarms me greatly. Like the river's floods, it's a force that's rising with increasing frequency, and potency.

*　*　*

Though the defined border coincides with only one of the Severn's 220 miles, it is a frontier river from source to sea. Stretches of it have served to define borders ephemeral – customs, tradition, language – and borders literal but long gone: tribal divisions, Roman legions, Marcher lordships, medieval kingdoms, ecclesiastical sees, aristocratic estates and political hegemonies. Had Owain Glyndŵr succeeded, and the kingdom divided according to his Tripartite Indenture with Mortimer and Percy, the Severn would have been the eastern boundary of his independent Wales, its great county towns of Shrewsbury, Worcester and Gloucester fulfilling their destiny as true frontier cities, where two nations meet, trade and tipple. And where they sometimes come to blows.

Every era has its battle scars at the Severn's edge. Nowhere is the palimpsest so acutely present, clustered like re-creations in a living history museum, as it is along the eastern bank of the river at Montgomery. Oldest is the massive Iron Age hillfort of Ffridd Faldwyn, hunkered high above the valley on the cusp of two tribal territories. Down below, on the flat fields by the river, are the banks of a Roman fortress, from where the troops sallied out to defeat Caratacus on that fateful day in 51 CE. In one corner of the fort, there is evidence of a substantial ninth- or tenth-century Saxon hall; intriguing when you consider that it is a mile or so to the 'wrong' side of what was then a fairly new Offa's Dyke. A couple of fields away is the Hen Domen, a motte-and-bailey castle built by the first of the

Norman lords immediately after their conquest. In 1223, the English crown decided to replace it with a far sturdier stone fortress on a nearby crag, and to build a walled town beneath it. It took the Norman motte's name, Montgomery.

Each defensive stronghold was there to watch the river, at a very specific and vulnerable point. Though it's now an obscure clearing below a sewage treatment plant, the shallow crossing of Rhyd Chwima (often anglicised as Rhydwhyman), 'the swift ford', was always the most incendiary flashpoint on the middle border. For a handful of decades in the mid-thirteenth century, it was the fulcrum of all English–Welsh diplomacy, a watery limbo land with no vantage points for ambush, a suitably neutral place to exchange hostages, negotiate truces and sign accords.

During the long reign of Henry III (1216–72), the ford was used regularly as a rendezvous, most notably on the day of Michaelmas, 29 September 1267, when the Treaty of Montgomery was signed there. With attendant heralds and hullaballoo, including a future Pope as Vatican envoy, Llywelyn the ruler of Gwynedd gave homage (and 20,000 marks) to the king, and in return was officially named as the Prince of Wales. It was the first time that the Welsh nation as a discrete polity had been defined and named, the zenith of Llywelyn's ambition. To that end, it remains the occasion around which much modern Welsh historiography revolves, an all-too-rare moment of success and unity, a touchstone of identity, of purpose and potential.

In September 2017, to celebrate the 750th anniversary of the treaty, a re-enactment was staged at the river's edge. The principal roles were played by strangely apposite updates of the originals: the papal envoy, the chief financier from afar, by a Powys county councillor; King Henry by a more lowly member of Montgomery town council; Prince Llywelyn by the grants officer of a Welsh language agency. Children from the Welsh-medium primary school in Newtown played Llywelyn's attendant troops; Henry's were portrayed by pupils from two local English-medium primaries. All sides came together that night for a banquet in Montgomery's diminutive town hall, and the next day at the castle there was a medieval fayre that included a mock battle, staged by one of the very many military re-enactment groups found along the borderlands. Describing the celebrations as 'magnificent', the *Shropshire Star* reported that 'among the most popular activities were the skirmishes where Norman knights were set upon by the Welsh forces and had to fight to the mock death'.

Far more haunting is Rhyd Chwima's other date with destiny, just five years and four months later. There'll be no re-enactment of that, for it is the absolute antithesis of the drums and trumpets, flags and banners of the Treaty of Montgomery; a day of absence and anger that set into motion a chain of events that cascades down to the present. King Henry had died two months earlier, and Llywelyn was commanded to appear at the ford in order to pay homage to his son, the new king, Edward I. Though Edward was still away on the Crusades, his attendance *in absentia* was perfectly acceptable. Llywelyn's was not.

Picture the scene: a freezing Friday in January 1273. Though the days are midwinter short, this one still dragged. At the Severn's edge from daybreak are the king's plenipotentiaries, the abbots of Haughmond, near Shrewsbury, and Dore, near Hereford. News of their arrival has reached local ears, for the ford is big business these days, but as soon as locals come to take a gawp, they are shooed away by the abbots' henchmen. The day wears on, and with it, the growing, gnawing certainty that they are on a fool's errand. Horses stamp and whinny impatiently, snorts of vapour curling into the cold air. All eyes are fixed on the Welsh bank opposite, for any sign of life, but it never comes. Occasionally, one of the party thinks they hear something – approaching hooves perhaps, maybe shouting – but it is only ever crows circling the oaks above them, or a shiver of wind across the exposed plain, or the shrill of the river as it roars over shale. Eventually, the thin daylight slowly dies, and mist begins to pool in the hollows. The ghosts are gathering; the day is over. He's not coming, and the consequences will be mighty. After so many hours of pent-up inertia, there's a sudden flurry of fury, as the party turns and gallops across frozen fields, to the blazing safety of the new castle on its rock, to civilisation.

That winter's day three-quarters of a millennium ago was the beginning of the end for Wales's brief and tentative autonomy. Though he had ample good reason to be cautious, Llywelyn continued to break the deal, refusing to pay homage on other occasions and failing to show up for Edward's coronation. To the new king, already a far less accommodating ruler than his father, it was all the provocation he needed to crack down hard.

After his no-show at the ford, Llywelyn began construction of a new castle and town at Dolforwyn, 5 miles upriver, on his side of the Severn. When Edward objected, Llywelyn retorted that he did not need royal consent to build on his own turf. In response, Edward hired pirates to kidnap Llywelyn's wife, attacked Wales and besieged Dolforwyn until the garrison collapsed. As the castle crumbled, Edward began a massive fortress-building project encircling Llywelyn's shrinking lands in north Wales. His 'iron ring' – brand-new castles at

Flint, Rhuddlan, Builth and Aberystwyth, and later, so as to turn the screw even tighter, at Conwy, Caernarfon, Criccieth, Harlech and Beaumaris – was then the grandest fortification programme in history.

Though the ford at Rhyd Chwima continued in use into the nineteenth century, its place on the political map evaporated almost overnight as Edward I's new power bases grew. Having been born on the frontline, Montgomery settled into its new life as a bit of a backwater, a role it has fulfilled with aplomb ever since. There was a last sting in the tail to come, though. With grim symmetry, it was from Montgomery castle that the troops were despatched on another winter's day, in 1282, to corner and kill Llywelyn as he attempted to rally his people in Breconshire. His head was removed, taken to the king and placed on a stake as a trophy outside the Tower of London. Within a year, it was joined by the head of his brother Dafydd. Even though he had turned against Llywelyn and allied himself with the English, first with Henry and then Edward, he was shown no mercy, having latterly returned to the native fold. After a show trial in Shrewsbury, Dafydd was dragged to the scaffold by a horse, then hanged to the point of near death, disembowelled alive, his entrails burned, and then quartered and decapitated. Parts of his corpse were despatched for display in some of the larger English cities, and his head went to London, where it was paraded with that of his brother through the streets, both clad in ivy crowns. Even by medieval standards, this was brutal stuff. The Welsh clearly succeeded in touching the rawest of English nerves.

Still today, I get glimpses of the thirteenth century peeping through the cracks of modern *realpolitik*. A nominally autonomous legislature, regularly reminded of its subservience, threatened with extinction and unceremoniously slapped down if it inches beyond its remit … what is devolution but Llywelyn's principality reminted for the twenty-first century?

In the early days of the National Assembly for Wales, even at a time of relative political harmony and both governments in London and Cardiff being of the same political hue, the old dynamics lurked just below the smooth surface, and occasionally seeped through. Before the institution had even met, Tony Blair responded to the Plaid Cymru leader in the House of Commons with a withering slap-down that said even more in tone than it did in content: 'We give him an assembly in Wales, and he still complains … It would be good once in a while to get a bit of gratitude.' A quarter of a century later, with intractable hostility and implacable ideological opposition between the two administrations the norm, there are turf wars over every area of policy, daily detonations of blame and a growing number of elected Conservatives – thus far mainly in England, but that would change in an instant given the right circumstances – calling for devolution to be rolled back, even abolished altogether. Blair as Henry III, a federalist undone by his barons, made way for the era of Boris Johnson as Edward I, the bellicose English supremacist, cheered on by a punch-drunk court.

As for today's Royals, they go where they're told. On the day that I'm writing this, there is a box in the corner of my computer screen broadcasting a livestream of the Queen in Cardiff, as she performs the official opening of the sixth session of the National Assembly (or Senedd, as it is now named). Unlike the annual state opening at Westminster, there is no constitutional imperative for the monarch to be there, and no limousine in the cortège dedicated solely to transporting their crown, but to give the impression that it is an occasion of real import, there are heralds, bugles and curtseys, and most out of kilter in a breezy Cardiff Bay of chain bars and restaurants, there is a full twenty-one-gun salute. At every bang, a *wooooh!* erupts from the modest crowd of well-wishers, and the windows of Nando's rattle a little.

Elizabeth II attended all six such occasions since the institution's inception in 1999. Charles, her heir, always accompanied her – it is, after all, probably in the otherwise brief job description for the Prince of Wales – and this last time a distinctly unamused Camilla was commanded to join them. It looked tortuous. Amid the high gothic camp of the Palace of Westminster, all this kind of flummery fits a treat, like a pack of playing cards come riotously to life, the full opiate rush of *Alice in Wonderland*. In the sleekit modernism of the Senedd, however, a building that does an excellent impression of a Scandinavian regional airport, it looks so forced, so incongruous, so *limp*.

In modern times, perhaps the only royal occasion to have looked even half at home in Wales was the 1969 Investiture of Charles as its titular prince. In the stone cauldron of Caernarfon castle, the theatrical pageant was presented as if it had been passed untouched down the centuries, directly from Longshanks himself. In fact, it was only the second such event. The first was in 1911, when the future Edward VIII was invested in a ceremony cooked up by David Lloyd George, then the ambitious Chancellor of the Exchequer, who also happened to be the MP for Caernarfon.

To be fair, the wily old goat could stretch some claim of provenance back to Edward I, and to Caernarfon. In the wake of Llywelyn's death, Edward had realised the political potency of the title of Prince of Wales, so appropriated it for his oldest son, and the oldest sons of all English monarchs to come. To further flatter the conquered Welsh that they were being treated heroically, the design of his new castle, the pearl in his iron ring of fortresses, echoed the architecture and ambition of the Roman Empire, specifically the great walls of Constantinople. True too that his son, the future Edward II, was born at this grand new castle, though there is no evidence that Edward duped the Welsh by promising them a prince 'borne in Wales and could speake never a word of English'. That was the invention of an historian three centuries later, though it was still relayed as hard, gleeful fact by my history teacher at school in Worcester forty years ago. My dad had been taught about savage Welsh bogmen, perpetually lurking and itching to pounce, while we were given them as easily bought off, the butt of a joke.

Despite its proximity, both physically and historically, that was the one and only time that Wales *ever* featured in our history lessons. We were never shown the stained-glass window – 200 yards away! – in Worcester cathedral, commemorating Prince Llywelyn's marriage there. We knew Hastings and Agincourt, Trafalgar and Waterloo, but not that the armies of Owain Glyndŵr and Henry IV had their week-long stand-off, the apex of the fifteenth-century Welsh uprising, ten minutes up the road at Abberley. Again and again, we learned about Worcester's fidelity to the Royalist cause in the Civil War, but nothing about its place in the March, or the border wars, or the string of settlements with Welsh-origin names along the Teme valley immediately to the city's west. Any mention of Bewdley came with a reminder that the name was a corruption of the French *beau lieu*, the beautiful place, but I never once heard it said that Malvern came from the Welsh *moel fryn*, the bald hill. Our eyes, and our young minds, were always turned east.

Of the twenty-two English Princes of Wales, the last incumbent, as well as being the longest in post, was the most assiduous, though it's not been much of a contest. Charles spent a term at Aberystwyth in the run-up to his Investiture in order to learn enough Welsh for the ceremony, and has shown some empathy for the country and its culture, particularly in its rural incarnations. Since 2007 he has kept a Welsh house, a first for an English royal, and used it as the base for occasional visits to his 'principality'. It has to be said though that it is mainly let out as holiday cottage accommodation, and that it only came about in the first place because his previous arrangement, to use Powis Castle as a sporadic Welsh sanctum, came to an abrupt end when the devoutly religious Earl of Powis refused to let him bring Camilla to stay before they were married.

Fewer than half of Charles's predecessors as Prince of Wales even deigned to visit the land that gave them their title. One who did really shouldn't have bothered. Just east of Melverley, the border peels away from the Severn to cross the old road from Shrewsbury. There by the side is a massive oak tree, a commemorative plate in the wall at its feet. This is the Prince's Oak, planted in 1806 to mark the only occasion in his fifty-seven-year tenure as Prince of Wales that the future George IV, that eternal playboy, was 'introduced to his Principality', as the plaque has it. The briefest of introductions it was too, a quick nod to this outstretched finger of Montgomeryshire, before he and his entourage galloped back into the ample bosom of regency England. For all the brevity of its origins, the tree has flourished in its royal status. Tall, proud and straight, with wide boughs and a plush canopy, it holds your gaze and would have the firmest of handshakes – if you could only touch it, that is, for it is locked in a fussy little enclosure of wall and railings. Like most royal offspring, it is imprisoned in plain sight and looks in dire need of a hug.

All along the frontier, the royal family crops up in the oddest of places. Through the twentieth century, the nearest thing to a Welsh royal residence was a railway siding at the western end of the Severn Tunnel, inches over the border, where they'd park the royal train for the night when their majesties were visiting south Wales. For Elizabeth II's 1953 coronation, the Forestry Commission planted three woods – at Monmouth, Knighton and near Welshpool – to spell out the letters ER, vast arboreal tattoos of loyalty stamped along the border as both order and incantation. Like the lonely Prince's Oak or the forgotten ford of Rhyd Chwima, these once-sharp pinpricks of royal authority are fading fast.

The area around Melverley and the Prince's Oak is where Wales pokes furthest into Shropshire, and the hills have retreated to an uncharacteristically polite distance. It doesn't feel quite right, as though a mountain bandit has been coaxed out into open country, and never to his advantage. A prominent Welsh nationalist politician tells the story of once canvassing here, and finding himself in the yard of a border farm. A Severnside farmer, rarely the most loquacious company, sucked impassively on his pipe as he let the MP set out his stall for a good ten minutes, before grinding to an uncharacteristic halt.

The farmer, as solid and red as his Georgian farmhouse, eventually broke the silence. 'You see those hills?' he asked, pointing his pipe towards the distant purple humps of the Clwydian and Cambrian ranges.

'Yes …' said the politician, a little too eagerly, as if this might presage a real conversation. 'Yes, yes, I do.'

Another pause.

'Well then, why don't you fuck off back to them?' said the farmer, and turned on his heel.

4.

FIREBREAK

/// coiling.packing.fermented

'It was pretty intimidating, at first. For a good few days, I was on the phone constantly. Dozens of them calling, from all over the world – America, Australia, Europe. And with no respect for time – Sunday night, someone rang me.' Siân Whiteoak, the secretary of Llanymynech golf club, is recalling the crazy few days in May 2020, when the first Covid-19 lockdown was coming to an end. The UK government, responsible for the rules in England, had given golf clubs a date to reopen. The devolved Welsh government had not. With fifteen holes in Wales, two in England and one straddling both countries, Llanymynech's dramatic golf course, spread over the summit of a limestone crag, found itself as an unexpected frontline, and global headline. 'All of a sudden, World War Two,' sighs Siân.

Until then, she says, their status was 'just a novelty', something to pop in the marketing brochures: 'Europe's only dual-country course', they sang; 'tee off in one country, putt down in another'. An unexpected by-product of all the publicity was learning that this wasn't actually true. 'A course in Scandinavia got in touch, can't remember where,' says Siân with the hint of a glare (I look it up; it's a club split between Sweden and Finland. Aside from the obvious difference that these are proper sovereign states, with Olympic golds and Eurovision *nul points* alike, they are also in different time zones, so that the fairway that spans the border offers 'the longest hole-in-one in the world', taking a full hour and a handful of seconds). 'Well, never mind,' she continues, 'we just changed the publicity to "the only dual-country course in the United Kingdom".'

This kerfuffle at the end of that first Covid lockdown seems almost quaint now. Days after the world's press were harassing Siân, the story erupted that the UK Prime Minister's chief adviser had broken the rules. On a beautiful late May day, he was hauled in front of the cameras in the Downing Street rose garden and forced into a graceless justification of his actions. It was the moment that the Covid consensus shattered, and for good. The border began to show real teeth.

That autumn, when the Welsh government decided to go it alone and impose a two-week 'firebreak' lockdown, all hell broke loose. The London media seemed to take it personally. From topical comedy shows to engorged tabloid editorials, the Welsh government, and First Minister Mark Drakeford in particular, became the object of everything from haughty condescension to undisguised loathing. Much focused on the decision, after lobbying by smaller retailers forced to close, to ban supermarkets from selling 'non-essential' goods. People were enraged by footage of fenced-off aisles, and 'Do Not Cross' tape stretched over kitchenware displays and clothing. In Bangor, one man was filmed rampaging around Tesco, shouting 'Rip the fuckers off!' as he stripped the tape and plastic sheeting. Nearly 70,000 signed a petition against it, the largest ever presented to the Senedd. Scenting political opportunity, the opposition Welsh Conservatives positioned themselves loudly against the measure. Their health spokesman tweeted sixty times in the first four days against it, in tones of rising apoplexy. The policy was, he thundered, a 'socialist's wet dream'.

A week later, Boris Johnson had to announce live on Saturday-night television that, in an (ultimately doomed) attempt to 'save Christmas', England was also having to go into immediate lockdown. Tweets were hastily deleted, history swiftly rewritten. Yet all the UK administrations had received the same unambiguous scientific advice: the only hope of stemming a fast-accelerating second wave of Covid, months before the appearance of a vaccine, was to instigate a 'circuit breaker', a short, sharp shock, a firebreak. Wales did, England did not, and in that one schism can be found so many of the cross-border differences – political, pragmatic and temperamental – that the pandemic has so remorselessly illuminated between the two countries.

At almost every turn, the Welsh government acted more cautiously than the UK administration, acting on behalf of England. In the first year of the pandemic, through the first and second waves, the strategy bore fruit, for there were markedly fewer excess Covid hospitalisations and deaths in Wales. Since then, and the arrival of the vaccines, the numbers have evened up, as have the restrictions. Yet still, a difference remains, a clear and palpable divide that has taken us all by surprise.

I had the conversation countless times with neighbours who travelled to England in that first year and a half: how chaotic it had seemed, with an undertow of resentment, even anger, and a reckless disregard for the rules, especially around masks and distancing. Some found it terrifying, and vowed to stay put in future. Some found it both alarming *and* appealing. I get that. We love to return to the soft cocoon of Wales, back to our well-meaning nanny statelet, but how intoxicating it was to take a walk on the wilder side, feel our blood flow faster, the electric pulse of the streets, to inhale the freedom to shop or sup or just *be*.

How swiftly, how *obediently*, the two sides of the line fell into character. Without consulting a map or sign, you could pretty much trace the border by clocking the behaviour in the towns and cities close to the line, on either side. As a resident of a Gloucestershire village put it to the *Guardian*: 'Our nearest supermarket is in Monmouth, and even though it's only a ten-minute drive … you're very aware you're in Wales. There are fewer cars and people, even in that very short distance. The atmosphere is very different.'

The difference manifested politically. At the beginning of 2020, the Yes Cymru campaign for Welsh independence had 2,000 members. By the end of the year in which the border had hardened so unexpectedly fast, there were 16,000, and the possibility of secession had moved from the esoteric fringes right into the mainstream. Not, though, on the breezy greens of Llanymynech golf course. Secretary

Siân Whiteoak assures me that 'the Welsh north of Merthyr have never been happy with the Welsh government anyway. I don't think Mark Drakeford's ever been north of Merthyr Tydfil, has he? That's what most people think round here.' She was more impressed with their Conservative MP. Hard on the heels of the controversy, he came to see them, and said that at the start of the pandemic the choice had been made whether to treat Covid as a civil contingency issue or one of public health. 'If they'd chosen to go down the civil contingency route, then it would have been done on a national basis. They decided to go down the public health route, so it was a devolved issue. Lesson learned.' I put it to her that many people on the Welsh side of the border have been glad to be there, that they have felt, whether justified or not, safer in Wales. 'Well yes,' she replies, 'some of the older folk do say that.'

As I leave her to go and explore the 160 acres of the course, her use of the word 'national' echoes in my head. To Siân, and to many others on both sides of the border (a number that increases markedly the further up the age demographic you go), it will only ever mean one thing: British. So freighted with history and emotion, 'national' is one of those words that seems carved out of stone, unyielding and permanent. It's anything but. If not quite a mirage, then it is certainly a projection, spun out of whatever light is shone upon it at any given moment. The challenge is to see where that light, and more importantly its shadows, might yet fall in the coming years. It cannot, will not, be stilled.

As I stride across the clipped fairways, combed by lines of poplar and birch, the sun is streaming down, and today the shadows could not look more benign. The views, too, brim with gold, over the floodplains of Shropshire and the mottled hills of Wales. From the clubhouse, particularly after an hour in the bar, it might look like one contiguous landscape, all of the same flavour and flag, but anything more than the most cursory of glances says otherwise. There facing you is a sweeping panorama of the upper Severn valley. Five separate hills, each topped with an Iron Age fort, sit in the immediate view, and down there too are castles, fortified churches, turrets, dungeons and defiles, radar stations, army bases and the furthest point of the

Second World War command stop line from London. All the front-lines are here.

At the twelfth hole, perched heroically on the edge of a cliff, a topo-scope tells me that I'm 218 metres up, and that it is 9 miles to Welshpool, 155 to London and 3,986 to the Augusta National golf course in Georgia, due west, beyond Snowdon. At the famous fourth, I sit on the commemorative stone bench with a plaque at either end: 'Drive in Wales' and 'Putt in England'. It's damp and uncomfortable and I have only the vaguest idea of what they mean.

Siân's open affability, the course's spectacular setting and the radi-ant autumn day all combine to soften my customary antipathy towards golf, but even now that I'm in my fifties I'm still clearly not of the clan. On three separate occasions, men of a particular bearing shout at me 'Are you lost?', to which I just smile and wave and call back, 'No, not at all, thank you!', and bustle on my way. After an hour of faintly frosty interactions, even the sunshine is cooling, and I'm surprised by the leap of joy when I spot stomping over the tidy lawns a party of children and their teachers, all kitted out in hard hats and truly filthy overalls. *Ogof Llanymynech*, of course! The cave! For deep in the heart of the golf course is a gaping hole in the limestone, a prehistoric portal in the middle of the Pringle shop: the entrance to a vast subterranean labyrinth. The national boundary is not the only frontier running through this rock.

Everything in Llanymynech appears to be on the brink of some-thing else. Below the golf course, the cliffs, stacked so high in horizontally bedded layers, trumpet their quarrying heyday, the bang-ing, shouting and clanking, the boom of explosions and crash of rockfall, the heat, and the dust and the danger. Everywhere you go, there are ghost wharves, truncated sidings, tunnels and inclines – one English, one Welsh; pits, paths, nuggets and remnants; cinder tracks, scars and humpback bridges over thin air. So present is that past that its silent encore aches with poignancy, a hush only heightened by the wintry flute of the jackdaws that nest here in their thousands.

This is no museum, though. In the village at the foot of the rock the border streaks down the main street, only adding to the hotch-potch that is Llanymynech. The former Lion Hotel, its front lounge in Wales and back bar and toilets in England, was always the go-to location for television crews doing a story, any story, on the border. Although long boarded up, there's no shortage of other drinking options: the Bradford Arms and the Cross Keys a few doors apart on the English side of the street, or the Dolphin Inn 50 yards away in Wales. The Indian and Chinese takeaways are Welsh; the chip shop English. More predictably, St Agatha's parish church, a Victorian confection, is in England, while a street away in Cymru is the Ebenezer Presbyterian Chapel ('OF WALES [ENGLISH]' says the sign, a little unhelpfully).

From the golf course media storm of the first lockdown, every single Covid cross-border rumpus mined precisely the same seam. Headlines were always about FURY, FRUSTRATION and CONFUSION. Instead of taking the time to illuminate their viewers about evolving regulations and different jurisdictions, TV news bulletins instead overflowed with vox-pops where journalists roamed shopping centres to prod people into saying how angry or bewildered they were. From the many radio phone-ins on the matter, you could be forgiven for thinking that almost the entire population runs either a caravan park near Rhyl or a border village pub.

Even here in Llanymynech, it didn't quite wash. 'Locally, people just get on with it, I think,' Siân at the golf club tells me. 'One of our members is the landlord of the pub that's in Wales [the Dolphin], bless him, and he was having to watch everyone going into the pub over the road. It didn't cause any animosity, though.' Conversations with other residents confirm the same; the 'confusion' was largely the creation of those with a particular story to frame. Even after eighteen months of the pandemic, with everyone rubbed increasingly raw, the only hint I see of grit is the oversized sign in the doorway of the village post office, erected so that customers have no option but to edge round it as they enter:

Welcome
you STILL have
to wear a

MASK
in the shop.
It is the law in Wales.
Thank you / Diolch ♥

A string of Welsh flags along the bottom underlines the point, and makes it almost – *almost* – celebratory.

* * *

Eleven days before the Scottish independence referendum of September 2014, *The Sunday Times* published a poll that had the Yes campaign in the lead. It was a hell of a shock: only a month earlier, Yes had been twenty points behind, and this first poll to show them pulling ahead blew the campaign sky high. In the ensuing spasm of shock, for just one skittering moment, the curtain fell away and gave us a brief and thrilling glimpse deep into the innards of the United Kingdom.

After all we'd been led to believe, we might have expected to see there a sleek and streamlined super-computer, humming efficiently, attended by a legion of purposeful people in bright white coats. In reality, we saw a startled old fella, nearing retirement and halfway through his lunchtime pasty, frantically tugging levers on a massive, clanking old machine and thumping every one of its Bakelite buttons. It was, though, just about enough to get the message out, and bang on cue, banks began muttering darkly about relocation, oil companies of collapse, supermarkets of higher prices and commentators of armed border guards. The Queen's severe displeasure was leaked; the terrorist threat raised. Unionist politicians and media painted themselves as brave, browbeaten underdogs, speakers of truth to intractable power – even though they comprised 635 out of the 650 MPs, 29 of the 30 UK and Scottish newspapers and almost the entire broadcast media.

For that split second, the full-beam glare was dazzling, and though it didn't light the path to an immediate Scottish secession, it shone a devastatingly clear shaft into some of our dustier, more inscrutable corners. The edifice of the UK was revealed to be tottery and leaking, in urgent need of overhaul, if not complete reconstruction, but in the adrenaline rush of the ten-point majority No vote the following week, that was quickly forgotten. And then came the wrecking balls of Brexit and Covid.

There will be another Scottish vote, sooner or later, and who knows, perhaps one in Wales too. They are very different prospects. With its own distinct political, legal and education systems, Scotland has always been semi-detached from the mechanics of the UK. Glasgow and Edinburgh are both well over 300 miles from London; the vast majority of the Welsh population is within an hour of Bristol, Birmingham, Manchester or Liverpool. Even the borders themselves are wholly different. That between England and Scotland cuts across a narrow neck of the island, and through a very thinly populated countryside. It is like the groove baked into a wheel of shortbread, to be cleanly and clearly snapped apart. If the Welsh borderland is a sweet treat, it is a moist slab of bara brith, half-and-half between a cake and a bread, invariably delicious but often a bugger to slice.

Even so, this border did once demand that its people decide on which side they belong. Parallel to the struggle in Ireland, there was in the late Victorian age growing pressure for some kind of Home Rule for Wales too. Wales-only legislation on the 'dry' Sunday was one result, so too the disestablishment of the Church of England in Wales. The Anglican church – land-owning, English speaking, Tory voting – was fast losing numbers to the Welsh-speaking nonconformist chapels, brimful of tenant farmers and workers who largely voted Liberal (and soon Labour). The divide between English and Welsh cultures was stark, and although ostensibly over matters spiritual, it was the cipher for far more prosaic questions of class and wealth, identity and language.

Disestablishment finally became law as the Welsh Church Act of 1914. For the nineteen parishes that straddle the border, the Act stated vaguely that 'reference to the general wishes of the parishioners' should be taken into account before deciding which way they might jump. This, it was decided by the church commissioners, should be in the form of parish referenda, which took place in the first couple of months of 1915. In one of the very first uses of universal suffrage, all parishioners over twenty-one, men and women, were granted a vote.

Despite happening in the dark days of the first winter of the Great War, the turnout was huge in every parish, from Lache-cum-Saltney in the north, a suburb of Chester, to Dixton Newton, near Monmouth, 100 miles south. Unsurprisingly at a time of conflict and greatly amplified British and imperial identity, almost every parish voted to stay within the Church of England. Consequently, some Welsh churches were transferred into English dioceses. Llanymynech voted more than two to one for the status quo, but in two parishes just to its north, the vote was so close that it was re-run the following year. One went with England, and one – Llansilin, Denbighshire (moved into Powys in 1996) – became the only cross-border parish of the nineteen to opt for the new Church in Wales.

At first glance, it's hard to see why. A mile from Shropshire, Llansilin looks much like any other border village: a string of Victorian cottages along a main street clogged with cars, post-war council housing around a tidy green, a new housing estate rising fast, a Victorian drinking fountain, a primary school (threatened), some chapels (three redundant, one tottering), a bus stop (the number 78, twice a week to Oswestry), a community shop (Tuesday and Thursday mornings), and centre stage, in solid and venerable communion, a medieval church and a Wynnstay Inn. All pleasant, if unremarkable, so … *why*? Why did Llansilin alone jump into the unknown?

If there is a single answer to be found, then it will perhaps be sat at the river's edge a field away. This little brown brook, skipping over stones and wriggling through the indifferent hills, is the Cynllaith, and a mile downstream are the mounds and moat of Sycharth. Suddenly, the sky cracks, the centuries evaporate and there is the Lord of Cynllaith and master of Sycharth himself, Owain Glyndŵr.

Over 600 years ago, a furious teenager, soon to be King Henry V, swept down this valley, intending to raze Glyndŵr's 'bounteous mansion' to the ground, preferably with the rebel himself still inside. But the Welsh prince was gone, folded into the hills from where he was leading the English army a merry ride. Fired up with impotent rage, Henry torched the place anyway, and then cantered off to do the same to Glyndŵr's other residence near Corwen.

The greatest irony is that Henry's petulance has served Sycharth so well. Had any trace of Glyndŵr's home survived, it would have been dug out and tidied up, fussed over by experts, packaged and parcelled for visiting coach parties of bored school-kids and wide-eyed Americans on their Welsh Braveheart tour. As it is, you have to do all of the work yourself. You need to feel the place, look at, around and through it, listen to it, run your fingers down the grooves of the bark of the vast oak trees, sit quietly in their roots, sniff the damp soil and taste the mossy air. There is nothing to mediate between you and Glyndŵr himself: it is eyeball-to-eyeball across six centuries.

Lovely though that is, it is extraordinary that this place of pilgrimage has been so thoroughly ignored by the tourism industry (the only concession a tiny car park, its sign spattered with Yes Cymru stickers). Entire heritage attractions, waymarked trails, visitor centres and inter-active experiences have been conjured from far less. Were they to try, though, I'd like to believe that the Sycharth spirits – and my god, they're a fierce bunch – would dismantle it every night as dusk fell and the builders went home, like those old tales of medieval churches and castles. Sycharth is just too big – as with its oaks, there's a hint of giganticism hanging in the ether – to be tamed by tin gods.

Glyndŵr or no, where northern Powys and northern Shropshire rub shoulders has always been the most clearly Welsh section of the frontier. The one remaining chapel congregation in Llansilin still conducts its services in Cymraeg, and at the last census over 30 per cent of parishioners recorded their use of it – the highest of anywhere on the English border, and higher than the Welsh national average. Not that the language stops at the line. For proof of that, we should hop on one of those two weekly buses to Oswestry – the Wednesday one, market day, is best. From Llansilin, the bus rattles over the border at Rhydycroesau, and then up a series of narrow bends. At 900 feet, we see the ditch and tree-line of Offa's Dyke side-stepping down from the hills above. At 1,000 feet, there's the old Oswestry racecourse, a sweeping figure-of-eight that runs for 2 miles across a high common.

Stand still long enough in the stumps of its Georgian grandstand, and on the whistling breeze you might just hear the raucous shouts, boozy cheers and filthy songs of two nations gathering in no-man's-land, come to flutter, flirt and fight.

Down, down the other side, down the long hill into town, and even the tarmac has turned suddenly Sassenach. Elegant and straight, faintly military, edged by grand trees and the long wall of a big estate, the road is a favourite of freewheeling cyclists, who hurtle past the number 78 as it coughs its way into Oswestry, and through the busy streets.

This is Shropshire, but not. Everywhere you look, we're in a parallel Wales. The bus drops us by the gates of Cae Glas park, bounded by the Welsh Walls, on the other side of which are the Brynhafod playing fields. Opposite the bus stop is Ivor Roberts-Jones's sculpture, *The Borderland Farmer*, clearly a man of two languages, even if he uses precious few words in either. By his side, a burly ram, its curly bronze horns gleaming with all the rubs they get given for good luck. Over the road is Booka, the town's ebullient bookshop. When I first read there, a dozen years ago, I asked the crowd of thirty or so how many of them spoke Welsh, and at least a quarter put their hands up.

It's market day, and in the cavernous 1960s Powis market hall there's almost only Welsh to be heard in the corner café next to Siop Cwlwm, 'Siop Gymraeg Croesoswallt / Oswestry's Welsh Shop', as the sign has it. Once, it was the chapels in English towns that knitted the Welsh diaspora together, and there are still a few left, with their creaking congregations and leaking slates. Siop Cwlwm and its ilk are the new chapels, bright little shrines of pastel shades and promise, knick-knacks and the lightest of nationalisms, and almost always run by fearsomely capable, affable women. In them, you can find your tribe and oil your mutations, dig out classes or lectures, or buy music and books, cards and toys, and a mishmash of home furnishings embroidered with words like CARIAD♥ and *Cwtch!* Stock up before you head home, perhaps to one of the new estates on the edge of town. In an act of bipartisan generosity, Oswestry Borough Council gave some of its cul-de-sacs, closes and groves Welsh names: Erw Wen, Llwyn Crescent, Nant Lane, though the gesture didn't go entirely to plan. Instead of the intended Cae Onnen, the 'field of ash trees', the signs read Cae Onan, or 'Masturbation Meadow' as the papers soon sniggered.

In the early 1970s, when the county map was being redrawn, it was mooted that Oswestry and its surrounding villages might officially be moved into Wales. A TV crew canvassed opinion on another market day, half a century ago. Almost everyone was in favour of the idea. The first interviewee, a cheery old dear clamped into a plastic rain hat, thought that the town already was in Wales. Even the two teenage girls who immediately answered 'English!' when asked their national-ity, gave an equally swift 'Yes!' when asked if they thought it a good idea to move the border, and said that they'd be happy to learn the language. The least enthusiastic interviewee, an elder of the town in dark overcoat and homburg hat, thought of himself as English more than Welsh and couldn't see the point at all of changing things. 'So you'd be against it?' asked the interviewer. 'Oh no,' came the reply.

A local film-maker, Barry Edwards, repeated the exercise in 2015, and found many of the same attitudes, though there was a distinct stiffening of identity on both sides. In 1972, the question was airy theory, of no great practical consequence, a bit of a laugh even. Forty-plus years later, in the age of devolution and referenda, hard-nosed economic and political realities had nudged all that out of the frame. In another sign of the times, the most passionate advocate of return-ing Oswestry to Wales was a Londoner who'd moved to the town; the strongest voice against, an elderly chap with an accent as clear and Welsh as a mountain stream.

'The March is thinning,' border poet Ben Gwalchmai tells me when we hook up for a walk near his home in a village a few miles south of town. Ben is in his thirties, and even in his lifetime he's perceived the buffer zone shrinking, attitudes congealing, and on both sides. Though from the Powys side of the line, he was at high school in Oswestry, when it felt to him 'far more mixed than it is today. Now they seem very English, and quite noisy about it.' But then it could be said that Ben has gone in the equal and opposite direction, as the founder of Labour for an Independent Wales, and former chair of Yes Cymru.

Ben happily ploughs two shallow furrows, as a Welsh independence campaigner on the border and within the Labour Party. It's hard for those from beyond to understand Labour's iron grip on Wales. Over the last century, even at the very highest tides of Churchill or Thatcher, they have won every single one of twenty-seven general elections, a run of one-party rule unequalled in the West. In England, outside of Tony Blair's victories, Labour has only ever won a majority twice, in 1945 and 1966. Labour in Wales are the establishment, the party of more-of-the-same and steady-as-she-goes, and never more so than in their Unionism. Though polls have shown that somewhere over 40 per cent of Welsh Labour voters are at least 'indy curious', none of their members in either parliament, Westminster or Cardiff, has ever committed to the cause, at least not publicly.

If right now 'internationalism through independence' appears to be a Sisyphean pursuit within his party, it's not a great deal less lonesome for Ben within wider Welsh nationalist circles. We last met Yes Cymru at the gates of Sycharth, with the wind in their flags, membership having ballooned in just a couple of months of the pandemic from 2,000 to over 16,000. That was the high point, and the descent came fast. As the lockdowns ground on, the clarity and sharp collective endeavour of the early Covid days dissipated, in the independence movement as everywhere. Ben and a cohort of radical campaigners were elected as the organisation's central committee, but their plurality and youth was a shock to an old guard whose politics had been forged thirty years before, and stayed there. He and the committee were all undermined to such an extent that they had little choice but to resign en masse. Half of the membership went with them.

I've marched with Yes Cymru and come 3,067 votes short of being elected as a Plaid Cymru MP. From my very first encounters with Wales, I've been certain that it holds something special, qualities we could all do with learning about, even emulating. The pandemic only highlighted them. Time and again, and despite vicious belittling by politicians and journalists, the Welsh government attempted to act according to older, deeper principles of egalitarianism, kindness and community-mindedness. To those of a libertarian bent, such qualities are anathema, but not to me. Within them is not just the blueprint for a healthier society, but one that holds as essential the revolutionary power of education and creativity, for their own ends and on their own terms, not solely as vocational training or economic tools.

I'd long fantasised that the best way for us all to flourish was for the UK to dissolve into its natural constituent units, a brotherhood of neighbours and friends. On our walk, Ben paints a vivid picture of what an independent Wales might be: small but expansive, sure of itself, content with its place in the world. It's a vision I share, but I'm struggling to see how we get there right now, with belligerent nativism setting the debate's increasingly rigid parameters, from whichever angle you take it. This is not the 1990s, and there is no Velvet Revolution waiting just off-stage. When that rogue poll came out just shy of the Scottish independence referendum of 2014, the UK establishment was caught napping. It will not be allowed to happen again.

Here in Oswestry, the 'Welshest town in England', things are stirring, and it's hard to see quite where they may go. In the tidy glades of Cae Glas park, I ask the statue of the town's most celebrated son, First World War poet Wilfred Owen, but he won't say. He stares past me, glassy-eyed, frozen in municipal bronze.

Some see him as a heroic cipher, martyred a week before the armistice, his statue a fuller version of those metal soldier silhouettes that have sprouted everywhere in recent years, the favoured symbol of militant poppy enforcers. To me, he is the beautiful doomed youth, an officer of principle and lover of men, a truth-whisperer and pure sprite of the border, Welsh in origin and inclination, Shropshire and Wirral by upbringing. I fell in love with him – that glint, those cheekbones, those *words* – decades ago, when he was still often considered with suspicion, not quite one of us. One far-off Remembrance Day, I was due to read in the assembly at my Worcester school, where lumpen militarism was worn polished and proud. My choice was Owen's lacerating *Dulce et Decorum Est*, though I had to fight for it. The teacher in charge that week, a peacock-in-khaki and something big in the Cadet Force, felt that the poem was 'a bit much, rather anti ...', and suggested instead a pinch of Tennyson or, at a push, Rupert Brooke. I flooded him with evidence from the Head of English, who was fully complicit in my mild insurrection, and floored him with persistence. When the day came, I gave everything I had to Owen's hot-cold, glorious fury:

> If you could hear, at every jolt, the blood
> Come gargling from the froth-corrupted lungs,
> Obscene as cancer, bitter as the cud
> Of vile, incurable sores on innocent tongues,—
> My friend, you would not tell with such high zest
> To children ardent for some desperate glory,
> The old Lie: *Dulce et decorum est*
> *Pro patria mori.*

Both sides can find what they want on this border, and that long co-existence is a welcome curiosity. I can have my fey boys, my shell-shocked Great War poets – Wilfred Owen, Edward Thomas, Ivor Gurney, David Jones – and overlording them all, the spiritual sirens of the borderland at war, Housman and his comely lads. And they can have the poppies and the parade grounds, the quick-march two-step and the veterans' clubs of age-old military outposts, riddled all along the border: not just Oswestry, but Chester, Shrewsbury, Hereford, Brecon, Monmouth.

Behind both of the faces of these Janus-towns are the very same qualities, which derive entirely from being on the border: a disjunction, a literal edginess, both inner and outer. Conflict is an inevitable by-product of course, but so too is creative energy. Even when the other side appears firmly in control, it still sparks and crackles, and in those times, an unexpected victory, entirely against the run of play, is all the sweeter.

In December 2021, after two almost unbroken centuries of parliamentary representation by a Conservative, Oswestry dealt the first blow in Boris Johnson's downfall, courtesy of a by-election that he unnecessarily provoked, and then proceeded to lose. Framing the

North Shropshire seat as an agricultural backwater, much of a muchness with Norfolk or Devon or Cumbria, London commentators failed to spot any of its unique Marcher characteristics, especially the old nonconformist Liberal tradition that bubbled up and bled over the border from mid Wales.

Were he capable of any sort of modesty or circumspection, Johnson might have seen it coming. The Liberal habit wasn't the only slumbering beast in the borderland bedrock; lying in wait too perhaps was the revenge, served icily cold, of an affronted Anglo-Welsh squirearchy. In 1987, Johnson married his first wife Allegra Mostyn-Owen at Woodhouse, her family estate 5 miles east of Oswestry. He arrived for the ceremony with no suitable trousers or shoes, lost the wedding certificate, misplaced the ring and told off-colour jokes in his speech. His wife later described the wedding as 'the end of the relationship instead of the beginning'. They separated a little over two years later, and divorced in 1993, twelve days before he married again, his new bride eight months pregnant.

All along the border are the houses and estates of the Anglo-Welsh aristocracy, many drawing a direct line back to the Marcher lordships. Like the March itself, they too are thinning, in power and purlieu, raw wealth and acreage. A few, like the Mostyn-Owens, have retrenched and relinquished where necessary in order to maintain their demesnes, and to keep them private. Many others have had to tart themselves out as tourist attractions, hotels, luxury spas, shooting estates, golf courses, conference centres and wedding venues. Plenty have vanished altogether, the houses long gone, the estates broken up, their residue only in names and ghost shapes on the map, like the chalk outline on a pavement of a murder victim.

Some were already on the way out, and the Great War was the final straw. In August 1921, a church bazaar at Lymore Hall, Montgomery, proved calamitous when the floor of the grand oak banqueting hall gave way, plunging the Earl of Powis, fifteen townsfolk and Miss Doris Tomley's fancy goods stall into the vaults below. 'Suddenly without any audible promontory symptoms, a knot of guests were observed to disappear outright,' squeaked the following week's *Montgomeryshire Express and Radnor Times*. 'Some of the ladies showed a tendency to faint,' it continued breathlessly, 'because it was feared that very severe consequences had ensued.' Thankfully, they hadn't, though the collapse rang a resounding death knell for the house, the Herbert family's fantastical replacement for the town's castle. After attempts to save it came to nothing, the half-timbered hall, the finest ever built in local oak, was demolished in 1931.

After the First World War, as estates collapsed or radically shrank, there was the greatest transfer of land ownership since the dissolution of the monasteries. The second war only hastened the process. In the 1950s and 60s, over 10 per cent of Britain's stately homes were demolished, and many mysteriously 'went on fire', usually in the dead of night. Their grandeur was entirely out of sync with the mood of the time, and some landowners embraced the iconoclastic mood. Shân Legge-Bourke of the Glanusk estate near Crickhowell told how her mother got so fed up with the vast gothic house and its endless needs, she went out one morning in 1953, armed with bags of explosives, 'and just blew it up'.

One great Oswestry house bucked the immediate post-war decline, becoming an unlikely outpost of the international jet set: Brogyntyn, whose long estate wall and classical gates we passed on the number 78 bus as it bounced down the hill into town. Until it was sold in 2001, this was the principal home of the Lords Harlech, and their story is that of the rise and fall of the Anglo-Welsh, and with it, the thinning of the March.

The hereditary title of Lord Harlech, named after the distant family estate on the north Wales coast, was created in 1876 to elevate Shropshire Conservative MP John Ormsby-Gore. Though his family wealth was largely the result of plunder and landlordism in Ireland, the increasingly strident – and electorally successful – calls for Irish Home Rule meant that other avenues needed to be consolidated. Wales has so often been Ireland's understudy, both as unionist bogey-man and nationalist totem, and Anglo-Welshism became the perfect proxy for the waning Anglo-Irish nobility.

To give his house, an indifferent pile called Porkington, some greater noblesse and a Welsh pedigree, the new Lord Harlech rechristened it after Castell Brogyntyn, a twelfth-century tump in the grounds that had taken its name from a prince of Powys. Within five months of his ennoblement, though, Lord Harlech was dead, a morbid premonition of how often the title would change direction due to sudden death and suicide. The second Lord, his brother, stayed mainly on the family estate in Ireland, making only rare forays to Westminster.

The third Lord, his son, was a military man, and a year into the First World War, with casualties mounting and conscription yet to come, was made commander of the brand-new Welsh Guards division. Rural Wales, fuelled on nonconformity, pacifism and imperial suspicion, was proving reluctant to join the war effort, and it was hoped that the new division might help change that. It was soaked in the trappings of *Cymreictod* – recruitment posters in Welsh, using unashamedly nationalist slogans and images – and the division launched on St David's Day 1915, with a leek in their caps and *Men of Harlech* as their marching tune. Brogyntyn and Oswestry were indelibly linked with the division; even now, on the town's old army camp is the Welsh Guards museum.

Like all of his predecessors, the fifth and most famous Lord Harlech, David Ormsby-Gore, was a Conservative MP, though he quit his Oswestry seat in 1961 to take up the post of British ambassador to the USA. In doing so, he rekindled a childhood friendship with the new president, John F. Kennedy. On Kennedy's assassination, Harlech became a close confidant of his widow Jackie, and after he too was widowed, proposed marriage to her. Towards the end of her life, she is said to have expressed regret for having turned him down.

Returning to Britain, he threw his energies into the world of TV and film, becoming the chairman – and name – of Harlech Television. In the biggest shock of the 1967 ITV franchise round, Harlech snatched the right to broadcast to Wales and the west of England from TWW, who'd held the franchise from the start.

For the last half of the twentieth century, the swivelling television aerials of the borderlands were their own referendum. When Channel 4 and Sianel 4 Cymru (S4C) were born in November 1982, many non-Welsh speakers turned their aerials towards the English service (and a few, mainly around Oswestry, did the opposite). Though much political capital was made of it, this was no new habit. Since ITV's inception in the 1950s, the service had been operated regionally. The difficult geography of Wales meant that most people near the border received better pictures from Granada in Manchester or ATV in Birmingham, a situation further compounded by the rather patchy and patrician offerings from TWW and its short-lived twin in west and north Wales, Teledu Cymru. In a 1962 editorial, Cardiff's *Western Mail* inadvertently nailed the problem: 'We are still speculating on how much of this network's output would be cultural and Welsh, and how much entertainment?' That they were taken as mutually exclusive is an issue that roared back to life twenty years later with the fourth channel, and still underpins so much lingering antipathy even today.

Harlech Television promised to bridge the gap. You *could* be Welsh and popular, it boomed, and we're going to show you how. Behind Lord Harlech, his transatlantic sheen still gleaming, was a stellar board of Welsh A-listers: Stanley Baker, Sir Geraint Evans, Harry Secombe, Wynford Vaughan-Thomas and the most famous showbiz couple in the world, Richard Burton and Elizabeth Taylor. The key criticism that had lost TWW the franchise was that its headquarters was in London. That changed under the new management, but it was largely window dressing. Harlech had mopped up *la crème de la Cymry*, but barely any of them were based in Wales, including of course his Lordship himself. The promise that its board of stars would be regulars on the new station also proved to be elegant embellishment. In 1972, Burton and Taylor finally made one film for HTV, the aptly titled *Divorce His, Divorce Hers*, but it was truly lousy, ate almost the entire year's drama budget, and had to be filmed in Munich rather than Bristol, as promised, on the insistence of the couple's tax advisers.

As far as Bristolians were concerned, the movie was just another snub from their supposedly local ITV station. They'd been deeply suspicious of Harlech Television from the word go, and a rebrand after two years, to the more neutral HTV, failed to staunch that. The station wanted to see itself as the broadcasting incarnation of the new Severn Bridge, sleek and ambitious, modern, confident, uniting the two banks. As it was, the greater intimacy afforded by the bridge was only making people on both sides more acutely aware of how very different they were. There was no love lost in a region described by one newspaper as 'a televisual Austria-Hungary'.

If this was the pinnacle of the Lords Harlech, the apogee of a particular kind of Anglo-Welsh squirearchy, it was a low and hollow summit. The descent has been swift and sad. On Lord Harlech's sudden death in 1985 – resulting from a car crash, like his brother and wife before him – Brogyntyn was mothballed. After being walloped by death duties, the next Lord, his youngest son Francis, moved down to The Mount, another property on the estate. Frankie, as he was known locally, was a regular in the pubs of Oswestry, the courts too, on charges that variously included drink driving, heroin possession and carrying a weapon. He died in 2016, aged sixty-one, at Glyn Cywarch, the old stone house near Harlech itself, traditionally the Lords Harlech's holiday home, but now the only remaining family property. Brogyntyn was long ago sold to developers, and The Mount – after one of those mysterious fires – has been rebuilt as a mock-Classical palace for the owners of a local scrap dealership.

With their estates in Ireland and England gone, all now rests on the Welsh property. To finance renovation of Glyn Cywarch, the latest Lord Harlech secured heritage grants and auctioned off family heir-looms, even selling his grandfather's sweet nothings from Jackie Kennedy for a cool £100,000. He rents out the estate for shooting parties and corporate events, and intends to run it as an upmarket B&B. On a recent trip, I noticed a steely ruthlessness in the damp Gwynedd air that I hadn't felt before. You used to be able to walk the estate woods unhindered, but now the (monolingual English) signs and warnings of extensive CCTV forbid it. Gates are padlocked and old parking spots blocked by boulders and tree trunks.

Harlech itself didn't lift my mood. I'd heard about the town's recent losses, but seeing for real the row of dereliction along the main road was heartbreaking. At the top of the hill, the wreck of the St David's Hotel stared hollow-eyed out to sea. Just below, the smashed-up student accommodation tower and the boarded-up Coleg Harlech. Founded as a second-chance education for those who'd slipped through the cracks, it turned so many lives around, people I know, have met and been wowed by, brilliant people reborn on this wild shore. Education being turned into a marketplace saw off this unique institution, and looking at it, my blood boiled. It threatened to blow at the next ruin: the bold and beautiful concrete crab of Theatr Ardudwy, now blanked out behind metal grilles, bolts and warning signs. They were all buildings at the very top of their times, high ideals made manifest, from an Edwardian arts and crafts heyday to post-war egalitarianism and the boisterous optimism of 1960s brutalism, and they've all been left to die.

Not though the next building at the bottom of the hill: the subur-ban clubhouse of the Royal St David's golf course. That was going great guns, its car park packed with expensive German machinery. From Llanymynech to Harlech, across the wide Severn basin and all the way to the sea, the sodding golfers have won. For now.

WIRRAL

FLINTSHIRE

Flint o

Shotton o

Neston

o

5

CHESHIRE

o Chester

Saltney

DENBIGH SHIRE

6

Holt o

o Farndon

Wrexham o

Whitchurch

Llangollen

The Maelor

R. Dee

8

o

7

Ellesmere

o Oswestry

SHROPSHIRE

POWYS

2
NORTH
DEE

5.

SEA / LAND

/// chin.clashing.waltzes

Sealand sounds delightful, a bubbling blue world of pristine coral and fairy-tale fish, but the reality soon detonates the fancy. We are not welcome. The signs, green with mould, make that quite clear: SEALAND ARMY RIFLE RANGE & TRAINING AREA says one, 'Danger Keep Out / Perygl Cadwch Allan' the other. Ah right, Sealand is Wales. On the other side of the locked gate, with another KEEP OUT sign on it, in case you hadn't yet noticed, sheep graze a slimy marsh, and around them, sullen crows stand and wait for pickings. In the distance, pylons lumber across a dark horizon.

Coming from the north, from the acrid Irish Sea as it ferments into the estuary of the River Dee, this gravel track at Burton Point is the very first border crossing of all. Technically, you could make an earlier one across the quicksands and tussocks, but you'd be pushing your luck. Even the national mapping agency can't call it. As the border trails out to sea, the label on the map reads 'Boundary between Wirral, Cheshire West and Chester and Flintshire / Sir Y Fflint adopted for the purposes of Ordnance Survey'. Borders are fictitious enough at the best of times, but this one, where tidal flats become sky, wrapped in fogs and rippled by watery hazes, is pure make-believe.

I cannot credit that I've never been here before, as it is exactly the kind of place that I've spent decades going out of my way to visit: lonely, straggling dead ends that peter out under big grey skies. On the OS, the English bank of the Dee estuary is a classic of the genre, a frill of inlets and channels, dotted with blue symbols for marshland and the stentorian clang of the label DANGER AREA in panic-button red. Ancient earthworks, embankments, tracks and sidings creep across the uncertain turf, pointing towards old mineshafts and a succession of quays, each abandoned in turn as the river silted up. The cheeriest is Parkgate, which still fancies itself as a bit of a resort, its brassy prom stocked with all the necessary seaside accoutrements (with the notable – but clearly not deal-breaking – exception of the sea). Miles away over saltmarsh and waders is Wales, and even from here you can see that it is different, with none of the la-di-da of the Wirral. The towns and smudge of industry strung out along the far shore seem to have their heads down, hard at work, perhaps a little browbeaten. Not even the low ruins of Flint castle, Edward I's gate-way into Wales, can quite lift the scene. It has none of the spectacle of his other conquering fortresses, the likes of Conwy or Caernarfon, and from over here is dominated by a set of 1960s tower blocks.

Samples from the bed of the Dee show that it has been silting up since at least Roman times. Chester, the primary port of England's north-west and gateway to the colonisation of Ireland, was always the town with most to lose. A document from 1377 records its haven as 'ruinous'; another in 1449 said: 'the navigation had been so much impeded by sands from the frequent changing of the channel, that it occasioned the total ruin of the haven'. The new harbours constructed further and further up the river were generally done on the cheap, and none lasted long. In the early 1730s, a radical solution was cooked up; one that had just as great an impact on the England–Wales border as it ever did on shipping.

Much is made of engineer Nathaniel Kinderley's project to dredge a new deep channel for the river, an attempt to keep open Chester's harbour. That was the stated aim, and that too has been its place in the history books, but from the outset there was a greater and grub-bier motive at work, one that has lasted much longer and forged so much more of the world as it is today. More than anything, the cana-lisation of the Dee was a massive land-grab.

Right from the off, Kinderley's original promises about the ship-ping channel were downgraded, by special acts of parliament if needs be. One such piece of legislation, in 1740, created the River Dee Company (RDC), 'for recovering' fertile reclaimed land from the estuary 'and preserving' the maritime trade. It was clear which was the priority. A lavish company map produced in 1770 for prospective tenants shows forty-five plots carved out of the polder, with very many more to come. In 1846, a report by the Tidal Harbours Commission criticised the company for 'attending more to the reclaiming and embanking of waste land for their own benefit than to the improvement of the navigation'. A subsequent Admiralty enquiry declared that the RDC had been criminally negligent. All the while, the sands continued building and the river silting.

In the saga of the Dee estuary, everyone wanted their share of the spoils. Sir John Glynne, lord of the manor of Hawarden, Flintshire, who took a slice of any tithes paid to the village's rector, was very keen that the new lands were recognised as an integral part of his parish. He cut a deal with the RDC, confirmed in a 1753 act of parliament (Sir John was also the local MP), whereby he forfeited rights to the land in exchange for a sizeable annual lump sum. It was his insistence that the border of Hawarden parish and Cheshire be fixed along the line of the river's old course, rather than be placed along the new one or – as had been the custom – defined only by the estuary and left to wallow in its shifting channels and wide skies. In support of the claim, and in an echo of the tiny land-grab in the Clun Forest, Sir John used an historic mass burial to prove that the new terrain belonged to his side, after Hawarden had buried the bodies from a shipwreck in the Dee, the opposite Cheshire parish of Blacon having refused. Consequently, the border was pinned along the estuary's far northern shore, a good couple of miles from the newly canalised Dee, making almost all of the reclaimed lands nominally Welsh.

It was a rare victory for Flintshire over Cheshire, the most unequal twin counties in Britain, and ever since, Cheshire has been quietly attempting to appropriate the land, whether by statute or stealth. Many Chester tradesmen purchased tenancies, and south of the new cut snapped up parcels of Saltney Marsh as they were enclosed in the late eighteenth century. The village of Saltney was developed, becoming a south-western suburb of Chester, despite being in Wales. It grew rapidly as the place for the city's less salubrious trades: its oil and grease works, chemical and fertiliser plants, anything that rendered the air thick with toxins.

In 1889, local government reorganisation made Chester the second smallest county borough in Britain – in effect, an administrative county all of its own. Though they were pleased with the status that came with the title, the city fathers immediately began to plot the borough's expansion. The flatlands to the west were an obvious target. Before the century's end, a government inquiry considered the absorption by the county borough of five surrounding parishes, three of which – Saltney, Sealand and Broughton – were in Wales. The imperative was both financial, for the borough was hugely in debt, and logistic, to build huge new sewage farms and a contagion hospital there. Instead, the move was couched as a favour to the people of Flintshire, an educational opportunity for their children, who would otherwise be ineligible for scholarships to the city's schools. There was a carrot dangled for their fathers too: swapping sides would mean the end for them of the Welsh dry Sunday, introduced in the previous decade. Although the *Chester Chronicle* records that they were repeatedly laughed at in the inquiry, the representatives of the Welsh side stood their ground, and the border stayed put. Chester's councillors tried again in 1954 and 1962, but to no avail.

A reprise of the old argument flared up over the festive season at the end of 2021. Thirty years earlier, when Chester City FC sold its ground for a retail park and built a replacement stadium half a mile away on the other side of an industrial estate, that the new ground was mostly in Wales was little more than a good pub-quiz question. Then came devolution and, in 2007, the smoking ban, when the split suddenly meant something. It came to mean a whole load more with the pandemic. In the first few days of January 2022, the club was summoned to a meeting with Welsh government officials and representatives of North Wales Police, and told that its two home matches over Christmas had breached regulations. In Wales, crowds were limited to fifty, but in England there was no restriction. Over 2,000 spectators had been at both matches. The club hastily cancelled the next game, and all hell broke loose.

As with Llanymynech golf club the previous year, the story went global (what is it with this particular border that ignites such excitement? Is Britain seen as a kind of ground zero, an international litmus test of shifting identities, or is the world simply enjoying its long laugh at us?). An article in the *New York Times*, headlined 'Is This Stadium in England or Wales? The Team Needs to Know', talked to Chester chairman Andy Morris, who told them that he was keen to have the border altered, to introduce a tiny hiccup in the line to bring them back into the English fold. To the BBC, he said that the location of the ground was no longer a joke and 'had become a very real problem'. 'It was never a problem before we had devolution,' he added pointedly.

The idea that it had ambushed them from nowhere, that – as some claimed – it was an issue they'd barely been aware of, was thoroughly undermined by another board member. He told the *NYT* that thirty years earlier when the stadium was being built, they'd gone out of their way to ensure that its main entrance was in England, even though that required angling the main stand to the south-west, a rarity in football as that means that spectators are dazzled on a sunny afternoon. Selective memory was at play too. When the stadium was built, bulldozers had to move two eighteenth-century boundary stones.

Being about football, and borders, and almost two weary years into the pandemic, the story travelled far, on oceans of online vitriol. English zealots exhumed all the old sheep and begging bowl clichés, while their Welsh opposites swore bloody revenge if Chester appropriated so much as a goalpost. Many mentioned the mirror example of The New Saints FC, who play in the Welsh league at their ground in Oswestry, England. Throughout the pandemic, they'd gone by Welsh rules, to fit in with the clubs they were facing. Why, said many, couldn't the same elasticity be shown for Chester?

Something similar will happen again, and the consequences could be enormous. As the *New York Times* had it in their report, 'in an era when once loose British borders are stratifying, a curiosity may become a crisis'. In the chaos and bad blood of 2020s Britain, the greatest ruptures to our political tectonic plates come not from orderly campaigns or incremental steps, but from freakish, furious and often apparently inconsequential flashes in the pan. The Chester FC chairman put it best: 'the United Kingdom might start falling apart because a sixth division football match could not take place'.

Even as one who instinctively comes down on the Welsh side of things, I'd say let them have the bloody stadium. Having been to visit, I'd say it only faster. It's at the back of a huge industrial estate, the kind that you notice with a sigh on satellite maps, a splat of grey boxes crusted to the rim of every town, bypass and motorway junction. The border across those sodden fields was defined in the fourteenth century using drainage ditches to stake its course. It now wanders aimlessly not just through the football ground, but also an auto-parts warehouse, a Swiss chocolatier's distribution depot, 'one of the world's leading manufacturers of gas loaded bladder, piston and diaphragm accumulators', a pharmaceutical wholesaler, a specialist cycle insurer, a printers, a contract cleaners, the offices of the Consumer Credit Association, and a park-and-ride that doubled up as the city's Covid vaccination centre. They are all Chester.

Turn the corner, though, and it's a different story. There, Ferry Lane runs a mile down to the Dee, and to what the sign tells us is the 'historic river crossing / *man hanesyddol i groesi'r afon*'. We're back in Wales for sure, and even the air seems to have slowed down. With some inevitability, first up is a holiday park, caravans in a field in the sixties morphed into lodges for £100,000 apiece today. At its entrance, stumpy palm trees bristle in a steely breeze – literally so; we're 5 miles downwind of the Tata plant at Shotton.

To the river, 90 yards wide and straight as an arrow, the inland end of the eighteenth-century cut that shoots the Dee out to sea. Twenty years ago, I came this way for a television series about the Welsh coast. To sail out of Chester, we had to find a boat with a sufficiently shallow draught and wait for one of the highest tides of the year. It was well worth it, to get views directly into the city's grandest villas, and catch the sapphire sparkle of kingfishers nesting regally at their feet. We crept out of town, following the curves of the river, and I remember so well the feeling of rounding that final corner and there was the canalised straight, stretching out before us like a runway. Our skipper, a local fisherman, slammed his boat up a gear, and we had lift-off.

Today, my route is a whole load more sedate. I walk the very first mile of the Wales coast path, along the cut, and then over the foot-bridge to Saltney, built in the 1960s to replace the ferry. Dispel any mental images you may have of the Welsh coast path, of cliffs, water-falls, kittiwakes and gulls, the slap-tang of salt and hunger. You'd never picture this, a smooth tarmac towpath gliding towards a distant vanishing point with all the charisma of an airport travelator. Yet there's something hypnotically appealing about it, pulling me forward, spurring me on.

So too the view from the footbridge, ugly-pretty in the Welshest of ways. The Dee below is sludge-brown, choppy and lapping at the edges of its channel. All lines point forward, to a distant futuristic fantasy: the bright blue Meccano of the bridge at Queensferry being sliced precisely by the soaring blade of the new Flintshire Bridge, even though the latter is miles further on around a bend in the river, and crosses it at an angle. Squaring up to each other on either side of the bridges, the blue-and-grey boxes of the steelworks and the four square chimneys of a power station, punching the sky in a fist, like a Soviet propaganda poster. Dotted around them a couple of dozen pylons, their wires threaded across the wide water in a brutalist cat's cradle.

Across these claggy meadows, the next set of battle lines is being drawn. Though Chester's attempts to bag these lands have regularly hit a dead end, there are other ways. Plans have been presented, refused, adapted, and re-presented to build a link road across the fields between the football stadium and the river. A new bridge would speed traffic over Saltney and on to the A55 dual carriageway a couple of miles further south. And though the arguments are all about speeding up congested traffic, the real impetus is that where there's a new road, and a new bridge, there will be new houses – 2,000 of them, if the developers get their way. It will happen; the only question is when.

Just one glance at the map will show you why. On its English sides, Chester is bursting out of its corsets. The only way is west.

It could be all kinds of disaster: a climate crisis floodbath on 400 acres of houses, almost all dependent on two cars, filling the new road and all of the old ones too. There would be the usual sour wrangle about developments in Wales that pay no heed to their location; the lacklustre compromise to give the new streets Welsh names, to be grumbled about and mispronounced for decades to come. Flintshire council has magnificent form here. When journalists have used Llanymynech once too often to illustrate their scare stories about the border, they come instead to Saltney, specifically to vox pop residents of Boundary Lane, where the line runs down the middle. Leading off it into Cheshire are the newbuild Beaumont Close, Lindfields and Stanley Park Drive. Opposite, their precise mirror image in Flintshire: Cwrt y Terfyn (Boundary Court), Llys Rhuddlan and – slam-dunking the point home – Ffordd y Dysgwyr / Learners' Way.

Let's however think positively, and imagine that this steroid injection might just be Saltney's big moment. Flintshire has only recently recognised it as a town in its own right, rather than merely as a boil on the plump arse of Chester. The newly minted town council have great plans for their collective future, of forging this dissipate parish, defined thus far by what it's not and where it isn't, into a cohesive whole. Plans are for a bit of landscaping, some boulevard gentrification, a piece or two of public art (almost inevitably involving a dragon) and to develop the graffiti-clad riverbank, up at the back of the trading estate, into a tourist honeypot. The nearby walls and cathedral of Chester can probably breathe easy.

I'd suggest instead that the town council should think big and campaign hard for Welsh independence, because more than anywhere else, Saltney is poised to become Wales's Gretna Green, perhaps even El Paso or Lake Tahoe if it's feeling especially giddy. The town's history, identity and income *is* the border, and there's nowhere better placed for a rash of petrol stations, duty-free shops, casinos, strip joints, souvenir tat and drive-thru restaurants to satisfy the voracious appetites of England's north-west. Saltney and Sealand beyond have long been where Chester keeps its dirty secrets. It's high time they got rich on it.

Poet and novelist Gee Williams grew up in Saltney, and the jagged identity of this border has haunted her ever since. Some of her earliest memories are of being strapped onto the back of her mother's bike as she pedalled up the hill into Chester, to an assortment of cleaning jobs in the grand, gated houses of Curzon Park. The Saltney of her child-hood was a noisy and sulphurous place, 'good practice for your immune system,' she says. On a Sunday, Saltney men hung around at the top of Boundary Lane, waiting for the pub to open on the other side of the railway bridge, in England. The Dee would sometimes overtop its banks, flooding the redbrick streets below.

I've always loved Gee's work for its acute sense of this border. She turns into an asset the awkwardness of never quite belonging, and has a glittering ability to cast a dispassionate eye over both sides of a place, an idea or an identity, and a fearless determination to share it. And it is very specifically *this* border, where Flintshire grit hits soft Cheshire sandstone. This is not the Marches, a mystical greensward for misplaced nostalgia, but a tight, thin-lipped line that sighs on the wind and vanishes into an indefinable horizon. For the last couple of decades, Gee has lived a mile the other side of the border, in one of the Wirral villages that used to be on the estuary before it was drained and the river canalised. As the waters receded, so too did any sense of its true hinterland. She and her husband wrote a fantastically lively village history book, and seriously offended some of their neighbours by pointing out how nearly Welsh they all are. Neither did they take kindly to being reminded that their lush and lovely Wirral villages – far older, wealthier and whiter than the national average – were built on the money from slavery. 'It's very pretty,' she tells me, 'but it's all soaked in blood.'

* * *

So to Chester. I've been guardedly circling it, catching glimpses and snippets, and now it's time to plunge in. As I head out of Saltney and under the railway bridge into the city, I picture baby Gee on the back of a sit-up-and-beg bicycle, as her ma puffs and strains up this same hill to go and scrub for strangers. Then and still now, the *Upstairs, Downstairs* symbolism of this road is remarkable, as if you're going from peeling cellars and steamy kitchens up the back stairs and into the salons and drawing rooms above. Even the vape shops and kebab houses look suddenly shinier. The contrast – and the speed of the change – takes my breath away, makes me laugh in shock. Saltney to Chester is I think the most graphic demonstration yet of the border, and just to make sure, I turn back and do it again. This time, going under the railway bridge and popping out the other side, I'm reminded of the scene in *Who Framed Roger Rabbit?* when Bob Hoskins drives through a tunnel, out of tough-nut, two-bit LA and into the lollipops-and-sunshine of Toontown.

That fits too. To generations of Lancastrians and north Walians, Chester is a cartoon, a gaudy playground of fantasy and fun, and to some extent it always has been. From its foundation as one of the largest legionary fortresses in Roman Britain, through centuries as a military and political headquarters, it has invariably been full of visitors and outsiders, who all needed watering, comforting and entertaining. Once the river had finally silted up beyond repair, the city turned away from its port, letting upstart Liverpool take the strain, and launched instead into a life of leisure, of racing and shopping, hotels and theatres, coffee shops, dining rooms and promenades.

Arriving in town, I feel like a bandit who's spent the last couple of years in hiding. This is my first time in a city, any city, since the outbreak of the pandemic almost two years ago, and it is simultaneously thrilling and terrifying. The week before my trip, news had begun to spread of a new coronavirus variant, one that was far more virulent in its transmission. True to form, the Welsh government had acted more quickly and cautiously than Westminster, and yet another gulf ripped open along the border. Masks were the most obvious faultline. In rural Wales, pretty much everyone had been wearing them in shops and pubs since the beginning of the first lockdown. In Chester, even with the new variant, they are very much a minority pursuit.

While pursing my lips in disapproval, I also feel some sneaking admiration for the attitude. Christmas is a couple of weeks away, the city is dolled up to the nines, and the sense of freedom, even if it is misplaced, is intoxicating. One evening in town, I head to choral evensong at the cathedral and then have dinner, a pint too many and some fascinating and funny conversations with complete strangers in the Albion, a backstreet boozer tucked under the city walls. It's a pub that trumpets its anti-modernism, eschewing screens and muzak, its walls stiff with William Morris wallpaper, vintage enamel signs and Union Jacks. In normal times, such places make me itch, but there's an authenticity to the Albion that sidesteps my cynicism. Or maybe it's just the beer, the food, and the sweet, sweet feeling of connections briefly forged by a roaring fire in an interminably long winter.

At one point in the warm fug of an evening, I call home. My partner Peredur, the son of a Welsh mountain farm, would struggle in there. The name, the flags and the wartime memorabilia would put him on edge immediately, and there'd be no coming back. He doesn't have the slithery luxury of dual identity that I, as a middle-class Englishman turned *Cymro o ddewis* (Welshman by choice), can deploy without thinking. He cannot pass, and in Chester that has always really meant something. This is after all a city whose *raison d'être* is as the place from which to hammer the Irish and the Welsh.

In establishing their military headquarters here on the plains between, the Romans split *yr hen ogledd*, the old north, from the west. They were never again united, and ultimately, through the following centuries of battles and retrenchment, it spelled the end for the Brythonic cultures of the north. If Chester could be kept armed and alert, went the thinking, it was only a matter of time before the British west – Wales – would shrink to extinction too. The animosity towards the Welsh was sharper here than on any other part of the border.

In the early seventh century, the Anglo-Saxon king of Northumbria 'led his army to Chester, and there slew countless Welsh' (Bede), including hundreds of monks, mid-prayer, from nearby Bangor-is-Coed. On the coming of the Normans, Chester became a pivotal point of control and the centre of a new earldom, under its charismatic

Earl, Hugh d'Avranches. For his savagery against the Welsh, including holding the king of Gwynedd hostage for twelve years and dragging him every week through the city market, he is remembered in England as 'Hugh Lupus', Hugh the Wolf. In Welsh, he is remembered as Huw Dew, Fat Hugh.

Through the twelfth century, the situation calmed enough for Welsh traders to be allowed into the city, but never on equal terms with their English and Norman counterparts. In the last few years of the century, a monk named Lucian penned an encomium on the city, *De laude Cestrie* ('On the Glory of Chester'), one of our earliest urban guidebooks. While acknowledging that the people of the city and the 'Britonibus' (the Welsh) are similar, he warned that 'The native [of Chester] knows how savagely our neighbour often approaches, and stimulated by cold and hunger haunts the place, and then cannot help but compare the difference in supplies. Yet he returns, but with hostile glance and evil thoughts envies the citizen within the walls.' It is a vivid picture of crushing inequality, where suspicion always falls on the already downtrodden.

The same attitudes percolate down the centuries. George Borrow began his *Wild Wales* tour in Chester, and tells us that The Rows, the city's famous elevated shopping arcades, were 'originally built for the security of the wares of the principal merchants against the Welsh'. If anyone raised the alarm, they could be swiftly sealed off, and 'missiles of all kinds kept ready for such occasions' would be rained on the intruders. The only blights on Chester, trilled a 1930s guidebook, were 'fire, floods, plagues and the constant raids of the Welsh'.

Symbolically, it was to Chester that Prince Llywelyn was ordered to come and pay his stipend to the English crown for recognition as the Prince of Wales. In 1275, the new king Edward I himself travelled to the city to receive not just Llywelyn's money, but his homage too. As happened at the ford on the Severn two years earlier, Llywelyn failed to show up, and the epoch of wary truce snapped shut. Within a further two years, Edward had launched his campaign against the Welsh from Chester and garrisoned his troops and later his stonemasons there. From the city came the men and machines to build the 'iron ring' of castles, and the walled English enclaves alongside them, most planted deep in the Welshest turf. Llywelyn's old lands were carved up into shires, on the English model.

Even that wasn't the zenith of cross-border tension; that came just over a century later in the aftermath of Owain Glyndŵr's uprising. His powerbase, in northern Powys and Denbighshire, was within an easy day's gallop, and the burghers of Chester were taking no chances. Welshmen were not permitted to enter the city in a group larger than three, and were banned entirely from being within the walls – on pain of decapitation – between sundown and sunrise. All Welshmen, even merchants and traders, were allowed to carry only one knife; any other arms were to be forfeited at the city gates.

Plus ça change … I leave the Albion pleasantly tipsy, and head out into the sharp night air. The streets sing of fun and light and the coming festive season. On the city side of the gates there's a boisterous crowd of youngsters, wearing far too few layers and not a mask between them, queuing for entry into a bar. Before letting anyone in, bouncers in black puffa jackets pat them down, arms out, back and sides, legs apart, all the way down to the ankles, and I wonder if the fifteenth-century city gatekeepers had much the same technique, and if their successors are giving extra attention to anyone with a Welsh accent.

Town is lively. It always is – if I close my eyes and think of Chester, I think immediately of the sound of souped-up cars roaring through its streets – but after the privations of the last two years there's an extra charge in the air. A little earlier in the evening, between the cathedral and the pub, I'd caught the annual Winter Watch parade. Even that harks back to Chester's suspicion of the Welsh, having its origins in a fifteenth-century ceremony, where the mayor and his retinue would tour the gates and walls, checking that there was no one from across the border lying in ambush. Once assured that all was safe, they'd hand over the keys of the gates to the City Watch, and have their Christmas feast. Today's parade is more generic, a multi-form celebration of winter, darkness, Yule, the solstice, Christmas, Hanukkah, you name it. There's an inevitable samba band, some animatronic puppets, jesters, angels, dragons (Chinese, not Welsh), reindeer, unicorns, Jack Frost, devils, crows and an Ice Queen, but outnumbering them all are people made up as corpses, cadavers, ghouls and ghosts. At the head of the parade, two enormous puppet skeletons writhe in and out of the crowds in a sinuous *danse macabre*. Death is on the menu. A virus lurks within these old walls, but no one mentions it and no key will halt it.

* * *

To Lucian the twelfth-century monk, Chester was a supremely blessed place. He afforded the city almost biblical status, staking its claim as a near equal of Rome and Jerusalem, even skewing its geography so that, wrote Robert W. Barrett, Jr., 'the city's streets and buildings become scripture made manifest'. As for the city, so too its county. Cheshire was one of the shires afforded palatine status by the Normans, giving it considerable independence and its Earl many of the powers of a king. 'The province of Chester', wrote Lucian with pride, 'is, by a certain distinction of privilege, free from all other Englishmen.' The status lasted far into the Victorian era, and has helped give Cheshire a most elevated sense of itself.

Another twelfth-century borderland cleric cooked up an even richer confection of superiority. In Monmouth, visitors to the old priory used to be shown a beautiful oriel window and told that beneath it, Geoffrey of Monmouth had written his *History of the Kings of Britain*, published in the mid-1130s. That the window is three centuries younger than the monk was just the first of so many fantasies in what was to become our national foundation story, of Britain not just as an island, a unit of geography, but as a calculated political construct.

Geoffrey claimed that he had translated the work from 'an ancient book in the British (i.e. Welsh) tongue'. In truth, he stitched together tiny snippets from earlier texts, and drowned them in myth and invention, including an entire lineage for the first Britons. Geoffrey had Brutus, who he claimed as our founding father, fleeing Troy alongside Aeneas, the founder of Rome; the two men – and the cultures they went on to found – were contemporaries, and equals. Brutus had three sons, Locrinus, Camber and Albanactus, who ostensibly each founded one of the British nations: Lloegr (England), Cymru (Wales) and Alba (Scotland). As the eldest, Locrinus, was heir apparent, his London the home of the one crown. Geoffrey's first three chapters tell of the disasters that will unfold should London's supremacy ever be denied.

More than any other single source, *History of the Kings of Britain* switched our understanding of the word 'British'. It had hitherto meant Brythonic, or Welsh ('Breton'), and was largely linguistic. By inflating it with bogus imperial credentials, linking it explicitly to Ancient Rome and implicitly to the island's new Norman overlords, the word began its long march to becoming a highly charged synonym for English. That became its default, the norm, a hard political and often overly racialised gold standard by which first the other inhabitants of these islands were judged and found wanting, and then too the rest of the world.

For the Welsh, there was at least a sop, a saviour in the story: Arthur, the once and future king. Though Geoffrey of Monmouth painted a pitiful tale of the original Britons acquiescing in their own downfall, his Arthur vanished into the ether, where he waits for the day when he will return his people to the throne of Britain. Everyone claims him, though, and sees in him what they will. Geoffrey's version of the tale washed across medieval Europe, and on this island his court of Camelot has been firmly placed at – among so many others – Glastonbury, Winchester, Tintagel, London, Cadbury Castle, Caerleon, Llangollen. Along the border, as befits the line between the two cultures that claim him most, the standing stones, caves, outcrops, bluffs, graves and hillforts named in his honour are legion. He is – as a medieval scholar in Caerleon once roared at me in a television interview, his words as rich and sticky as toffee – 'our greatest chronological prostitute'.

When in 1485 the Welsh Tudors came to the throne after the Battle of Bosworth, many – the new king Henry VII included – claimed that this was, at last, Arthurian prophecy made manifest. The Welsh flourished at court in London and over the next century enjoyed an apparent golden age. In the space of a few decades of the sixteenth century, the first printed book in Welsh was produced, the Bible translated into the language and a Welsh college was founded at Oxford. Chester loomed large in the Tudor story. Henry was a frequent visitor, and so too his son, Henry VIII. On the dissolution of the monasteries, the city's abbey, where Lucian had sung such fulsome civic praises three and half centuries earlier, was spared destruction, instead being given cathedral status and made the centre of a new diocese.

When we think of Cheshire, it is Tudor architecture that springs straight to mind. No other county in Britain contains such a plenty of black-and-white houses, including some of the very finest we have, though in the city itself so many of the half-timbered properties are in fact late Victorian fakes. And that, perhaps more than anything, is the spirit of Chester: mock Tudor incarnate, the very embodiment of sentimental parochialism.

Are they fakes though? What is 'real' when it comes to a cityscape? I admire Chester's shamelessness in this regard, and not just with the mock Tudor. Everything about the city is a glorious sham. Tourist guides talk of the city's ancient Roman walls, though they were built by the Saxons in the tenth century, then given battlements by the Normans, and further tidied and embellished by Tudors, Jacobeans, Georgians, Victorians and modern revivalists in turn. Below one section, the Roman Gardens appear to house an intact ruin of a fourth-century palace, but the antiquities were brought from digs all over the city in 1950 and rearranged to give the illusion of unity. The medieval market cross was installed in 1975. Even the cathedral doesn't quite ring true. Georgian diarist Hester Thrale sniffed that 'it seemed more like imitation than reality', and I'm right with her. To get to evensong, I walk through sandstone cloisters uplit in pink and purple, and scattered with white fairy lights for Christmas. If it gets me in the mood for anything, it's not the Blessed Sacrament but a boogie down memory lane to a 1990s gay disco.

The sleight of hand continues, as bronzed and brazen as a TikTok influencer. Walking the walls, whatever age they might be, is by far the best way to orient yourself in Chester. It's quite a ride. A paved walkway brushes along the top of sandstone walls, above meadows, the racecourse and the river frontage, but also through gaps in concrete car parks, shopping centres, flashy hotels and flatpack office blocks. All time is now.

Crossing over the street at Newgate, I'm suddenly aware of shouting in the street below. It gets louder, closer and more strident, and appears to be some sort of demonstration. A few other people stop to look, and we discuss what it might be. Anti-vaxxers most likely, we decide, with a sigh. The procession comes nearer and – oh my goodness – it's *kids* dressed as *Roman soldiers*. A guide in full centurion outfit is marching them around the city, getting them to wave shields and pretend swords as they holler bloodthirsty chants. A few of the children (and their teachers) look terribly sheepish, and my heart goes out to them, but others are loving it, roaring with what looks like genuine fury and an eagerness to be given the nod so that they can start walloping passers-by. It's *Lord of the Flies* on a pavement by the Premier Inn. The border is only 1.5 miles away, but I am definitely, conclusively in England.

For all its pretence of timelessness, Chester powers on, and nothing is so sacrosanct that it cannot be ripped down, rebuilt or repurposed. One large block of The Rows was entirely hollowed out in the 1960s to build one of the first shopping precincts. Even in these straitened days, when physical shops are melting in the heat of the internet, it seems to be doing just fine, though there's a sad old sign of the times next door: what used to be the famous Browns of Chester department store, all boarded up with pretty *trompe l'œil* hoardings, but boarded up all the same. Along with every other outpost of the Debenhams empire, the pandemic finally did for it.

Browns was the byword for Chester's retail elegance; a 1930s advertisement promises 'pincushions and pillowcases, tallboys and tweed suits, bracelets and Bokhara rugs', and reminds us that they also have an auction and estate department, beauty salon, two furniture depositories, a removals department and a restaurant. Hanging in our front room is a beautiful pair of curtains from Browns, as bright as the day they were bought fifty years ago by my partner's grandmother. As for many Welsh farm wives, a day's shopping in Chester was a prize annual jolly, though serious business too, their one chance to import a splash of ritz into the mountains of Meirionnydd. And now – it's only progress – their great-granddaughters come to the city for its bars, clubs and pamper parlours. Great-grandsons too; there are whole streets where almost every unit is some kind of men's salon. In the winter twilight, I peer through the windows into so many halls of mirrors, and marvel at the city's sheer number of tattooed young tups, sockless and squeezed into too-tight trousers, being busily crimped into shape for the weekend ahead.

This is, after all, the city of *Hollyoaks*, Channel 4's buffed-up teen soap launched in 1995 and set in a fictional Chester suburb. Though it's now filmed on a set in Liverpool, they do occasionally come back here for a few location scenes. If you see a film crew around the city now, they're more likely to be working on the area's latest small-screen incarnation, *The Real Housewives of Cheshire* (the word 'housewife' used here in its very broadest possible sense; so too the word 'real').

There will never be a reality series called *The Only Way is Flintshire*. Much though I've enjoyed a few days in Chester, I'm itching to get back across the line, one that seems – if anything – even more heavily inked in than before. It's partly my own prejudice, I know. I've never particularly warmed to Cheshire, something that goes right back to childhood and some step-family and friends that we used to visit there. Even then, the only topics of conversation among the adults were money, houses and cars, and, with my peer group, whatever the latest gadgets or trainers were. Having the wrong brand, or something that was too old, brought immediate derision, tinged with an aggressive quality that I could never quite fathom. The villages and countryside looked tame and flat, and long before the advent of CCTV, felt as if they were watching you, and not especially liking what they saw. I'd look towards the distant Welsh hills, fantasise about their rough, chipped beauty, and wish to god that I were there.

I have mellowed, though perhaps not much. On the last night of my stay in Chester, I sit by the river in the gloom of a December dusk, looking over at the city centre lighting up on the far bank. To the Welsh, this side was known as Treboeth, 'hot town', a reference to how often they razed it to the ground. I can almost hear the shouts of alarm and the city gates being hastily slammed shut again, though it's drowned out by the welcome crawk of crows as they slice the skies before settling down high in a rickety ash tree. At this point in its journey, even in the golden core of Chester, the Dee is gloriously unkempt. Boats lie prone on the mudbanks, ferns terrorise walls, crows and gulls and geese lord it over everything.

Most unknowing of all is the river itself, swirling its damnedest around the heart and history of the city. Of the three rivers whose watersheds are bisected by the England–Wales border, the Dee is the one I know by far the least. The ridge that separates the basins of the Severn and Dee sits between Oswestry and Chirk, and that too is the border of my familiarity. North of that, it's all interesting, and often beautiful, but it's not mine.

Four days earlier, preparing for this trip, I hiked to the source of the Dee, under a rocky scree to the south-west of Bala. I followed the water upstream for miles, through conifer plantations inhabited by wild ponies and then out over an ankle-twisting, tussocky bog. Though a tough hike, squelching slowly across hostile territory, it was magnificent. The winter light was lemony sharp, snow dusted the surrounding peaks and the bony ridge of Dduallt, the river's source, took on every possible shape and shadow. I walked all day, and met no one at all.

And now, sitting by the big brown beast as it muscles its way around Chester, I think of that excitable brook at the heart of a huge untenanted landscape, and find it thrillingly difficult to reconcile them. Culturally too: the Dee rises in the most stoutly Welsh corner of all, where the language is strong and the politics fierce. Those utterly foreign mountains are little more than 40 miles away from these placid English meadows, and I know that along this northern tranche of the border I will meet some of its sharpest contrasts and greatest secrets.

6.

GROS VENEUR

/// marriage.moods.premature

This is a first. I've been ordered out of plenty of places over the years, but never before by a bollard. I'm 50 yards off the road, on the drive to the main gate of Eaton Hall, and suddenly one of the stone posts lining the way roars into life. 'Can I help you?' it booms, a metallic light flashing in time with the voice. I tell it that I was just hoping to take a photograph of the splendid gates, but it doesn't want to know. 'This is private property. Please remove yourself to the public highway,' the bollard orders me, and I do, nervously eyeing up its fellows to see if any are doubling up as a tiny gun turret.

It was no great surprise. Less than 2 miles further back, the very first thing I saw in crossing the border was the Grosvenor Pulford Hotel & Spa, an Edwardian redbrick pleasure palace of ersatz Merrie England, attended by ladies in shades sliding out of jet-black Range Rovers. It was clear that I had entered not just England, nor even Cheshire, but the Land of Grosvenor, the family name of the Dukes of Westminster. This is their manor, and everything points, or rather genuflects, in their direction.

In Chester, 5 miles up the road, the name checks are so common that they become white noise: drive in over the Grosvenor Bridge, to take a room at the five-star Chester Grosvenor, next door to the Grosvenor Shopping Centre, before going for a stroll around Grosvenor Park or to visit the Grosvenor Museum. For a little variety, why not get some fresh air in Westminster Park instead, at the end of Westminster Avenue, off Grosvenor Road, or shop in the new Westminster Arcade, fashioned out of the exuberant terracotta Westminster Coach & Motor Car Works? Should your budget not stretch to a night in the Grosvenor, down towards the railway station are the Westminster Hotel (three star) and the Belgrave (two), another family handle that has spread far and wide. It's the name of an estate village, home of the fine drive and aggressive bollards. Most famously, it's the name that went down south, polished its vowels and mutated into Belgravia.

Asked for advice on how young entrepreneurs might succeed, the sixth Duke of Westminster, who died in 2016, once replied, 'Make sure they have an ancestor who was a very close friend of William the Conqueror' (the original *gros veneur*, 'the fat huntsman': Huw Dew, Hugh the Wolf). He might have added that it was also handy to have had a forebear who bid highest in the auction of the eleven-year-old heiress of a large farm in west London. In developing their new acquisition, the Grosvenors of Eaton Hall turned the estate into Belgravia and Mayfair, and themselves into Britain's wealthiest family. After her husband's early death, the young bride tried to challenge the arrangement and reclaim some of her inheritance, but the Grosvenors had her declared insane and put away.

Their honorifics ballooned alongside the riches. On the 1677 marriage that launched the dynasty, they were mere baronets, passing the title of Sir from one generation to the next (itself a paid-for upgrade of a single knighthood, bestowed when the king visited Cheshire in 1617). In 1761, the title baronet was plumped up to Lord, then Earl in 1784, Marquess in 1831 and finally in 1874 to the very top drawer itself, as the Dukes of Westminster.

In west Cheshire, they are everything. As I noted in the last chapter, the city of Chester is bursting at the seams, which is why westward expansion, into Saltney and Wales, is almost inevitable. There is another direction in which the city has ample breathing room: to its south. But there lies the 11,000 acres of the Grosvenor Estate, off-limits to the authorities – and off-limits to us too.

Within the entire estate, there is only one public right of way, squeezed along the bank of the River Dee as it meanders around Eaton's eastern edge. The path connects two of the main estate villages, Eccleston and Aldford, and though signs at either end warn that the river can rise rapidly, there is 'No alternative access available for the next 2,500 meters [sic] should flooding occur'. Neither is there, at any point along the long and muddy path, a single place to rest or even sit down. Through the double fencing, the walker gets an occasional peek at Eaton's Victorian clock tower, and hears it chiming every quarter of an hour in an almost identical peal to its big brother, Big Ben. It's hard to remember which is the one that sets the real time and timbre of the UK: the Westminsters at Eaton, or the Etonians at Westminster.

Dotted around the edges are classic estate villages, neat as buttons and wildly desirable to the property pages. The houses are trim and red, with mock-Jacobean flourishes, immaculate gardens and identical white gates. Summer flowers and winter wood smoke hang on the air, but neither can quite outdo the fusty tang of feudalism. They are Stepfords-in-sandstone, and though they take a lovely photograph they squeeze the living breath from me.

Of the villages, Eccleston (from the Welsh *eglwys*, church, and Old English *tūn*, town) sees itself very much as *primus inter pares*. Here is the main entrance into the Eaton estate – the grand avenue from Belgrave is kept only for Sunday best – and here too the church where the first six dukes lie in their vaults. It was the first duke that got the old church demolished and this one built, in the nick of time for his own interment. The exterior is regimental, the interior sombre, all high pointed arches in dark sandstone, a dusky hush and the faint smell of polish. It feels like a public school chapel, and through the stiff gloom I squint at the memorials. All those riches, but they don't live long, these Grosvenors. Only two of the dukes made it to seventy.

In Aldford, a few of the mock-Tudor houses are flying the English flag, making it look even more like a Hornby train set come to life, but in the churchyard it is remarkable how many of the dead are Welsh. There are whole clusters of them bunched up together in holy and eternal communion, their headstones carved with whispers of love and longing in the old tongue. Like so many more of their comrades (a word from the same root as Cymru) they came to be part of the army of servants at Eaton Hall, over 300 strong, and stayed, and died so near yet so far from home.

There's another entrance drive to the Hall in Aldford, guarded by gates emblazoned with two big Ws and a PRIVATE sign. I take some photos, and sit on the adjacent wall for a few minutes, watching a cadre of jackdaws dart through the trees along a stream, and off into the estate. It's a windy day, and their ghoulish cries bounce on the gusts, curdle in mid-air and make my blood dance. A black Range Rover purrs down the drive on the other side of the gates. They glide open, he pulls through and stops by me. The passenger window slides down. The driver is all in black too, tooled up like a policeman. He looks at me with studied blankness. 'Can I help you?' he asks.

Is it the Grosvenor estate motto? My mind drifts back ten years, to the Duke of Westminster's stalking and fishing estate, a massive slab of moor and mountain in Scotland's far top-left corner. A friend had taken up a post there as the estate gardener; her main job was to fill the house with flowers whenever The Family came to stay, even if that was out of season and meant a six-hour round trip to Inverness to buy some. We went to visit. I took a walk, and had got all of half a mile before being challenged by a man with a gun and a 'Can I help you?' On being assured that I was staying with one of his colleagues, he pulled back, and wished me well, but I couldn't help but wonder what the response would have been otherwise – and this on a remote estate of 150 square miles, in a country with an ostensible right to roam. I returned to our friend's house, one of a tight cluster of buildings where all the estate staff lived. CCTV blinked on every corner, feeding back to a central command headquarters at Eaton Hall, 400 miles away. Never before had I realised that you could be simultaneously walloped by both agoraphobia *and* claustrophobia.

Back on the Cheshire plains, the more mannered suffocation of the Eaton estate fades fast on the Welsh border at Pulford. That, too, was a tied village, clear not just from the Grosvenor Hotel and Spa, but also from its lodge houses, neo-Jacobean cottages and heavy sandstone church. Since the estate relinquished the village in 1919, the stays have loosened; new housing and new businesses have made it feel like a real place, or at least Cheshire-real, like its housewives. The hotel trumpets its success at the English Wedding Awards (North), and up the street there's a performance-car showroom and a Thai massage parlour in the old post office. You won't find that in Eccleston or Aldford.

Crossing the border, the change is immediate and the relief palpable. In the very first Welsh village, Rossett, *yr Orsedd*, people are strolling, chatting and happy to greet a complete stranger with a smile. If anyone were to ask 'Can I help you?', it feels like they might actually mean it.

The swiftness of the change in these northern borderlands is dizzying. After the baggy ambiguity of the central Marches, the ducking and diving of the border itself and the wide corridors either side, I'm blindsided by how sharp the cut is here. A tough-nut rivalry between the two sides lurks just out of focus, fuelled by history (English and Welsh of course, but Irish and imperial too), by football, language, politics, religion and recreation: Chester and Liverpool for Welsh shoppers, north Wales for holidaying Scousers and Mancs. Sometimes, inevitably perhaps in such populated areas, it boils over.

In the first month of Covid lockdown, we all retreated into our chosen comfort blankets. Some took to cakes and chocolate, some to books or box sets, others gave up giving up smoking or hit the bottle a little earlier each day. Racists nailed everything about the pandemic on foreigners and immigrants, capitalists blamed socialism and vice versa, and conspiracy theorists found that if you spent enough time online, the threads between Covid and 5G and 9/11 and the Illuminati manifested like a string of magic beads. And those whose main hobby is cross-border sniping found plenty to keep them busy.

The possibility of sealing the border was much discussed during the pandemic. It was demanded by some in response to every twist and turn of the saga, and became *de facto* policy at times when the rules were significantly different on either side. Travelling the border for this book, I repeatedly heard stories of people not going to their usual shops because they lay on the other side of the line, or steeling themselves to make lightning raids on favourite supermarkets and garden centres at their quietest times, hearts thumping all the way. Gee Williams told me that on Christmas Day 2020, she and her husband left their car on the English bank of the Dee and walked over the Saltney Ferry footbridge to visit her sister and sit for an hour in her garden.

From a public health perspective, it was essential to keep holidaymakers from coming to Wales. In the north, middle and west of the country – the very areas tourists and second-homers flock to – hospital provision is so patchy, and so easily overwhelmed. I was, though, deeply uneasy at the old narrative that quickly resurfaced, with its clear implication that the only way the virus – an *airborne* virus – might arrive in Wales was for it to be physically imported from over the border. It was the latest manifestation of that sickly but stubborn Welsh self-image, of poor, pure Lady Gwalia being overwhelmed by diseased hordes from the east. It is a trope that needs burying, not resuscitating, especially in a globalised age when it is so easily exploited by the darkest of forces. I aired my disquiet in a piece written for a Welsh news website, was thanked by some, but shouted down by more. The piece 'make[s] me wonder whose side he is on?' someone responded.

Whose side am I on? Not that one, not ever. It's a question that continually prickles though and always makes me anxious, which is perhaps why I'm pleased to feel such unambiguous joy to cross the line at Pulford, and into Rossett. The fog clears. Though I have never been here before, I am home. We're still on the flatlands – the scarp of Wales is looming large ahead – but Cheshire has already evaporated, like its eponymous cat. The grin that it leaves has perfect, and very pricy, teeth.

With my back turned finally on the Grosvenor lands, I look at Denbighshire and Flintshire. There's no shortage of big houses here either; this north-eastern corner of Wales is home to its greatest concentration of grand estates. The stone, coal, fireclay, lead, zinc and iron industries that provided the literal bedrock of the Grosvenor riches across the border also seeded many near neighbours in Wales, with all of their own tied housing, home farms and society etiquette. So many are gone, though. The casualty rate among big houses in north-east Wales has been massive, far exceeding that of neighbouring Cheshire or Shropshire, and for myriad reasons. There was industrialisation of course, which did for lots in the unsentimental pursuit of coal and profit. Roads and railways, of which there have been many, took out others. Beyond the purely practical, though, there's something else here: a far less advanced sense of deference perhaps, a more egalitarian mindset, a commitment to broader values. I see it as much in the Rossett smiles as I do in the gaps on the maps.

It may of course just be my wishful thinking. Those of us who were drawn to Wales for its apparently unbreakable left-of-centre outlook, who cheered so deliriously when the country returned not a single Conservative MP for almost a decade around the millennium, have had to recalibrate our rose-tinted specs of late. Rossett is in the Wrexham constituency, which for the very first time elected a Tory MP in 2019. Over the Pulford Brook, the people of Chester, which includes Eaton Hall and all of its fastidious little villages, voted Labour.

* * *

The closest Welsh equivalent to the sheer scale and scope of Eaton Hall is Wynnstay, a mock French château at Ruabon, 5 miles the other side of Wrexham. It is a name you cannot avoid in north Wales. If you go for a pint on the English side of this border, chances are it will be at a Grosvenor Arms. On the Welsh side, it'll likely be at a Wynnstay Hotel. The two dynasties, each founded on the wealth tugged from the ground beneath Flintshire and Denbighshire, once eyeballed each other across the border as equals, though that illusion is long gone now. In their contrasting fortunes, and the ever-widening gulf between them, is almost everything about Wales and England, Britain and the UK.

Lords of the manor of Wynnstay were the Williams-Wynn dynasty. Through canny marriages, they forged a massive estate and, just as importantly in Wales, an impeccable pedigree. You could ride from

Ruabon to Aberystwyth, 60 miles distant on the west coast, without leaving their land. In my patch of mid Wales, I'll often find boundary stones carved with the letters WWW, for Sir Watkin Williams-Wynn, the name since 1719 of every successive baronet.

Like Eaton Hall, Wynnstay was built for maximum effect in relation to the curves of the River Dee. Various picturesque flourishes – a column, a folly tower, a hermit's cottage, a mock Doric temple, a cascade – made the most of the spectacular views down the river valley, towards Llangollen and the stumps of its hilltop castle, the heathery mountains above and the sensational new eye-catcher of the Pontcysyllte aqueduct. By the end of the eighteenth century, encased in its Capability Brown parkland, fringed by a dozen lodges, 8 miles of perimeter wall and four of river frontage, Wynnstay was the largest and finest estate in Wales.

For all the grandeur, and unlike the Grosvenors on their meteoric rise through the ranks, the eleven Sir Watkin Williams-Wynns have remained stuck on the lowest rung of the nobility, as baronets. And that despite being the 'right' kind of Celt: proudly and loudly Welsh, but also staunch Tories, Unionists and imperialists. Four Sir Watkins in a row sat as Conservative MPs for Denbighshire between 1716 and 1885, and other sons for neighbouring Montgomeryshire too. They were good Royalists as well, though perhaps the suspicion lingered that their fondness for reciting a family tree back to the kings of Gwynedd was code for potential treachery, a proclamation that their blood was at least as blue as anything flowing in Buckingham Palace.

There are so many stories of the benevolence of the Williams-Wynns. They were patrons of the Welsh arts, helping to foster national sentiment at a time when it was ignored or disparaged. Richard Wilson, the often-overlooked father of landscape painting, was their protégé, as were poets, harpists, composers and playwrights. Adjoining the house was a purpose-built theatre, thrown open to the local public for free every winter. For all their dyed-in-the-wool Toryism, there was political rootedness too: in 1831, as MP and Lord Lieutenant of Denbighshire, the fifth baronet was summoned to the Prime Minister to explain his public sympathy for striking miners.

Their support for the Welsh language was constant, and practical too. Giving locals affordable chances to buy their tenanted farms kept many young families in north Wales, at a time when emigration seemed the only option. My partner's grandfather was one such young man, on his way to America before the opportunity arose to buy an estate farm near Bala. He went for it, settled there, and almost all of his sixteen grandchildren and thirty great-grandchildren are still in north Wales, many in agriculture.

By 1883, the Williams-Wynn family owned 145,770 acres across mid and north Wales, bringing in an annual income of £55,000. In sharp contrast, just 300 acres of the Grosvenor Estate in Belgravia and Mayfair – described as 'swampy meads' when they married into it two centuries earlier – was by then netting them £250,000 per annum. The Wynnstay holdings became even less profitable as their mines and quarries closed, while the value of the Grosvenor real estate rocketed. Acre for acre, in 1883 their London land was worth over 2,000 times as much as that of the Wynnstay Estate. Since then, the gap has only grown stratospherically wider.

Death duties, wars and divestment did for the Williams-Wynns in a long and tortuous decline. After burning down in 1858, the house was rebuilt by an architect that the Sir Watkin of the day met on a train. 'A High Victorian version of French Renaissance,' sniffs Pevsner, 'it has much of the coarseness and little of the gusto associated with the genre.' William Condry, the kindliest of nature writers, agreed: 'from a distance it looks fine, but close to is less satisfying'. It's a cheerless lump of a place, but the family sold up long ago, in 1948. It became a private school, which itself went bust in 1994, and has since been turned into apartments.

Most of the outlying estates were sold off even earlier, but never made enough to staunch the haemorrhage. The waters have risen on the Williams-Wynns, leaving them with ever smaller disconnected islands of property dotted around north-east Wales. The eleventh baronet, now in his eighties, lives alone in one of the last estate remnants on the other side of Denbighshire; his son and heir in a remote cottage with no gas or electricity.

The melancholy is no less marked in the once grand park that made their name. Most of its finest features are long gone or inaccessible. Ornate gates to nowhere are rusted shut, the windows of its lodges barred or broken. The folly tower, once a famous Picturesque viewpoint down the Dee valley, has mostly fallen down the cliff. What remains is choked by trees and firmly out of bounds, but even were it clear and accessible, the view now would be a close-up of lorries thundering over a massive concrete viaduct, built in 1990. In routing its bypass through the middle of the parkland, and building a junction on top of the tree-lined avenue from Ruabon to Wynnstay, the village severed its connection with its upbringing.

The fast road is the key to Wynnstay's new life, as a nowhere place from which to commute. After the school went bankrupt, the buildings were bought by Manchester developers. Odd-shaped apartments were squeezed into every corner and cupboard, lavishly promoted in the property pages, and sold on 999-year leases at the height of the millennium property boom. Many of those that have since come back on the market have been resold for less, often much less. The brochures still call it luxury living, and the park a Capability Brown masterpiece, but really, both the house and its gardens feel like the rehab hospital in a low-budget wartime drama.

No such degradation for the Eaton estate down the road. Over the same twenty-year period, average property prices in Belgravia and Mayfair have more than quadrupled, their wedding-cake compounds irresistible to those who shelter behind opaque identities in tax havens. Wynnstay's cheap cynicism and Belgravia's pitch-dark plenty feel like worlds apart, yet the thread between them is direct and sturdy. Over the last forty years, London's status as a safe stash for dirty cash, and its consequent ballooning unaffordability, have pushed the worst of property greed out across the land like ripples on a particularly effluent pond. Casino economics collided with kleptocracy, and rewarded only the most venal. The poison has swamped our housing supply, job market and democracy, and seeped into our individual and collective understanding of worth and value. It could well be what chokes the UK to death.

The ripples wash ashore right here at Wynnstay. Wales as land of cheap property, more-bang-for-your-buck, the place to plunder, patch up and flog off. It has long been the default image, in the media especially. Shamefully, that includes much of the Welsh media, whose self-esteem has always overly depended on comparisons with the neighbour in a pathetic and permanent game of catch-up. Galloping house prices are easily quantified, so become the yardstick by which they measure success. You cannot plot on a graph community cohesion, quality of life, or a more collaborative political culture.

You can feel it, though, in conversations, observations, little wisps of insight that flutter quietly by. The villages around Wrexham still have it, all scruffy swagger in red Ruabon brick, so to be told – as they routinely are – that their best hope is to hitch a ride on the coat-tails of Chester, to look and sound and act as much like that as they possibly can, is such a dull and derivative insult. It's nothing new, though. Go to Gresford, the pretty old pit village known for two extremes: its splendid fifteenth-century parish church and its terrible 1934 colliery disaster, when an explosion underground incinerated 266 men in fiery hell. Almost every writer visiting the church sings the same tune as the 1940s *Archaeologia Cambrensis*: 'the perfect Cheshire church in Wales', it gushed. The disaster, though, that's wholly Welsh. Inside the church is a memorial book to the victims, all but eleven entombed underground when the threat of further explosions meant that the pit had to be sealed. Nearly every dead man came from this side of the border, a line only 3 miles away. There are so many names, a legion of Griffiths, Evanses and Thomases, three separate John Williamses and four Thomas Joneses.

For Wrexham and its villages, it is hard to withstand the lure of copycat development, the idea that the only future has to be an off-the-peg version of what might have worked elsewhere. They always get told that, these places with little historical or cultural capital, the ones rarely allowed to speak in their own voice, those that have to be prefaced with an excuse or an explanation before being allowed onto the stage with the big boys. Almost all of this north-eastern corner of Wales falls into this category. Our collective sense of it is vague, defined more by what it isn't than what or where it is. It's clearly not Cheshire, with its acutely elevated sense of self, not Wirral (ditto), nor Liverpool and Manchester, the cocky shoguns of England's north-west.

It's no less muddied in a Welsh context. To outsiders, it's raced past en route to the honeypots of Eryri (Snowdonia) and the coast, and for the Welsh, it's too redbrick to make much of a dent on the eisteddfod circuit, and even in English, is suspiciously Scouse and semi-detached, at best, from its own capital city. 'The region has not had its share of Welsh institutions,' hectored the late historian John Davies at the opening of the 2007 National Eisteddfod in Mold, Flintshire, 'not because it is an unsuitable place in which to locate such institutions, but because we in the rest of Wales have connived in the region's marginalisation'. With the added provocation of the area's rapid industrial decline, the temptation for hollow gestures or second-hand solutions is hard to resist.

It is, though, an area with resistance pumping through its veins, and in that is its real flavour, and hope for the future. I meet up with Marc Jones, a Wrexham councillor, who's been at the forefront of a very specific recent act of resistance, campaigning against the council's fourth attempt in just over twenty years to secure city status for the town. His argument is nuanced and reasoned, and I think right – such a title is 'a distraction when we need a laser-like focus on improving our town'. It's also a brave stance in an age when foghorn populism drives most public policy. Entirely predictably, the council leader accused Marc and his fellows of 'talking Wrexham down'. I'm heartened though that Wrexonians seem to agree with Marc. The council undertook a public survey, and found that 61 per cent of the borough's population didn't want to bid yet again, at some cost, for city status. The ruling Conservative–Independent administration went for it all the same, and was successful. In May 2022, Wrexham was announced as one of eight new cities to celebrate the Queen's platinum jubilee.

When I first came to Wrexham, almost thirty years ago, there was a chip on its shoulder moulded precisely to the size and shape of

Chester. The English city, only 12 miles but a psychic galaxy away, exercised such a pull on the Wrexham mindset. It's that force – if *they* have it, then so must we – that has driven all four bids for city status, and so much more besides. For shopping, eating, drinking or dancing, a day out or a bit of a treat, Chester was assumed to be effortlessly, almost inevitably superior. There was one glorious exception, though, the one that often sparks the greatest flashpoint of all between the two: football.

Wrexham–Chester matches are legendarily fierce. They're guaranteed box office: a local derby that spans a national border, between two towns each a little chippy about their place on the map, and two teams that have both endured more heartbreak than heroics. For once, though, Wrexham has the upper hand. The two sides first met in an FA Cup tie in 1888, which Wrexham took 3–2, and they've won a roughly similar proportion of their 156 cup and league encounters since.

More than that – and despite never having risen higher than their four seasons, forty years ago, in the old second division – the Welsh side has a strut that far outweighs the stats. In 2008, dogged work by a Wrexham fan paid off when Guinness World Records accepted that the team's Racecourse stadium was the world's oldest international football ground still in use as such, Wales having first played Scotland there in 1877. A couple of years later, more intrepid digging turned up new discoveries about the origins of the club. As a result, the foundation date on the WFC crest was changed from 1873 to 1864, making it the third oldest professional football club on earth. Then Hollywood came knocking.

In the autumn of 2020, having scoured western Europe for a suitably down-on-its-luck sports club to take on as both investment and reality TV project, film stars Ryan Reynolds and Rob McElhenney alighted on Wrexham. The talk was big and bold, of returning the club to the football league and making it 'a global force', but also of reinforcing 'the values, traditions and legacy of this community'. Though the slick hand of expensive PR was always evident, their interviews and social media output showed genuine empathy, and it was no shock that when the buyout was put to the 2,000 members of the Wrexham Supporters' Trust, who'd owned and run the club since it almost went under a decade earlier, 98.6 per cent jumped with them.

Though initially sceptical, Marc Jones – a lifelong WFC fan – is up for the ride. 'It's a rollercoaster,' he says, 'but you've got to be on it.' There's no doubting the interest that the showbiz spotlight has given his beloved club, nor the excitement that it's generating in the town. 'The last year before the pandemic,' he says, 'there were around 2,000 of us season ticket holders. This year, there's been over 6,000 applications. You can't argue with that either.'

Even before the stardust was sprinkled over Wrexham, the latent strengths of the club were clear: 2,000 season ticket holders in a league where many clubs routinely attract crowds only in the hundreds. It might have been luck that brought Reynolds and McElhenney here, but as they quickly came to appreciate, this corner of Wales is ripe for a revolution, and football its most likely – and potentially most positive – catalyst. Though the area struggles to get noticed, even within Wales, passion and talent for the game has always been its hallmark. So many of the biggest names in Welsh football – Ian Rush, Mark Hughes, Gary Speed, Neville Southall, Billy Meredith – came from here, played here, managed here. For all of its first few decades, the national team was based here; not until 1900 did a Wales international take place in the south. When, in 2019, the National Museum of Wales agreed to open its eighth site and dedicate it to football, there were some half-hearted claims from elsewhere, but never much doubt that it was going anywhere other than Wrexham.

This matters in more than just sporting terms, for what Welsh football has come to mean is key to what might lie ahead. Rugby is always assumed to be *the* Welsh game, its national obsession and holy grail, yet on any given winter Saturday there are fewer people across Wales at rugby matches than there are at the football. The assumption is partly geographic; so strong in the national identity is the gravitational pull of the south Wales valleys that other places get entirely eclipsed, even those – like here – that also dug and smelted and sweated in the dark bowels of the earth, and who died for it too. Rugby may be a religion in south Wales, but like most state religions it is looking increasingly bloated and behind the times.

Welsh football, on the other hand, is roaring. There are the successes on the field – none more thrilling (or more Welsh) than the 58-year wait for qualification for a major tournament, then a headlong canter into its semi-finals at Euro 2016 in France – but equally important is the mirror that it holds up to the country at large. The Welsh Rugby Union, a phalanx of stuffed blazers and royal hobnobbery, looks and acts like something from the Welsh game's glory days in the 1970s. The English Football Association is all that too, riven with pomp and lacquered in backhanders. The Football Association of Wales looks very different to either: slick, nimble on its toes, with an easy diversity and cheerful confidence in its bilingualism. It's a far more appealing version of the modern country, a potential blueprint for something lasting, and it was born in Wrexham.

* * *

In the Covid lockdowns, I took to the map. I usually do. In my 2009 book *Map Addict*, I wrote that 'my route of escape has long been thrusting my head into a map and staying there until the deafening buzz recedes'. At a time when travel was proscribed, that need became even sharper. The border explorations that I had planned in pursuit of this book, three-day walks and leisurely drives down high-hedged lanes, were postponed. Like so much else at the time, the only way to travel was to do so virtually, poring over Ordnance Surveys at home with the intensity of someone looking for coded messages buried within. I stroked contours and conjured old holloways, imagining them for real in vivid meditations, and lost happy hours jumping between the paper map and its plentiful online brethren.

Even from the map, it's clear that there are some parts of the border more aesthetically blessed than others: the curves and folds of the Clun Forest, threaded by tracks and the dyke's deepest gouge; the tightrope ridge on the far edge of the Black Mountains to the south of

Hay; the seductive meanders of the Wye as it heads through wooded cliffs on its last hurrah to the sea. Yet one map, and one bit of border, kept pulling me back for perusal, where the frontier runs along the Dee either side of the twin towns of Holt (Wales) and Farndon (England). It's not an especially celebrated stretch, nor one I'd explored before, but Ordnance Survey made it look fascinating. The pale blue river wriggles and squirms like a puppy and – judging by the number of places where the border leaves the water to scoop out fields on the opposite bank – the Dee has changed course regularly over the last few centuries. Online searches, where you can toggle between old maps and a contemporary aerial view, show that this dynamic change continues. As you'd expect on a floodplain, there are few dwellings, but plenty of streams and gullies, footpaths too, in random patterns that spoke of old tracks for farmhands, postmen, midwives and schoolchildren. In the middle of such a busy landscape, the map of the gap in its middle promised big skies, sliding waters, a breather.

North of Holt and Farndon, the map shows numerous solitary riverside dwellings, and they looked the most intriguing aspect of all. Along both banks of the Dee's ample meanders are a few dozen build-ings, dotted regularly every 100 yards and stretching out for miles. Most appear to have no direct access to a track or road. Online I read that they are chalets of the plotlander movement that were originally built there in the interwar years. Such ramshackle clusters of sheds, caravans and old railway carriages were once commonplace on the coast or along rivers, though most have long vanished, eaten up by developers or squashed by councils who take a very dim view of the kind of planning anarchy that they represent. The Farndon chalets are a rare survivor. There in lockdown, I planned my route to Arcadia-on-the-Border, and couldn't wait.

That the journey, when it finally came, started in Aldford, the Eaton estate village where every gatepost and window frame is identi-cal, only made the prospect of plotland even more delicious. It's a hefty walk; there is no easy access, which perhaps explains both the appeal for chalet owners and their survival. Being divided between two countries, on the brink of both, must also have a bearing.

Plotland was every bit as odd and beguiling as I'd hoped. Some chalets are the originals, patched up lovingly over decades or, in some cases, quietly surrendering to the floods and the elements. Others have been resurrected, rebuilt or replaced by Baltic log cabins, central European dachas or very British static caravans. Each is entirely its own, personalised with gardens and jetties, loggias, verandas and roof-top terraces. Solar panels and wind turbines jostle with wheelbarrows, wood stores, gas bottles, bikes and boats, lace curtains and Tibetan prayer flags. A spirit of defiant independence floats in the air, that of an overgrown childhood den perhaps, or an adolescent lair. It is all very *Swallows and Amazons*, though there are a few hints – howling dogs, glinting binoculars, the crust of real poverty – that it might occasionally get a little bit *Hunger Games*.

I get chatting to a lady exercising her daughter's dog, and we end up walking together to Farndon, where she lives. She and her husband moved down from the west of Scotland ten years ago to be near family, and though cheerfully unsentimental, she clearly misses the old place and its stronger sense of fellowship. I ask if, when house-hunting, she ever considered going a few feet further into Wales. Yes, she says, they looked, but having heard so much bad press about the Welsh health service (this was the time of David Cameron's 'line between life and death' speech), decided against it. She's content enough in Farndon, if slightly mystified by the English ways of life, and noticed during the pandemic a good deal more community spirit and mutual help going on across the river in Holt. 'I think that may be a Welsh thing,' she says; 'it's more like it was at home there.'

I'm glad to hear her say this, because I've noticed it here too, and wondered if I was just wishing it to be so. The two little towns are almost clichéd embodiments of their countries: Holt with its chapels, redbrick terraces and air of chipped pride; Farndon its villas, delis and – until very recently – royal gossip Paul Burrell's antique empo-rium. Linking them is the border crossing straight from a nursery rhyme, the handsome fourteenth-century sandstone bridge over the Dee. Today it's all queues of delivery vans growling at the traffic lights, waiting to be steered across in single file, but half-close your eyes and there are pennants fluttering from its ruddy piers, and a knight on one bank professing his love for a princess on the other.

Fairy tales are usually as dark as dungeons, and so it is here. Bloody ambushes were commonplace on both sides of the bridge, a fierce Civil War battle raged over it in 1643, but the most enduring ghosts are those of two small Welsh princes, thrown over the parapet and drowned by their Marcher lord guardians. A hoodoo still lingers. As my Scottish friend and I walk into town, she says suddenly, 'Oh, there's something I think you'd like to see,' and points out an ash tree on the riverbank. Apparently growing out of the bark are clusters of mossy fabric and pockets of cloth bulging with gravel. 'I've no idea what it is,' she says, but suddenly I see. It's the remains of a teddy bear, its head and one arm reduced to limp rags, the other arm, its legs and feet swollen and sticking out of the trunk. It must have been tied to the tree years ago, perhaps in memory of someone, and the ash is slowly swallowing it, limb by limb. Was this too the grievous memory of a child, one perhaps lost to this water between two lands?

Up and down the border, there are places that trigger unexpected sensations of childhood. So much part of their enduring appeal, the between-lands conjure up halcyon days, eternal summers, fresh air, freedom. This is the buried treasure of our upbringing, the jewels that we might spend the rest of our days trying to rediscover, with only some patchy memories and a fading map to guide us. So dazzlingly bright are they, and so compelling the search, that we often overlook the gunk and gore in which they lie buried. Perhaps that's the very point. What we search for is not a direct rekindling of the moment or the memory itself, but the incandescent power that even the most fleeting of pleasures had in our young minds to blot out so much else.

Even that light might not be enough, though. Down the road is Bryn Estyn, the former approved school that became a byword for systemic sexual and physical abuse of hundreds of boys between the 1960s and 1980s. Twelve former pupils are known to have killed themselves, and countless others struggle with the aftershocks. One survivor, interviewed in 2012, told of repeatedly trying to whistleblow about what was going on there, but never being believed by anyone in authority. Several inquiries, each casting a wider net than the last, have put numerous men in prison and revealed a staggering network of corruption, right the way across north-west England and north-east Wales. In politics, education, administration, the police and judiciary, entertainment, sport, the press and broadcasting, in every damn area of a supposedly civilised society, it was this region that time and again proved to be the shelter and hunting ground for some of the very worst of humanity.

Bryn Estyn still stands, though perhaps not for long. After being renamed and repurposed as Wrexham council offices, it closed for good in 2015, and plans were announced for its demolition as part of a scheme to build hundreds of new homes and a school. Reading about it, I'm instinctively against the idea – a building is not, after all, guilty of the heinous crimes committed within it. On visiting, my opinion shifts.

After seeing its mock-Tudor frontage so often on news reports, to come across it in reality is a shock, even though it seems to be shrinking from view, returning to a better nature. The lane has been recently truncated, so that the house is now a dead end, and weeds carpet the car park. Ground-floor windows are covered in wooden boards and metal grilles; those upstairs – pretty bays and fake mullions supposed to evoke knights and fair maidens – are broken and blank. A neighbouring staff house built in the 1960s has almost vanished into the undergrowth. It all looks beyond redemption.

Something else falls into place for me. Bryn Estyn was built in the early twentieth century for a wealthy Wrexham brewer, 'a replica of a Cheshire Manor House' as it was billed when sold by his widow in 1928. Pretending that it comes from not just another time, but another place too, that it's not on the edge of workaday Wrexham, is symptomatic of so much more, and as I soak up its curlicues and crenellations, its liquorice beams and gingerbread chimneys, the gulf between its architectural whimsy and the gruesome reality makes me choke. And though Bryn Estyn is an extreme example of that awful gap, it's one that I've seen too much of on this bit of the border.

It's there in the airless villages fringing the Eaton estate, the gothic clock tower at its heart, its black gates and bellicose bollards. There too in the nearby imperial city, its tinhorn emporia, kids as Roman centurions and copious curtsies to the richest family in the land for sparing the odd copper. And most disconcertingly of all, it's there in the source of that unprecedented fortune, the sale of another child's virginity, who was also later discredited, disbelieved and put away by absurdly powerful men.

Not to be outdone, it's there on the Welsh side too, in the flattest of flatpack châteaux at Wynnstay, the Arthurian never-neverlands and the ever-decreasing returns of competitive genealogy. Whatever your version of Britain – Britannia, Brythonia or Prydain Fawr, Albion or Blighty, the UK, GB or just plain England – you'll find all your prejudices expertly polished here.

Your hopes too, though, never forget. For all the damping down of dissent and gradation, the painstaking reinterpretation of the past to fit the politics of the present, you need only refocus your eye and look again, as a child, and see that there is nowhere beyond redemption.

Even in Cheshire at its most *Footballers' Wives*, there is filthy, ancient magic spilling out of the landscape, breaking through its manicured veneer in crags as wild and green as their names: Peckforton Point, Stanner Nab and the Table Rock, Maiden Castle, Mad Allen's Hole, The Cloud and Alderley Edge. No one has voiced these places, nor their spirit, with greater alacrity than Alan Garner.

Though rooted in the east of Cheshire, Garner is a writer who has always spanned the border, both as a line on the map and as a state of mind. His first book, *The Weirdstone of Brisingamen* (1960), played with the ubiquitous legend of the sleeping hero, placing it in a version passed down to him by his grandfather on the wanton outcrop of Alderley Edge. The Edge, he later wrote, is 'a Celtic cosmos not an English one', and when as a boy he found the Welsh programme on the family wireless, he listened spellbound through the crackles: 'it was as if I were hearing the knights, who lay in the cave with their king under the hill behind our house, talking in their sleep'. J. R. R. Tolkien had a similar epiphany on seeing the coal trains, with the names of Welsh mines emblazoned on their wagons, steaming through his Birmingham suburb.

Garner's life-work has been to repair the torn fabric of our collective myth, and to place it in its rightful cultural and linguistic context. For him, it is in the vernacular tongues of Britain, Welsh and his own Cheshire dialect included, that the richest loam lies. But that was never allowed to be, by those who made the rules. 'Our folk memory was dubbed a heresy,' he said in a lecture in Canada in 1983. 'The Ancient World was the pattern for men of letters, and the written word spoke in terms of that pattern. Education in the Humanities was education in Latin and Greek. English style came from the library, not from the land; and the effect, despite the Romantic movement, has continued to this day.'

The myths are hard as iron, and truthful as the seconds before death. They will outlast any given reality of the moment, even this land of make-believe on the northern end of the border, a quarter of the way through the twenty-first century. The hero sleeps on, and there is work to be done.

7.

INVASION

/// upon.giants.hopping

The wooden border post is the only thing to break the bleak skyline. ENGLAND carved vertically down one side, the letters picked out in paint still sufficiently intact to read. On the other side, slap into the prevailing winds, the paint has faded on WALES, but the post clearly serves as a predator's look-out, for white excreta is dribbled down the side and has pooled in the hollows of the letters. The harriers and owls, casting their beady eyes over the vast expanse, have shat a fine job of it.

Here, all the borders collide, undecided. The two countries in flux, but so too the three states of matter: solid, liquid, gas. Walking across Whixall Moss, the black peat underfoot is spongy and springy, sucking hungrily at my boots. Off the designated tracks, the ground is even less stable. Pools and runnels have no clear edges; their dark waters imprinted with clouds. And now, at the end of winter, the grasses are bleached and birches pale, as they haze imperceptibly to a horizon that might be land, or sky, or water; perhaps each in its turn. Across these 2,500 flat acres, distance is almost impossible to gauge.

This is the border at its most disorienting, a dull throb rather than a clean cut.

Poet Gladys Mary Coles (also the most dedicated keeper of the flame for Mary Webb) wrote a sequence, *Kingdom of Sphagnum*, about the Mosses, 'a wilderness between Wales and England'. The 'fixed lines on the map' she called:

> False frontiers, invaded by winds,
> by seeds, spores, germs.

Her words chime true, perhaps more than on any other part of the border. And not just because it runs here in a straight line across a vast peat bog, dividing only puddles and the call of curlews, nor even because the Mosses are a secretive and self-contained land already, one that pays little heed to the outside world. Even were this a regular landscape, it would still be odd, a world of false frontiers, for this is the Maelor, a calloused Welsh toe stretched out and poking deep into plump English ribs.

Before the local government changes of 1974, the Maelor was marked on maps as 'Flintshire (Detached)', the final remnant of the many exclaves that once littered the county plan of Britain. In its time, it has been a queen's dowry and a king's playground, part of the Saxon kingdom of Mercia, the Welsh princedom of Powys Fadog and the Marcher lordship of Maelor Saesneg, the 'English Maelor', before settling for nearly 700 years as a remote – and sometimes reluctant – outpost of Flintshire. On the wrong side of both the Dee and the dyke, the 46-square-mile relic of history sits detached still and floating among the meadows and pony paddocks of Cheshire and Shropshire.

I cross the Mosses and plunge properly into this little Welsh curio. On the bog's edge, the first parish is Bronington, its handsome church converted from a redbrick tithe barn in the early nineteenth century. Not everything fitted. For decent sight lines and ease of movement, the altar had to be built on the south wall, rather than the customary east, facing Jerusalem. No matter. The altar's position is still officially counted as liturgical east, with all the other compass points shifted accordingly to fit. Once inside its stout walls, you must accept as an article of faith this altered reality, and much the same goes for the Maelor as a whole. The compass reads east, but the evidence suggests otherwise.

Its position on all the borders has long been its calling card. As detailed in an 1883 book, *Overton in Days Gone By*, there was one particular corner of the Maelor where: 'One may stand in England and Wales, in the provinces of Canterbury and York, in the dioceses of Lichfield, Chester, and St Asaph; in the archdeaconries of Chester, Salop, and St Asaph; in the deaneries of Wrexham, Malpas, and Ellesmere; in the [court] circuits of Oxford, North Wales, and Chester; in the counties of Shropshire, Flintshire, and Denbighshire; in the hundreds of Oswestry, Maelor, and Bromfield; in the parishes of Ellesmere, Overton, and Erbistock; and in the townships of Dudleston, Knolton, and Erbistock. A truly suitable place to elude the officers of the law.'

Not that the district's palpable otherness comes only from lines on the map drawn by far-off administrators, nor even as an inevitability of its place in the between-lands of England and Wales. It is inherent. The curious landscape of the Mosses gives a clue to an unusual geology, of young sandstone rocks buried deep below a glacial drift – clays, gravels and sands – that got stuck. That produced poorly drained swamps that became the Mosses, but also a profusion of lakes and ponds that formed in its dips, and some very rich agricultural land. Alongside the natural pools are a stack of old moats, testament both to past wealth and the contested territory of borderland, now mostly mouldering away in quiet fields, their houses long vanished. According to Lorna Sage in her fabulously scabrous memoir *Bad Blood*, the Maelor – a 'little rounded isthmus of North Wales sticking out into England' – is 'a time warp, an enclave of the nineteenth century'.

Even today, that feeling hangs heavy in the air, alongside the ever-present hum of manure and hint of possible insurrection. Places apart, those at the far edge of their territory, or defined by fluid demarcation, are habitually restive. On the northern edge of the Maelor, the settlement of Threapwood – née Thieves' Wood – is now in Cheshire, has been in Flintshire (Detached), both at once, and neither. For centuries it was extra-parochial, a vast common 'reputed to be in no County, Parish, Town or Hamlet' as the MP for Chester wrote to the Lord Chancellor in 1753, alarmed that the couple of hundred inhabitants did not 'pay any rate or tax whatsoever except the Ale sellers' (and that only recently, and forcibly). At a time when an increasing amount of land was being enclosed, Threapwood was a free-for-all, people from miles around coming to exercise common rights for their cattle, and themselves too. 'As neither the Sheriff of Chester or Flint were ever known to exercise the office in this place, so no offence, criminal or capital, committed in this place can be tried in either of those Counties or anywhere else I apprehend,' he continued.

In his reply, the Lord Chancellor said that he had heard whisper of such a 'debatable land' in this corner of the kingdom, and although 'it is surprising that one has not heard more complaints' about it, such a swamp 'must be the seat of much Disorder and Irregularity and the asylum of many disorderly persons'. Though much of the land was eventually parcelled up and enclosed, and a church built there to tame its wild energies, Threapwood continued to be famous for its bull and bear baiting, cock-fighting, race meets, assemblies and balls, drinking, swearing and poaching. Today, even if the licentiousness has cooled, there's still a palpable anarchy to the place, in its warren of lanes and tracks, patchwork of paddocks and small, scrubby fields, its rough scatter of farms, cottages, sheds and lock-ups.

Romani gypsies and military deserters found their place in Threapwood's scattergun hierarchy, though its most enduring reputation was as a place where unmarried mothers ended up, often the subjects of harsh movement orders enacted by the elders of their more upright Christian parishes. In 1778, Thomas Pennant wrote that it was 'from time immemorial a place of refuge for the frail fair, who make here a transient abode, clandestinely to be freed from the consequences of illicit love. Numbers of houses are scattered over the common for their reception.' Over a century later, newspaper reports show that this was still a regular aspect of local life, and despite the best efforts of the Church and politicians, often with little sting. For many, the place of enforced and shameful exile instead became one of rare and welcome sanctuary.

It's a different story just down the road in Hanmer, the setting for Lorna Sage's *Bad Blood*, which tells of her own teenage pregnancy at the very end of the 1950s. At first glance, the village looks to be the epitome of hearty good health, its fine, solid houses stretched out along the bank of the Maelor's largest glacial lake, Hanmer Mere. Above the water is the church of St Chad, standing grand on its great green mound, next to a primary school straight out of the Ladybird books. On the stiff March day of my visit, lake and village alike glitter in cold sunlight.

On a previous trip, I picked up a twelve-page booklet in St Chad's, entitled 'Hanmer Village Memories of Lorna Sage and the Story of her *Bad Blood* Autobiography'. It was a polite but seething hatchet job. Sage, who wrote the book while terminally ill and who lived only just long enough to see it published in 2000, poured into it the unsparing truths of someone looking death square in the face. The gothic portrait of her grandfather, vicar of Hanmer for twenty years until his sudden death in 1952, was rooted in his own words, from his diaries. Brutal though it is, *Bad Blood* is one of the finest, funniest and most well-honed literary memoirs ever published.

Not according to the booklet, written by a lay reader of St Chad's. The stall is set immediately in his opening words: Sage's grandfather, Thomas Meredith-Morris, 'is still remembered with respect and affection by the older people of Hanmer', while 'those still around from that time say that Lorna's story is mostly exaggerated and often untrue'. The priest, whose fondness for the bottle saw the Church cut his supply of communion wine and who seduced a schoolgirl friend of his daughter, among others, is described variously as 'a good friend to all' and 'this wonderful man', whose 'marvellous preaching ... drew crowds from far and wide'. Lorna, by contrast, is described as 'always a day dreamer' and 'a loner' who 'never seemed to have or be taught any domestic skills' and 'caused a great deal of strain on her mother and father by her wayward behaviour'.

An 1834 topographical gazetteer described Threapwood as 'long the resort of abandoned characters of every description, and especially of women of loose or blemished morals'. Next door, twenty-first-century Hanmer nods in righteous agreement.

* * *

With no hills to dam or define it, this is the most porous bit of border yet. The Maelor itself is leaky enough, but so too the heaths, moors and meres that surround it. Around its edge are a rash of Cheshire and Shropshire villages in disguise (Welsh Frankton, Welshampton, Welsh End) and more that prefer not to commit themselves either way: No Man's Heath, Belt o' th' Hill, Gravel Hole, Baggy Moor, Criftins, Trench. There too are hints of strife; the shapely town of Malpas – literally 'the bad or difficult pass' – was first dubbed as such in the twelfth century. It is a name found elsewhere, a note of caution, usually in valley communities prone to mud and flood. This Malpas though is a sturdy hill-station; the warning is not of natural peril, but of potential ambush by the Welsh, brought unexpectedly far into the flatlands by the Maelor.

In my wanderings, I've been asking people I meet about their sense of identity, their loyalties and habits. The pandemic has changed so much, from the obvious questions such as which rules you are obliged to follow (and which ones you'd prefer to follow), to more idiosyncratic allegiances of things like the weekly supermarket trip at the height of lockdown. Here though, people look at me as if I've lost my mind when I start asking them where they go shopping. They go where they've always gone, and no virus was going to change that (and certainly no government diktat, whether from Cardiff, London or the moon). It's entirely understandable. For someone in the eastern part of the Maelor, their official hometown is Wrexham, 15 miles away; the busy Shropshire borough of Whitchurch, with its lovely high street and multiple supermarkets, all of three or four.

My questioning is beginning to sound crazy to me too, but for an entirely different reason. The pandemic has been blown off the front pages by the Russian invasion of Ukraine, and suddenly border talk – and there's *always* some kind of border talk – is no longer about putting on a mask as you cross a nebulous divide, but about things infinitely more urgent and visceral. We've watched for weeks Russian military hardware being massed at the border, then trampling it with tanks and troops, bombing it to dust; we've heard the demands for altered borders, entirely new borders, for re-alignments and safe corridors. Helpless and horrified, we've witnessed families divided at borders, the men – taxi drivers, chemists, musicians – returning to the fray in their burning country, the women and children, the young and the old, tentatively crossing the border, red-eyed, into a terrible unknown. Poking around in the hinterland of Wales and England suddenly seems so dusty, so small.

Just as with the pandemic, those with axes to grind immediately did so. Having already stated – even after the annexation of Crimea – that Vladimir Putin was the world leader he most admired, Nigel Farage weighed in, telling anyone who would listen that the invasion was 'a consequence of EU and NATO expansion'. Prime Minister Boris Johnson jumped in too, saying in a speech, 'I know that it's the instinct of the people of this country, like the people of Ukraine, to choose freedom, every time. I can give you a couple of famous recent examples. When the British people voted for Brexit in such large, large numbers, I don't believe it was because they were remotely hostile to foreigners. It's because they wanted to be free to do things differently and for this country to be able to run itself.' And, sounding horribly like a descant version of the same tune, a Plaid Cymru MP wrote in his local newspaper a week after the invasion, 'For us in Wales there is a particular menace in Vladimir Putin's words. Ukraine is not a real country he says. It does not have a right to exist. It is he, far away in Moscow, who has the right to rule. We in Wales are familiar with these arguments.'

Damn them all, those that look at other people's bloody agony, and in it see only themselves. They take us all down.

That's not to say 'a plague on both your houses', as if they are equal and opposite. They are not. The British supremacist position, weaponised for Brexit and sprayed around by Farage and Johnson with the finesse of bullocks, has behind it the full crushing weight of loaded history, power and filthy money. It changed the world. The Welsh version, the force that underpins too much of its patriotism, relies on a trophy cabinet of shoulder chips, brought out if anyone asks (and even if they don't) and buffed to a proud shine.

To try and understand more of what was happening in Ukraine, I turn once more to maps. From a starchy Victorian school atlas to online digital wonderlands, I see borders wriggling across the Eurasian mainland, retreating, renewing, re-emerging after decades, even centuries of slumber. They define and divide populations by geography, geology, race, culture, language and, all too often, the predilection of despots. They mark the ebb and flow of empires: those that could never hold, such as Austria-Hungary; those that overreached, like Prussia; those – like France and the UK – that kept their dirtiest deeds far from view in distant territories; and those that preferred to keep their psychopathy comparatively local, like Russia. The lines on the map come, they go, but they never quite die.

Between those lines, identities grow and solidify into nations and empires. To those of us brought up in the UK, a nation-state explicitly created for imperial expansion, it's too easy to forget that this is not the global norm. For all the nations, sub-nations, former nations and emerging nations of the world, there is one unassailable divide: on which side of imperialism do you lie? Did you do it, or was it done to you? The UK is clearly, massively one side of that line, and that version of the UK is very much Greater England, fuelled by its mighty capital city.

What of Wales? Thirty years ago, I was told more times than I care to recall that racism was practically non-existent there, that it was 'an English problem', a product of colonialism from which Wales was entirely apart. It took the brutal racist murder of a Neath shopkeeper to silence the first fatuity, but the second lingered stubbornly on. As recently as 2018, as a way of introducing himself to voters, the new Plaid Cymru leader published a book of his essays and speeches under the title *Wales: The First and Final Colony*. He talked of 'channel[ling] … into hope rather than resentment … some of the elements within what has come to be known as populism', and suggested that Wales, alongside former colonies in Africa, Asia and the Caribbean, should be paid reparations by London.

By then, the old tune was sagging. Awareness of the real costs of colonialism and racism was growing fast, and no amount of verbal dexterity could disguise the fact that much of Wales, and many of its people, had done well out of the Empire. Its capital city, an insignificant village at the beginning of the nineteenth century, had ballooned in size, status and wealth entirely on the back of its coal trade for the colonies. The narrative turned, and now mostly comes almost entirely from the other direction. To say that Wales was colonised at all, to place it on the same continuum as nations in the global south, now sparks only opprobrium in some quarters.

That both could simultaneously be true, that Wales could be both coloniser and colonised, is not a terribly hot take right now. We might perhaps swing back towards it eventually, I hope, for there is a fuller, more textured and far more important picture to see if we can. So much of the geopolitics still employed today, in its reasoning and methodology, was forged by British imperialism. And so much of that very same imperialism was first formulated and finessed in campaigns to conquer the Welsh. This patch, this border, was a significant seedbed for the modern world.

If we hold the notion that two equal and opposite forces can simultaneously be so – and we should, for it's a hard-won truth right now – then the Maelor is as good a place as any to hold it. It is nuance itself in territorial form, looking both ways and keeping its counsel; as quiet as its gentle landscape, but as rich and odd as its geology. Here then is the riddle: could you – should you – ever ask a place this ambiguous a question so binary as 'to which side of the line do you belong?'

It has been asked, of course, and will be again. In 1887, as preparation for the creation of the first county councils, Boundary Commissions met to tidy up the often-chaotic borders of the traditional shires. At an inquiry in Overton, a newspaper reported 'that the opinion of the people [of Maelor] themselves was unanimous in favour of their uniting with Shropshire', before an enigmatic coda, 'but they since found that it was not quite so unanimous as represented'. A meeting of local magistrates favoured the move, together with the amalgamation of the rest of Flintshire with Denbighshire. None of it came to pass.

In the local government reorganisation of the early 1970s, the possibility of Maelor being placed in England was once again floated, once again assumed to be the popular will, but once again dismissed. Flintshire and Denbighshire were finally amalgamated to form Clwyd, so ironing out the odd exclaves, the Maelor included. Twenty years later, it was all change again, when public dissatisfaction with the new counties had reached boiling point. 'The only option not presented to the people of the Maelor was the one that they probably wanted the most – namely to be transferred over the border and into Shropshire or Cheshire,' a local historian told me, fifteen years ago when I filmed a travelogue in the area. 'Very few people here feel any real affinity with Wales.'

His 'probably' is shouldering some weight there. And there's no science to say either way, but even were it largely true, I think things may have shifted since then. Whether that's devolution, sport, the pandemic, the UK's palpable breakdown or what, who can say, but something is changing. Polling now suggests that a majority of people in every constituent country of the UK do not believe that it will still exist in its current form in ten years' time. Some big decisions may lie ahead, and fences – long sat on – climbed off.

If it comes to the crunch, if people are ushered into village halls some time in the next few years in order to vote on massive, fundamental constitutional change; if the standard of our leadership, and with it the status of the nation, continue their remorseless slide into the gutter; if Scotland has opted out, and Ireland is in the process of reuniting; if our world keeps on warming and flooding and splintering and being ruled by algorithms that polarise us ever further … what then? It's hard enough to imagine what then for Caernarfon or Cannock, burrowed deep into their respective nationalities, but for the Maelor, in the teeth of such conflicting winds, where might they blow? How big the storm? And how much damage?

It is not difficult to imagine that at some time, possibly quite soon, there may be a rump UK that consists of just England and Wales. If that transpires, the dynamics change utterly. The pressure to hold an independence referendum in Wales will be immense, as will internal

tensions in England. It sounds extraordinary, but such things have happened throughout history, and we are not exempt.

The unhappiest analogy, one that will be ruthlessly replayed by those most fiercely advocating the continuation of the Union, is former Yugoslavia. Its demise in the 1990s was one of the very bloodiest, with the re-emergence on central European soil of death camps, rape, torture and bottomless spiteful brutality. It is not, though, an inevitable model. Even there, Slovenia slid painlessly out of the federation right at the outset, with barely a ripple, and at the same time, only 100 miles north, appeared the poster boy for amicable separation, the Czechoslovakian 'Velvet Divorce'. In the context of the Wales–England border, that's an instructive comparison: the frontier between the Czech Republic and Slovakia is almost the exact same length, and it too divides partners of quite different size, power and wealth. Not as wide as the gap between England and Wales, and narrower now socially and economically than thirty years ago, but there's still a clear mismatch.

The similarities though are outweighed by significant differences. Czechoslovakia had only existed for seventy-five years, since the end of the First World War, and with a further interruption for the duration of the second. The border between them, in incarnations such as Bohemia, Moravia and other Austro-Hungarian provinces, was older and scored more deeply than the one that penned them in together. Furthermore, it hardly went near any populated areas, hopping mainly from peak to peak through forested mountains like a fugitive. Anyone who wanted to move to the other country was helped to do so, without question. So too individual communities; in a neat exchange, one village on either side duly swapped to the other.

Most germane to the success of their divorce was that eleven years later both countries joined the European Union. Any potential tensions were duly sublimated, as was the need for very much border apparatus, although that has changed during some of the migrant crises of the last few years, when the line has periodically hardened. We of course opted to throw away the safety net of the EU in June 2016, and as we have witnessed since with the UK–Ireland border, there is no frictionless separation to be had.

Both England and Wales voted to Brexit. Beneath that bald fact lurks a pit of vipers, of why it came to be, what it has meant since, and how it may play out in the years to come. For people of my generation and politics, Wales and the EU seemed like such a tidy fit. At last the country had a wider platform, and a focus other than next door. In the sweet, brief years between the falls of the wall in Berlin and the towers in Manhattan, we sang in lusty pubs, and raised our glasses to Europe's stateless nations, as they emerged blinking into the spotlight, like hostages kept for years in a dark cellar. Out of the cold and into the fold came Estonia, Latvia and Lithuania, Slovenia and Slovakia, Moldova, Montenegro and Macedonia. In the wings hovered Catalonia, Scotland, the Basque Country … and might that be *Wales*? As a new millennium loomed, we fired up our bodhráns, practised our verb endings and got another round in, waiting, hoping.

Clues that the mood had moved on were there all the time, if only we'd chosen to look. Just down the road from the Maelor, where the flatlands buffer suddenly into the first mountains, is a fine redbrick metaphor. In 1988, fanfares rang out along the Dee valley when Llangollen was chosen as the headquarters for the EU's new European Centre for Traditional and Regional Cultures (ECTARC). A stout Victorian chapel, repurposed as a multi-media space for exhibitions, talks and gigs from Europe's folksier fringes, quickly became a regular stop for every professional Mac, Ó, Ní and Ap in the phone book, and their many continental cousins. In the new century, as the world hardened and the EU sharpened its suits, ECTARC was scaled back, moved to a less commanding site around the corner and had its acronym repurposed as the European Centre for Training and Regional Co-operation. Essentially, that meant a language school; it was even rebranded for a while as the Mulberry School of English. Since Brexit and the withdrawal of the UK from the Erasmus+ scheme, that work has drifted away too, principally to Ireland.

From heady early days of music and theatre in a happy cacophony of minority languages, to monoglot dealer of English for hard cash, is quite the business model and political trajectory, one that many Welsh republicans would prefer not to contemplate. They hold to the notion of *Cymru yn Ewrop*, the small nation in a continent of comrades, and are cold certain that they were bounced out of it against their collective will and judgement. When the narrow Welsh Brexit vote was broken down into its constituent identities, the categories that were most and least inclined to have voted leave were those who identified as English (72 per cent) and, in a precise reverse, Welsh speakers (28 per cent). These figures were given great prominence in 2019 when an Oxford academic stated on the back of them that Wales voted for Brexit only because of its large number of English retirees. In augmenting this assertion, he referred to the high leave votes in the border counties of Wrexham, which includes the Maelor, and Powys.

Though there's truth in it, this is far from the full picture. For that, we need to remember that the parts of Wales where the leave vote was highest were not the borderlands but the old industrial areas of the south-east, districts with the highest proportion of Welsh-born inhabitants, and very few downshifters from Surrey. Then there's agriculture.

In the run-up to the referendum I had so many conversations with farmer neighbours, most from families that had tilled the same fields for centuries and all mustard keen to be 'rid of Brussels paperwork'. That their unions and advisers were saying the same, particularly in private, was dispiriting. It may have been a concept hatched by English nationalists, but Brexit was by no means only theirs.

* * *

A common (and occasionally deliberate) misunderstanding is that Maelor Saesneg means 'the English-*speaking* Maelor', and so comes loaded with an implication that this has always been the case. In fact, the 'Saesneg' refers not to the language, but to geography, and tells us nothing more than that this is the part of the old Welsh province of Maelor that is physically closer to England. The assumption powers on, though, eternal and evergreen.

Almost every conversation I have here about people's sense of identity quickly pirouettes into their takes on the Welsh language. Two different people tell me the tale of when the Queen visited Overton in 1992, and they had to get the village's solitary Welsh speaker to raise a toast to her (one of them also tells me about another Welsh speaker in the village, rather undermining the story). Everyone conflates ability to speak the language with 'real' Welshness, and that it is therefore a standard they cannot help but fall short of.

This is something you hear all the time, not just here on the border but throughout Wales, the way in which the linguistic self – like any other 'minority' identity – gets turned inwards. I've regularly noticed that people habitually, and often massively, underestimate their ability in Welsh. Those who have a pretty good grounding from schooldays or within their community say that they cannot speak it at all; nearly fluent speakers call themselves beginners, sometimes for decades; even those that use the language every day worry that they are not 'good enough' or that they cannot read it or write in it.

Combine this with the Maelor's strange geography, surrounded on three sides by England and cut off by the Dee on the fourth, with the word (Detached) appended to it on the map for centuries, and it is no wonder that people here feel like they don't quite belong. Those with the loudest voices keep declaring the Maelor an anomaly, that it belongs across the border, and that everyone thinks so, but then the soil is prodded a little more rigorously and, just as in 1887, it transpires 'that it was not quite so unanimous as represented'. For all the snags and contradictions, many appreciate the piquancy that being Wales's oddest outcrop gives to what would otherwise be a distinctly unremarkable part of the world.

Power speaks *Saesneg*, of course: most of the grand old manors and moats look and sound English, though the field names and land measures, the stuff of the earth, are mainly Welsh. Even on the Maelor's easternmost flank, some of the oldest farms are Iscoed, Maesy-groes, Pen-y-bryn. But language is far from the only measure. When I ask people about sporting allegiance or other indications of identity, there's no question that for all its ambivalence the Maelor is weirdly Welsh.

Flamboyantly so in its own way too, as shown by Flintshire's finest, Emral Hall, near Worthenbury. First built in the thirteenth century for the widow of a Welsh prince turned English informer, the house spent most of its days in the hands of a single Shropshire noble family, one of whom was Edward I's chief taxman in newly conquered Wales, another who married the sister of Owain Glyndŵr and joined his uprising. Tudor, Jacobean and early Georgian reconfigurations produced a house that was gloriously idiosyncratic, 'of strangely haunting beauty' (Pevsner) that reflected 'not just fashions in architecture, but the social and economic history of a whole area', said *Country Life* magazine in 1910.

Emral's fortunes fluctuated as wildly as its fashions, but the road finally ran out in 1936, when it was sold off at auction, and demolished. Looking at photographs of the house is a strange sensation, for there is something so familiar about it, like spotting your own nose and chin in the sepia shot of an ancestor. Clough Williams-Ellis raced across north Wales to get to the auction in the nick of time, and bought (for thirteen pounds) the elaborate seventeenth-century barrel roof of the banqueting hall, a plasterwork riot of the Labours of Hercules and the signs of the zodiac. He bought other parts of the house too, and rebuilt it all as the Town Hall at Portmeirion, his 'home for fallen buildings' on an Eryri promontory. The remnants of Emral sit happily in this Welshest of settings, between the sea and the mountains, lapping up the love and dazzling in the crystalline air. They were meant to be there all along.

Owain Glyndŵr himself, the very apogee of *Cymreictod*, also married into the Maelor. His bride was a Hanmer in both name and purlieu, their wedding in the village church above the mere. Some 500 years later, in the same spot, the Reverend Thomas Meredith-Morris cajoled and canoodled, while his little granddaughter Lorna watched and waited for her stone-cold revenge. He in turn – entirely inadvertently – helped cultivate another Welsh icon, when in 1940, in the words of Byron Rogers, 'the paths of two of the strangest priests in the Church in Wales' crossed, and poet R. S. Thomas showed up as his new curate. Fresh from their marriage, Thomas and his wife Elsi were housed in the parsonage at Tallarn Green, a subsidiary church to Hanmer, where they would watch German bombers going overhead on their way to hammer Liverpool. Many bombs were dropped short, near enough for him to feel, he writes in his autobiography *Neb*, 'the occasional puff of wind going through his hair and lifting his wife's skirt', for the vast expanse of the Mosses, a few miles away, doubled up as a decoy. When a raid was imminent, a network of fire baskets was lit across the bog to simulate already burning streets in Merseyside, and encourage the Luftwaffe to bomb that instead of the real thing.

Maelor helped to fire up R. S. Thomas's burgeoning sense of Wales, and his place within it. Thus far, he'd clung to its perimeter: born in Cardiff in one corner, brought up in Holyhead at the other, and now in Flintshire (Detached), 'one of those strange bits of Wales that got stranded on the other side', as Elsi later wrote. With the war raging, Thomas resolved to find himself a proper Welsh parish, deep in the fond hills, and set about learning the native tongue. In 1942, he was appointed vicar of Manafon, 35 miles south-west in the swollen green of Montgomeryshire, and he continued for the next four decades moving west into ever more Welsh-speaking parishes until his last one at Aberdaron at the far end of the Llŷn peninsula, where he could go no further without falling into the sea. Though he ministered in Welsh, wrote prose in it, campaigned for it and scolded people in the street for not speaking it, his poetic output, as chiselled and sharp as the finest slate, was forever in English.

In learning the language denied him, Thomas hoped to connect with 'the true Wales of my imagination', something perhaps destined to remain just out of reach. Not that it will ever stop us trying, and sometimes rather too hard. Every Welsh class – and I've seen a few – includes someone who's changed their name to something out of the *Mabinogi*, an American trying to excavate a lineage, someone plastered in badges for every Celtic cause, and a ragbag of goths who think that *Game of Thrones* was a documentary. I walked into one class with a copy of the *Independent* and was roundly ticked off by my fellow students for bringing a 'papur newydd *Llundain!*', a London newspaper, into the hallowed hall of mangled mutations. We badly need to relax on the issue.

If the Maelor teaches us anything, then it is to embrace contradiction, subtlety and perhaps even an inevitable modicum of human hypocrisy. R. S. Thomas remains one of the greatest poets of the twentieth century, and the communicator nonpareil of the Welsh condition to the wider world, even though he was a snob whose overbearing needs almost killed stone dead his wife's artistic career. Equally telling, for all his fierce words on (and in) the Welsh language, he denied his only child Gwydion knowledge of it by sending him away to English boarding schools. I knew Gwydion slightly, and it was a dislocation that he never overcame.

One person I meet in Overton tells me that she has noticed a very particular change locally with regard to the language. 'I've invigilated exams at The Maelor high school in Penley for years,' she says, 'and it used to be the case for Welsh exams that quite a few of the students would turn their paper over, write their name on it, and then sit back, arms folded, looking quite grumpy, for the rest of the duration. That just doesn't happen now. They get stuck in.' Someone else though tells me that there are plenty of parents so desperate that their offspring avoid the Welsh language entirely that they send them over the border, at considerable inconvenience, to the high schools in Ellesmere, Whitchurch or Malpas. Things are moving, but in both directions at once. The March, after all, is thinning.

In Tallarn Green on the northern edge of the Maelor, the Thomases' old rectory sits between the now closed Victorian church and a wartime hut that has been repurposed into the village hall. Covid dealt its blows, but it's tiptoeing back. Posters advertise a bingo night, a book club, a litter pick and a planning meeting for the village's contribution to the Queen's platinum jubilee celebrations. The hall is also the parish polling station where someday, perhaps someday soon, people will trickle in, thoughtful, fearful or hopeful, in order to cast a vote on the future of the two countries that they straddle.

For all those that have weighed up the arguments and listened to the debates before deciding, there will be many more who knew from the outset, deep in the pit of their belly, exactly how they were going to vote, and have never wavered from that. And there will be some – probably more than we think – who will either have no firm idea which box they are going to place their X in, or who change their mind at the last second, their stubby pencil poised over the ballot paper and then steered by a giddy shock of adrenaline.

There are flames on the horizon, a throb in the sky, and a puff of hot wind makes me gasp. I strain my eyes to see. Something is happening at the thin border on the black bog, out there on the great canvas of the Mosses. Is it a decoy, or might it be the real thing?

8.

INTERCOURSE AND UNION

/// ladder.gripes.mourner

In the gloom there are spiders lurking; metaphors too. The first gulp of Welsh air is damp and bronchial, the soundscape a metallic staccato of drip-drip-drip into black water. The dog is cowering, and I have to coax her on, into the dark, deep into the tunnel, even though I'm not keen either. We're on the towpath of the Llangollen Canal, but it's narrow and rutted, awash with oily puddles that I don't see until I'm in them, and the angle of the wall means that I'm continually scraping my shoulder on clammy brickwork. For ages, the distant aperture of light never seems to get any larger ... still not ... still not ... and then suddenly it does, much to everyone's relief.

Here at Chirk, an aqueduct is followed immediately by this tunnel, making for a border crossing of rare pungency: first vertiginous, then claustrophobic. On opening in 1801, Chirk was the tallest navigable aqueduct ever built, and walking across it still packs an unexpected punch. Heart thumping, it's straight into the tunnel, and once finally out of that, on to a dramatic towpath walk. Within an hour, you pass through a wooded cutting of exceptional beauty, a further tunnel, and along a massive embankment that commands the Dee valley, bookended by another viaduct and another aqueduct. Not just any aqueduct either, but the mighty Pontcysyllte. On opening in 1805, it took the title of world's highest from Chirk, and has held it ever since.

The first glimpse of Pontcysyllte stops you dead in your tracks. That though is nothing to crossing it, whether by boat or on foot; 'it gives me the *pendro* sir, to look down,' George Borrow's guide told him in 1854, and so it still does. Walking it this time, I had to keep my eyes fixed on the back of the person a few yards ahead of me, for when I looked over the parapet at the foaming river 130 feet below, my stomach leapt and scrotum clenched, pulsing pure nausea to every agnostic limb. Fifteen years ago, I steered a narrowboat over, something I doubt I'd manage now. The shallow cast-iron trough, over 300 yards in length, has the towpath and railings on one side, but nothing on the other. Its rim is only six inches above the water, so from the top of a boat there is a sheer drop tugging at you, playing havoc with your perspective.

Even in the 2020s, stuffed with adrenaline thrills, Pontcysyllte astonishes. Walk over it, of course, but under it too, its columns soaring skywards, their iron and stonework as crisp as yesterday. How utterly miraculous, a vision of the impossible, it must have seemed 200 years ago. Sir Walter Scott called it 'the most impressive work of art' he'd ever seen, a 'stream in the sky' where the fishes swam above the birds. Some 8,000 people showed up for its official opening, on a wintry Tuesday at the end of November 1805. To the roar of cannon and the flourish of brass bands, all amplified by the surrounding hills, a ceremonial flotilla of boats paraded across the aqueduct, laden with local bigwigs and investors, officers and employees of the canal company that had built it. In the second boat was Thomas Telford, the engineer who had masterminded the project, alongside Lady Williams-Wynn of Wynnstay and the Ladies of Llangollen, an eccentric and celebrated Irish lesbian couple who'd eloped to the Dee valley nearly thirty years earlier. Symbols of romantic Wales, embodiment of the new appetite for the Picturesque, the Ladies were now thrilled to be shaking hands with modernity and industry.

The speeches made it bulldog plain. In his oration, Rowland Hunt, the Shrewsbury industrialist who'd been central to the canal project since its inception fourteen years earlier, started with a rousing verbal tour of the great classical aqueducts of Europe (many of which 'I have myself visited'). None, he declared, 'can compare with Pontcysyllte'; far better 'the Triumph of modern arts and British invention and industry, over the antient or later performances of Foreign nations'. He was similarly gung-ho about the bridge as a symbol of 'the eminence of patriotism' in the new United Kingdom of Great Britain and Ireland, minted just four years earlier on the abolition of the parliament in Dublin.

For Ireland, as so often, see also Wales. It too, thundered Hunt, was to be brought fully out of its Celtic half-light and clamped securely into the Brave New Britain. 'Wherever the Spirit of Commerce has touched the mountains on the whole borders of Wales, they begin to smoke,' he roared to the cheering crowds. On the side of the bridge, an inscription was unveiled that celebrated:

The Nobility and Gentry of
The adjacent Counties,
Having united their efforts with
The great commercial interests of this Country
In creating an intercourse and union between
ENGLAND AND NORTH WALES

That the air that day was charged with such jingo is no surprise. Only a month earlier, the French had been beaten at the Battle of Trafalgar, though at the cost of the loss of Admiral Lord Nelson. Even Thomas Telford, a man rarely given to shows of patriotic ostentation, was full of it, enthusiastically waving a Union Jack in each hand as his barge edged over the aqueduct. Excitement was everywhere. Walter Scott was far from the only Romantic to be enchanted by Pontcysyllte, and all that it represented. Many of those that waxed most lyrical about nature saw it only as an embellishment. Poets and painters flocked to capture the bridge's exquisite fusion of form and function, as it strode so elegantly across the valley and into the new, British century.

In one of the most famous paintings of the aqueduct, it is not the main subject, but an elegant *capriccio* in the background of the 1822 portrait of its maestro, Thomas Telford. Of all the dozens of canals and roads, bridges and tunnels, docks, drains and churches that he built during a career of over fifty years, it was Pontcysyllte that he most wanted to show off, his zenith and his chosen epitaph. The appeal was not only aesthetic, nor even strictly pragmatic. It was almost spiritual – not that the plain-speaking Telford would ever have put it so himself. To him, the aqueduct, like so many of his finest and fondest projects, represented the literal bolting together of the new kingdom. With every strut and rivet, he was helping to forge the future.

As a Scot also working in Wales and England, and living wherever the job took him (he didn't have a permanent address until the age of sixty-four), Thomas Telford had a clear and perhaps unique sense of Britishness. His version of it is very appealing. It was a kingdom united by principles and practicalities designed to connect its populations, a crucible of ambition and curiosity, of scientific advancement and political progress, but also modest, shrewd and above all egalitarian, driven not by hunger for money or power. It is a long way from the state of today.

Telford's sense was rooted in his humble Scottish Lowland upbringing, in Eskdale, near the English border and the 'debatable land' that lay in neither country. On the map, Eskdale looks to be a textbook backwater, but it had a rich culture that greatly prized knowledge, science, literature and craft, and young Tammy took to it all. The lessons learned in those unheralded hills stayed with him. His passion for universal education was lifelong, so too his diligence and eagerness to collaborate and to encourage the next generations of talent. Though a committed modernist, at a time of such rapid change, he never wanted to sweep away the past, but rather incorporate and enhance it with his work. Similarly, his childhood had inculcated a deep love of nature, and that too was essential to his thinking.

Having made his name as the county surveyor for Shropshire, where a fascinating legacy of bridges and buildings survives, Telford found in the Dee Valley something of a second home. Literally so, perhaps, for it rings with echoes of Eskdale: the first valley over the border from England, clearly and immediately different, and for all its remoteness, on one of the main routes between London and its outpost capitals, Edinburgh and Dublin respectively. Five years after the opening of Pontcysyllte, Telford was back, this time to survey the road to Holyhead, newly chosen by parliament as the main port for Ireland. The rebuilding of the route in order to bind the new kingdom together became the single biggest piece yet of government infrastructure, and for him, a crowning glory.

Getting his road from London to Shrewsbury was straightforward enough, for it just took the wholesale improvement of the Roman Watling Street. Beyond that, and into Wales, was a much tougher call, yet he managed the whole route, through the crags and peaks of Eryri, without ever exceeding a gradient of 1:20. Taking the traffic over the Menai Strait, a narrow but notoriously fraught sea channel separating Anglesey from the mainland, was even more of a challenge, one that Telford achieved with another astonishing piece of engineering, the longest suspension bridge in the world at the time. More than two centuries on, boats still cross Pontcysyllte, cars and buses the Menai Bridge.

His Holyhead high-road has had as many lives as a city cat. Stagecoaches vanished practically overnight on the arrival of trains, and when George Borrow walked the route in 1854, only six years after the railway had opened to the Irish port, he found 'the way was broken and stony; all traces of the good roads of Wales had disappeared'. Through the remainder of the nineteenth century, the route deteriorated further, until the arrival of bicycles, and then the car. The road roared back to life, was tarmacked and named as the A5, one of the prime meridians of the land, speeding business traffic, holidaymakers, freight and locals through increasingly congested bottlenecks. In the early 1990s came the dualling of the coastal expressway to the north, taking all of the Irish traffic with it, and much else besides. The A5 retreated into another semi-retirement.

There it is in Chirk, two fields away from the aqueduct, its wrought-iron 'Welcome to Wales' sign a homespun portal from another time. On a certain summer breeze, you can still smell the wheezing queues of holiday traffic, and hear the rip of flesh as youngsters prise themselves from the hot plastic of the back seat to holler in their parents' ears, 'Look! We're in Wales now … it can't be much further. Can it?'

Oh, but it can.

Generations of English children have crossed the border here, and never quite come back. Travelling from one side of the line to the other, the difference is usually soon apparent, but here it is so whip-crack quick that it makes you dizzy. The trunk road across the plains morphs suddenly into a mountain pass, serpentine and green, dripping with intrigue. Only 6 miles into Wales and you're at Llangollen, Lilliput-on-Dee, with its hilltop castle ruins, Alpine river, steam trains, canal barges, trinket shops and tearooms. You're not just in another country, but another dimension.

Along Telford's highway the wonders keep coming, and never more beguiling than when glimpsed at an impressionable age from the back of a stuffy family car. This is where it begins, that lifelong pull of Wales. For some, it's the mountains, woods or lakes, others the stocky grey villages and solitary white cottages on impossibly green slopes. For many, it's the air and the space, the caves, cliffs and coves, the potential to run, swim, jump and ride. For the more sedentary of us, it's the tang of wood smoke or a mountain stream, the final rays of the day across an eternal landscape, or an overheard smatter of Welsh in the street, levering open the thrilling realisation that there is an older other right beneath our noses. Often, it's nothing specific; just a sensation of home and *hiraeth* that cannot be calibrated or quantified, much less explained, but which is every bit as real as Mr Telford's stream in the sky.

* * *

Thrillingly real it is, but even as the crowds cheered and 'Rule, Britannia!' rang out across the hills, Pontcysyllte was already a white elephant. Halfway through the aqueduct's construction, plans for the canal across it were radically scaled back. Originally, the intention had been to connect the River Mersey with the Dee at Chester and the

Severn at Shrewsbury, via the iron and coal areas around Wrexham. In the brief orgy of canal mania in the early 1790s, when money was pouring into schemes everywhere, it had seemed an absolute banker of an idea. A plaque in the Ellesmere Hotel, in the small Shropshire town of the same name, records how in a packed launch meeting for the canal in September 1792, 'the books were opened about noon and ere the sun set, near a million pounds of money was confided to the care of the committee'.

It was in this intoxicating spirit that the two aqueducts at Chirk and Pontcysyllte, plus the huge embankment and two tunnels between them, were conceived. That spirit though soon collided with the growing political and economic uncertainty pulsing from the continent following the French Revolution, and the wars sparked in its wake. Work started on the greater aqueduct in 1795, but within a couple of years, with the enormous pillars already striding across the valley, doubts were surfacing as to whether the waterway would – or indeed should – be continued north, through the hilly terrain towards Ruabon, Wrexham and Chester. In 1800, that extension was abandoned in favour of a longer but easier lowland route far to the east, and a proposal put forward that the aqueduct might be better used instead as a horse-drawn rail-road. In 1801, it was agreed to proceed as a canal, but to terminate it in a basin at the northern end of the bridge. There, rails would bring the minerals and coal in, and send the products out. A feeder arm, bringing a constant supply of water to the canal, would connect the basin with the River Dee a few miles to the west.

Telford continued with all his customary care and thorough attention to every last detail, but it was only half the project he had signed up for. His vision of can-do Britain, a meritocracy of equals, had collided head-on with the other version, the one that we know so well: the country of bitty thinking and bottled schemes, of landed interests and haughty disparity between its peoples and regions. The spirit of commerce had indeed touched the mountains on the borders of Wales, as Rowland Hunt had it in his grandiloquent speech at the aqueduct's opening, but instead of them beginning to smoke, the truth was that the flames sputtered and went out with indecent haste. They usually did.

A towering physical presence, magnificent from every angle, but relegated at the outset from its promised place on the main drag, to eternity as a sleepy cul-de-sac: Pontcysyllte could replace the leek or daffodil as Wales's national emblem. And like so many other Welsh totems, its only rebirth has been for the tourists. Following the Second World War, the waterway was rechristened as the Llangollen Canal, after the area's biggest draw, and the feeder channel originally built to siphon the Dee promoted as a picturesque route for pleasure boats.

The industrial impetus for the canal and aqueduct, represented at the opening ceremony by Telford and Hunt, turned out to be a fleeting fancy. Far longer lasting was the influence personified that day by their fellow travellers, the Ladies of Llangollen, those romantic retirees to the hills. When Telford was back a few years later planning his great highway to Dublin, they were most put out by the idea. As it was, it turned the town into an even more favoured overnight stop en route, and brought them fame and a modicum of fortune, as it became custom for the most esteemed travellers to beat a path to their door, bearing gifts. Pilgrims of the Picturesque came too, ticking the old spinsters off their lists between a cave, a waterfall and a ruined abbey.

In his speech at the ceremony, Rowland Hunt came to an inevitable crescendo of praise in memory of Nelson, and in celebration of Trafalgar. 'The prosperity of the British empire,' he boomed, 'owing to its firmness and good principles, has withstood the trials of scarcity, the temptations of sedition, the difficulties of credit, and, above all, the gigantic foe that has threatened its annihilation.'

There was rather more to it though than firmness and good principles. There too, present, correct and making a great deal of noise, was the hubris of empire. The ceremonial cannons that fired the fifteen-round salute had been looted from the Indians six years earlier, at the Siege of Seringapatam. A surprise ambush, the battle was a vicious crackdown against the one local ruler that had succeeded in resisting the East India Company, British imperialism's mercenary and murderous vanguard in Asia. He and countless others were slaughtered, and vast amounts of prize money were given to the Europeans who pillaged the palaces and temples, including during his funeral. The cannons now sit outside the Officers' Mess at Sandhurst.

Thomas Telford's patriotism rarely broke out in the flag-waving seen at Pontcysyllte. He was far more of a rationalist than that, and more too of an outsider (in a recent biography, *Man of Iron*, Julian Glover lightly – and plausibly – posits the theory that he may have been gay). For all his sterling work in uniting the kingdom, the engineer from Eskdale was never really part of the establishment. The canal mania that had launched his career had transferred almost overnight to railways, without him.

His last canal project was disastrous. The Birmingham and Liverpool was one of the final big builds of the canal age, and Telford was tasked with taking it across Staffordshire. All too symbolically, the lord of the manor at Norbury Park refused to allow the upstart canal anywhere near the wood where his pheasants were kept, necessitating a detour and the construction of a massive embankment, sixty feet high and over a mile long, out of inherently unstable marly soils. As Telford's health deteriorated, the canal repeatedly slipped and breached. In September 1834, seven years after commencing the work, Telford died, aged seventy-seven. The canal finally opened six months later, and a railway covering exactly the same route only two years after that.

Synchronously, as the building of canals largely came to an end with Telford, they were saved from dereliction by the actions of his first biographer, L. T. C. (Tom) Rolt. Another borderman, Rolt was born in Chester in 1910, and raised in Cusop, on the Herefordshire side of Hay-on-Wye, and in Gloucestershire. His book *Narrow Boat*, detailing a 400-mile canal tour through the summer and autumn of 1939 as the world tumbled into conflict, was published five years later. Its hearty evocation of a hidden England chimed deeply with a population weary of the war. Like the works of A. E. Housman in the First World War and the Reverend Kilvert earlier in the second, it was that quality over all others that propelled the book to surprise success, but it was no mere bucolic whimsy. Although unintended as such, *Narrow Boat* was a call to action.

After its publication, Rolt received a letter from conservationist Robert Aickman. The two men and their wives met on the Rolts' canal barge, and from that was born the Inland Waterways Association. Though the canals had been long overtaken by the railways for most purposes, many were still in use for heavy freight, but with the increase of motor traffic that was waning fast. The IWA was astonishingly successful in its aim of halting the decline of the waterways, and perhaps even more importantly, changing the public perception of them. To a largely urban population, canals were little more than oily ditches sidling through the grimier parts of town. Few thought of them as ribbons of rurality, places of beauty or havens of wildlife. They, and the largely invisible (and dwindling) community of people who lived and worked on them, were an anachronism.

With his portrait of their four-month grand tour of the Midlands, Tom Rolt changed that almost single-handedly. Throughout the book, his passion sparkles for the landscape and its histories, in passages of immense beauty and tenderness. There is though in his writing, and in the work of many others who aim to conjure a sense of Britishness, an undertow as dark and reedy as the most mothballed branch canal, and it is one that always seems to need cutting back.

For starters, it is almost always a sense of Britishness filtered only through its majority viewpoint, that of England, and a very specific kind of England at that. This is one of the reasons that Thomas Telford's take on Britain was such a refreshing one, for it was forged elsewhere, both in terms of geography and social class. Rolt's came from a family 'dedicated to hunting and procreation' (in the words of his autobiography) and his years as a boarder at Cheltenham College, one of the most military and muscular of the public schools founded by the Victorians.

The first ingredient, the unguent that binds it all together, is blind and blanket nostalgia. In the second paragraph of *Narrow Boat*, Rolt tells us that in undertaking his canal voyage he wanted to find 'what is left to us of that older England of tradition which is fast disappearing'. Isn't it always? It matters not what era we start in, the one that is just vanishing from view was better. So frequent is this refrain in his story, so welded to every conceivable angle, and expressed in such withering terms, that the reader, unless they have a constitution as iron as Pontcysyllte, soon wilts in the fusillade of woe. In a country inn, the Rolts are greeted 'with kindliness and natural courtesy, two qualities which the townsman of today has lost'. Discussing the illiteracy of many canal dwellers, he still finds it 'preferable to a "culture" born of the cinema and the Sunday newspaper'. Enjoying some ribald medieval misericords in a country church, he calls them 'a voice that has been stilled forever by that new spirit of joyless sanctimony which was a product of commercialism'. 'When shall we see their like again?' he concludes plaintively, to which the invited answer is clearly – and wearily – 'never, sir, never'. So it always is, to every Tom Rolt, in every era.

Central to this tendency is an inability to see others as anything more than convenient ciphers, or in the case of Rolt's canal folk, as picaresque wallpaper. In *Narrow Boat* canal and country people are invariably salts of the earth, while clerks, commuters and those living in new urban developments are routinely sneered at. There is little real curiosity, and no empathy. One evening in a lonely canal pub miles from anywhere, he and his wife talk with a boatman, travelling alone with his three young children. There had been a fourth child, but she had drowned in a lock, and the man's wife had recently died too. Rolt can only marvel at how cheerful he seems, and when the landlord later notes that the boatman was drinking more than he used to, the author's only response is 'one can hardly blame him'. On the outbreak of war that September, his sole concern is that petrol is now too expensive, so he converts the engine to paraffin, and is most put out that the part he needs goes missing ('characteristically') on a railway system buckling under the weight of troops and evacuees. 'After a fortnight of vain telephone conversations with helpless or apathetic clerks' it is found, one station down the line from where he thought it should be, and the Rolts can finally sail away.

This is not to diminish his very real achievements, not just in igniting the spark that led to the preservation of the canal network, but then repeating the trick a few years later as a formative player in rescuing the Talyllyn Railway in mid Wales, and making it the world's first preserved steam railway. In his book about that, *Railway Adventure* (1953), he has mellowed slightly, but the cast of others is still a parade of lightly drawn cut-outs. Particularly of interest here are his takes on the differences between the Welsh and the English.

Here too, barely anyone breaks free of their caricature. The Midlands tourists, on whom the little railway depends for the bulk of its income, are crude and common; the locals, many still reliant on the Talyllyn for transport to town and the main line, all have 'soft Welsh voices, quiet good manners'. Naturally, Rolt convinces himself that he is more the latter than the former. While acknowledging that he is 'an invader myself', he feels 'that a childhood spent at Welsh Hay gave me some sort of passport', and is convinced that they see that in him too. Perhaps. He is sympathetic regarding what he perceives to be the plight of rural Wales: the risk of too much tourism, the loss of traditional ways of life and the decline of the Welsh language. As on the canals, though, there is no solution offered, beyond that things should stay the way they are, or better still go back to the way they were.

We could dismiss all this as harmless enough, the wheezings of the perennially bilious, were it not that in Britain this force is an urgent and apparently infinite power that mutates for every age. Most alarmingly, the generalisations and snobbery slip all too readily into darker tones. For a few months in the spring and summer of 1939, Rolt lives on the boat in a wharf in Banbury, while fitting it out for the journey ahead. He loves the weekday market, full of 'gaitered farmers and their plump, bustling wives', selling 'great baskets of eggs and golden farm butter'. Not so the town's Saturday market, where 'the wives of the men from the factories' with 'the discordant, clipped speech of Birmingham ... crowd round the Jew vendors of shoddy clothing and gawdy ornaments, clutching their string bags and shrilly admonishing their grubby children'. That he wrote that in 1939 is startling enough; that he left it in for publication in 1944 quite extraordinary.

Having managed a more measured tone throughout *Railway Adventure*, in its final few pages he cannot hold back. Post-war society, repairing a blitzed and battered country, is 'flattening all inequalities, even of speech and thought'; in this 'new Dark Age' the wrong people are getting the idea that education is some sort of a birthright; welfare is encouraging the feckless; our cars, buses and trains all look the same, so too all that we 'use, wear or eat', which must 'conform to the same shoddy common denominator of suburban values'. Look closer, and there are far too many flecks of spit in the well-clipped moustache.

Rolt was born in 1910, so would have had only the sketchiest memories of life before the Great War. It's not hard to see where his nostalgia came from, nor why it manifested so thoroughly as a furious hunger for the Edwardian age. For most people, the strongest emotional pull is to a mythical golden era just before they were born. Fuse that with a worldwide wistfulness for the certainties that had been shattered by war, together with the prevailing imperial mindset and an unshakable white Anglophone supremacy, and you have a highly toxic combination. We've seen the same with the generation that were children around the Second World War, who proved so susceptible to the nostalgia and exceptionalism of the Brexit campaign, and voted for it in droves.

'A product of his time' is the verdict of Steve Haywood, whose *One Man and a Narrowboat* fuses his own contemporary barge journeys around the English Midlands with an appraisal of the life and influence of Tom Rolt. Though acknowledging 'the uncomfortable right-wing vein of some of his thinking', he largely forgives it: 'who's to say we wouldn't all have been up for a dose of nostalgia after six years of having the crap bombed out of us by the Nazis?' Aside from the fact that *Narrow Boat* was written in 1939 and 1940, a process Haywood himself details exhaustively, such an observation places nostalgia as a *product* of conflict, rather than its cause and key ingredient.

Another book from the same year saw it clear. George Orwell wrote his fourth novel, *Coming Up for Air*, through the winter of 1938–9, and it was published in June, a few months before the war broke out. In it, Orwell is utterly sure about what is coming – 'Houses going up into the air, bloomers soaked with blood, canary singing on above the corpses' – and why. He skewers Hitler and Stalin alike, and at home the jingoists and tub-thumpers, idiot politicians, the public schools and the popular press, and is merciless towards the appeasers and apologists on all sides, his own included. The depiction of a Left Book

Club meeting, a nest of dusty factionalism in a dingy church hall, is faultless. Most of all, the entire plot is a witty but raging debunk of the English addiction to nostalgia. Sold to us as the elixir of life, our very essence, it invariably transpires to be the most thin and watery of milks, and always just on the turn.

Though no less potent a force, Welsh nostalgia is a different beast to its English cousin. There are no World Cup victories to hark back to; indeed precious few victories of any kind. Glyndŵr's couple of wins provide some spark, but far more potent in the Welsh national psyche is that he was ultimately defeated and then vanished into thin air, where he waits, like a dragon of legend or an Old Testament prophet, to return and rescue his people. English nostalgia is for its virility and successes; Welsh *hiraeth* for its losses and – best of all – agonising near misses. English victory and Welsh defeat alike have been worn smooth and shapeless in their endless retelling, yet their power remains undimmed.

We can even plot these yearnings on a map, for every nation has places that hold the nub of its dreams. London aside, a city-state with a global gravitational pull, for aspirational England it would be the Cotswolds or the Chilterns, chocolate box and plump with abundance. In countries defined more by their mountains, rather than honeypot hills commutable from the capital, it is those high, wild places that hold the numen. This is very much so in Scotland; for all that the vast majority of its people live in the central belt, the key to the country's soul is in the Highlands. So too in Wales, where it is also found in the north, in Eryri, the land of eagles, Snowdonia.

Even to someone in Cardiff or Carmarthen, and even if they've never been there, Eryri is key to Welsh identity. The linguistic and spiritual heartland, its rocks are some of the oldest and some of the hardest on earth, qualities we are encouraged to think are shared by the region's inhabitants. And from those crags came gold and silver, copper and zinc, but most of all slate. On the many days of damp and rain, the quarries and spoil heaps, slate roofs and walls growl with dark intention, but then suddenly the clouds break, the sun bursts through, and they glitter regally. That too mirrors its people.

As many of us first sensed on a far-off childhood journey as we inched across the border at Chirk, we were heading into a new dimension, a place with a sweet yet sharp power we'd never before encountered. The irony was that by using Thomas Telford's grand highway, built to bolt the kingdom together, the most immediately apparent truth was how very different and divisible it is. 'Chirk is the oddest place,' writes Byron Rogers in his biography of R. S. Thomas, whose very first parish it was, even before the Maelor. More than anywhere else on the border, he says, the village 'occupies a sort of hairline fracture between Wales and England … Like Missouri in the American Civil War, Chirk was a place for a man to define his loyalties.'

Or to change them.

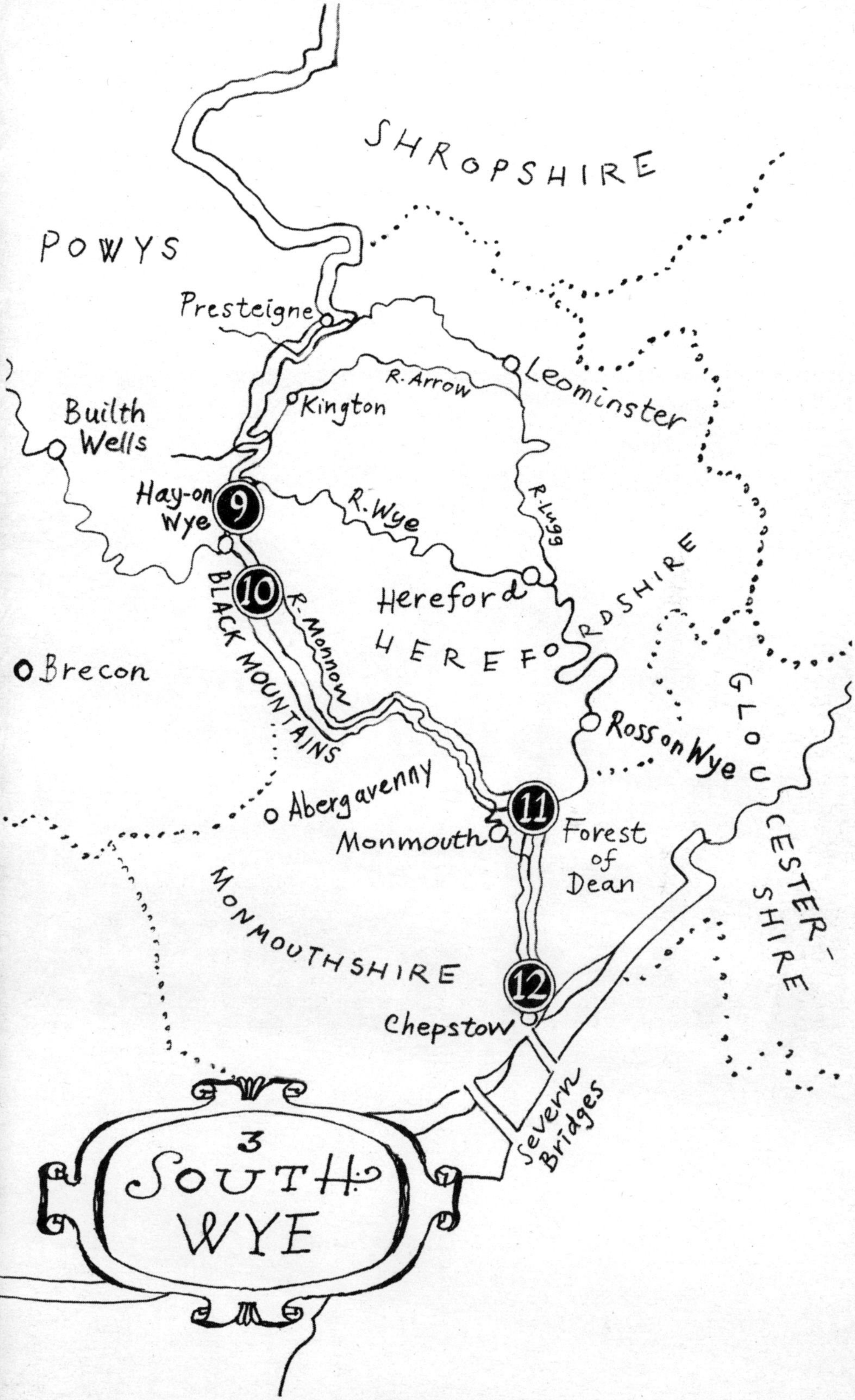

SHROPSHIRE

POWYS

Presteigne

Leominster

R. Arrow

Kington

Builth
Wells

R. Wye

R. Lugg

Hay-on
Wye **9**

10

R. Monnow

Hereford

HEREFO   RDSHIRE

Brecon

BLACK MOUNTAINS

Ross on Wye

GLOUCESTER-

Abergavenny

Monmouth

11

Forest
of
Dean

SHIRE

MONMOUTHSHIRE

12

Chepstow

Severn
Bridges

3
SOUTH
WYE

9.

INSELAFFEN

/// roosters.ghost.ambushes

The red-and-white-striped barrier, symbol of borders the world over, is refusing to rise. Out of the car window comes an arm at full stretch, the clunk of a pound coin into the box, and then ten long seconds of silence, a little birdsong, but no movement. The hand at the end of the arm jabs the touchscreen, gingerly at first, then with an increasingly random ferocity, but still nothing. Eventually, and in an understandable flap, the driver has to reverse away from the tollhouse, nearly hitting the car waiting patiently at the lights behind her. Another car appears tentatively from the other end of the bridge, peeping to see what's going on, and then reverses tactfully back out of sight. The river is glassy calm, the morning spring-bright and beautiful, but here it's genteel chaos.

The toll bridge over the wide and lovely Wye is the cutest way into Hay. There's a perfectly serviceable main road that covers the same few miles for free, but the old bridge, with its wooden carriageway and arches, its stripy barrier, table of Georgian toll charges and more than a hint of *Chitty Chitty Bang Bang*, perfectly sets up the mood for entry into the self-styled 'world's first Town of Books'. *Welcome to Ruritania!* it beams, even if today the barrier won't budge, and instead of a kindly tollkeeper appearing to sort it all out, all we have is a malfunctioning touchscreen and eight CCTV cameras.

It's all illusion anyway. The bridge looks the part, and usually acts the part, but this isn't even the border. That comes a couple of miles further on, and is so understated that you'd never normally notice it. As you enter town, past a new housing estate, warehouses and a super-market (*Croeso i Co-op Y Gelli*, says the sign), you're clearly led to believe that you've finally arrived in world-famous Hay-on-Wye. Only a roadside notice board headed CUSOP PARISH COUNCIL hints that you're somewhere else, and if you know your county map, that you're still in Herefordshire, and have not quite left England. Just ahead, the tiny Dulas Brook burrows under the street; that is the border, and only then are you into Hay, Breconshire, Powys; into Wales. For a place that makes such a lot of noise about almost everything, it is an astonishingly low-key entry.

The street ascends into the heart of town, gleaming like a well-groomed show pony. My anticipation ratchets up too. Even though on every visit I invariably reach the point where I can take the place no longer and feel an urgent need to flee, before that moment is reached it is always a pleasure. There is good food to be had, creaky pubs, odd shops and unexpected conversations, and if things start to flag I can just head into one of the bookshops, inhale the infinite musty pheromones and abandon myself to a deep dive of the shelves. I am looking forward to a very Hay day.

It starts well, bumping into Lisa and Judith, a couple of social media friends that I've never before met for real. They have recently moved to the town, and are having a great time of it, even though they laughingly call it 'a tinseltown theme park'. We go for a coffee and sandwich down by the Wye, and watch canoeists, kayakers and paddleboarders alternately wobble and glide along the broad – but terribly low – river. All I've read about the Wye lately has been bad news: banks denuded, trees ripped out, increasing pollution, habitat and species loss. Powys and Herefordshire councils' weakness for giant chicken sheds is usually posited as the main culprit, though some say that things are improving. My B&B landlord is a fisherman, and tells me that pressure is starting to break through from all the river's many users, the swimmers especially. Hay is – of course it is – a hotspot for 'wild' swimming, particularly on a languid bend of the Wye ten minutes' walk from town, a grassy common known as The Warren. It's a lovely dip, one I've done often, and it's good to know that it's still much used.

Between them, Judith and Lisa share Welsh, English and Dutch heritage, and I'm keen to hear what the border means to them. Their new place is actually in England, one of the newbuilds by the Co-op, though they'd prefer to be on the Welsh side of the line. To some extent, they feel like they are already, for Covid has made a real difference to people's sense of identity, they say. Until only a few weeks earlier, well after the second anniversary of the beginning of the pandemic, there were still signs in most shops reminding people that they were in Wales and needed to follow the policies of Cardiff, not London. They also mention a phenomenon that may be unique to Hay: a Welsh border town whose English citizens are keen to be as demonstratively Welsh as possible, in order to stick it to the Tory government in Westminster. 'Someone said to me the other day that Mark Drakeford looked like "a boring sociology lecturer",' Lisa tells me, 'but that they'd far rather that than the buffoon in Downing Street.'

This is, I think, part of a wider shift. I've been coming to Hay for thirty years, and have noticed a sea change in its identity. The bookshops put their Welsh and Celtic stock front and centre these days, sometimes even in the window, not in the dark and dusty corners that I remember back then. The gift shops are full of CWTCH and CYMRU tat, and the Welsh language has a far higher visible profile than ever before. Though the window of the estate agents is full of houses in somewhere called 'Hay-on-Wye, Herefordshire' (to be fair, it is the official postal address), the Eirian glass studio, Tŷ Tân gallery, Twmpa cycles, Welsh classes and choirs suggest otherwise. More surprisingly, on the streets and in the shops, I catch regular snatches of Cymraeg.

To the Farmers Welsh Lavender Shop, and its owner, the ebullient Nancy Durham. She's in deep conversation with a Lithuanian tourist who's over for a long weekend's fishing trip. He has a lot to say, and is quite clearly traumatised. The war in Ukraine is now in its third month, and Lithuania is also slap in the firing line. Putin's troops have been poised on their border for years. Just as the Russians are trying to blitz their way across Ukraine for a land corridor to Crimea, Odessa, perhaps even Moldova, so too are they angling to force one through Lithuania to the Russian exclave of Kaliningrad. Lithuanians are terrified and angry, including the one buying his wife some upmarket face cream on a spring day in Hay. If anything, the sheer sweet prosaicism of our setting, with its wafts of lavender and bursts of laughter on the pavement outside, only makes the contrast even starker. 'I just want this for us,' he says, gesturing to the essential oils, candles and Welsh blankets. 'A nice life. We were getting there, but it's all gone backwards so fast.'

Even in his sore state, and even though he has only been in Hay since late the previous night, he has noticed, and is intrigued, by the Welshness of the place, and asks Nancy and me if we can demonstrate the language to him. Though she is a Canadian, and I'm from Worcestershire, we muddle through a few sentences, and he hangs on every word. Small nations, their languages and their culture are so important, he says, and we must never lose sight of that. It's what held his country together in the Soviet times, so too its Baltic neighbours of Latvia and Estonia. Wales has a larger population than any of them; should it also therefore aspire to independence? I ask him. He shrugs. He doesn't think so, mainly because he is such a fan of the bigger unit – for us, that is, not them. 'The UK has been the number one support for Ukraine,' he insists.

Nancy's shop opened on the twelfth of April 2021, the day that the Welsh Covid border restrictions ended. 'It was busy!' she remembers. 'And when they came in, I'd say to the people from England, "So you're enjoying a little international travel today, are you?" There was a lot of laughter about it.' Like her customer, she has some rather sharper experience of borders, most notably the ones that emerged and splintered as communist eastern Europe disintegrated in the early 1990s, when Lithuania and the others became independent. She was then a European news correspondent for the Canadian Broadcasting

Corporation (CBC), a 'one woman band' as she describes herself, digging out and filming her own stories, with the help of a network of fixers. There were real horrors, especially as former Yugoslavia imploded. Even before the bloodshed, though, Europe's spaghetti bowl of frontiers seemed crazy to her, coming as she did from a continent divided between just two enormous countries. 'I had to get an extra-big passport to accommodate all the stamps,' she says.

When I tell her what I'm writing about, her immediate response is: 'I don't like borders'; unsurprising perhaps with that background. She's had more of a think about it by the time we meet up later, at the farm. Nancy is an accidental and unlikely lavender farmer. With the help of a small agricultural diversification grant, she planted half an acre in 2003 as an experiment, which succeeded far beyond her wildest hopes. Way beyond everyone's expectations too, for the farm, which they bought derelict in the 1980s, sits at well over 1,000 feet up a rough Breconshire hillside. In summer, the fields of brilliant purple and their heady perfume come as such a shock down a sheep-bitten back lane.

Finding Nancy and her philosopher husband down this track is equally surprising. 'I felt immediately at home here,' she says. 'I felt completely safe.' As she had to do sometimes in her journalism, playing the 'Canadian card' helped settle them in to rural Wales. 'We'd joke [to the neighbours] that we're also colonised, as Canadians, and people would laugh, but I'm sure there *was* some of that somewhere. We hadn't come from England. It's a fact.' Brexit has only reanimated her antipathy to more borders, but Covid made her very glad to be west of this one. 'It made us all really realise that we have a different government in Wales,' she says, and one for which she was grateful. 'They seem far more caring. I feel like I trust that they're trying to do their best.' As for Welsh independence, 'Yes, I can imagine that, and I'm not afraid of it. The United Kingdom is in trouble.'

Back at her shop, the town clock is chiming and the Lithuanian heads for the river. I've been in Hay only a couple of hours, and already I've had animated conversations about war, climate, economy, history, identity and culture. My brain is bouncing like a lamb in the fields, but they are only a couple of months old, while I'm halfway through my fifties and need some hush. It is bookshop time. At the turn of the century, there were around forty in the town, and although the internet has inevitably scythed through their ranks, there are still almost twenty. Their survival is guaranteed, I hope, for however accurate the algorithms become, however precisely they manage to recreate our urges or anticipate our needs, they will never replicate the synapse-crack of happenstance, the perfect joy of a surprise find. Second-hand bookshops exercise an intelligence that can never be artificial, one that relies entirely on the inexplicable alchemy of people and words. After an hour, perhaps more, I emerge blinking into the sunshine and the singing tills of a bank holiday Saturday, a fair few quid down but laden with treasure.

Many of the earlier bookshops have now mutated into restaurants, boutiques, galleries and souvenir shops. Unlike most comparable small towns, there are few empty units. Hay seems almost impervious to downturns, and in the gardens beneath the castle it's a pleasure to see the reason why: the face of the late Richard Booth (1938–2019) squinting out from a new bas-relief memorial. The old bugger has not been forgotten.

In April 1977, aged ten, I was thrilled by the kerfuffle created by Booth when he declared the town an independent nation, with himself, naturally, as king, 'Richard, Coeur de Livres' no less. 'The British Isles needs a Liechtenstein,' he boomed to the television crews, showing them the new country's flag, the same green and white as the Welsh one, but with a lion instead of the dragon (nothing heraldic, it was the logo of Booth's Gin). The cameras rolled as he hoisted the flag proudly over his castle, an oh-so-Hay hybrid of Norman keep, Jacobean mansion and twentieth-century fire damage (twice).

Booth's antics fitted like a glove, for Hay *is* a place apart, and always has been, far more so than any other border town. It straddles two countries, three counties, a broad river and very many miles to anywhere else. The walled town had two castles, nearby Cusop a third, and there were four more within a couple of miles. It has belonged to both England and Wales, alternately *and* simultaneously, to neither, and been attacked by both sides too. Even its names imply a definite swank: the English coming from the Norman French: La Haie, The Hay, 'the enclosure', and in Welsh, Y Gelli, 'the grove'. Those definite articles have a lot to answer for.

Commentators didn't quite know how to play Booth's UDI. Some treated it like a superannuated student Rag Week, and there was plenty for them: crown jewels fashioned out of a ballcock and copper piping; souvenirs, from Hay passports (75p) to a full dukedom (£25, including a T-shirt); a cabinet 'picked in five minutes in the pub', he wrote in his autobiography, including a Welsh Office 'occupied by a vaguely nationalist telephone engineer'; the country's First Lady, pioneer transsexual April Ashley, rechristened the Duchess of Offa's Dyke, perfectly coiffed and resplendent in a sea of beery yokels.

Some were more suspicious. In a long segment on BBC1's *Nationwide* magazine show, the voiceover called him 'Hay's own Ian Smith', after the breakaway white apartheid leader of Rhodesia, and placed his ideas within the wider debate on devolution raging at the time, noting that the new flag 'may prove something of a green and white rag to the Welsh assembly, if there ever is one'. The *Daily Mail*, predictably, could see only the worst: STORM CLOUDS OF BELFAST LOOM OVER HAY, its headline shrieked.

Even if the answers were wrong, commentators were right to ask questions, for behind the larky photo-ops, the stamps and edible bank notes, was some deadly serious intent. Booth had come to Hay in 1961, and opened his first bookshop the following year, in the old fire station. By the time of the declaration of independence in 1977, there were over a dozen, and in their wake came visitors and money. During that same period, other shops and services had declined sharply: the railway had gone, and so too many of the basics of small-town life. Booth railed against the quangos and committees, the Development Board for Rural Wales especially, which had failed to staunch the flow, and had – in his words – only 'encouraged foreign imports and subsidised London property deals'. Local, unusual specialisms were his answer, and the booktown was proving it. Booth's monarchy was anarchy, a creed that sat well in Hay.

Without Booth, there would be no Hay as global brand, no litera-ture festival, no Clintons or Tutu, no Groucho Club pop-ups, Michelin-starred restaurants, glamping resorts and acres of London newsprint oiling the wheels of his cranky capitalism. Big money has sluiced through the stubborn streets of his kingdom; even his moth-eaten castle, where I once had the pleasure of being knighted by King Richard in a television documentary, has been glammed up to a quite unrecognisable extent. Though he fell out with plenty of his fellow citizens, he usually patched things up and the town remembers him now with gruff affection (and a canny eye on his marketing potential). There's the new memorial, and a room in the revamped castle showing off the tatty old emblems of his little kingdom, now much polished and housed in display cases. His name still sits above his flagship bookshop, also much smartened up and including a café and even cinema, and on the edge of town, yards short of the border, is a tidy close of new executive homes named Gerddi Booth / Booth Gardens. It's the last in Wales, and so was he.

* * *

A cup of tea, and as ever I'm piqued by the feeling that if I stay in Hay any longer I might start shouting at people in loafers. Best to go. In deciding where to base myself for this initial research trip to the Wye, it had come down to a choice between the first three border towns on the river and its tributaries: Presteigne, the diminutive old county town of Radnorshire; Kington, Herefordshire's westernmost borough, or Hay. Being more familiar with the Welsh side of the line, I opted for Kington, and was very glad that I had.

The three towns are textbook lessons in the various stages of gentri-fication: the base, middle and apex of a pyramid that has long become practically the only model available. Hay sits at the top, a royally entertaining but ruthless machine for splitting visitors from their cash. It is the country town that so many others look up to and try to emulate, even if that means a tacit acceptance that the hallmarks of success will include eye-watering house prices and ostracised locals.

In the middle rank is Presteigne, its handsome streets much buffed up these last few years, but still with its scruffy heart beating strong. Once its Ruritanian civic status evaporated when Radnorshire was absorbed into the new super-county of Powys, the town slowly began to make a name for itself as a faintly counter-cultural centre for music and art, which, though nowhere near the scale of Hay and books, has given it a substantial bounce. 'It's not the real world, is it?' a friend's mother once said to writer Ian Marchant, a long-time resident of Presteigne. 'No more it is, thank Heaven; it's the land of milk and honey, and I've run out of both,' he wrote in response. Next to Hay, though, it's a shambling amateur.

By far the least gilded is Kington, which might come as a surprise, it being the only one of the three in England (a cliché it may be, but the sudden jump in visible wealth from Wales to England is almost constant. Even Hay goes up several further notches when you cross the line into Cusop Dingle). In Kington, St George's flags fly over numerous buildings and in a fair few front gardens, even though the town lies west of Offa's Dyke. Presteigne, 6 miles north and across the border in Wales, is east of the dyke. Nothing is quite as it seems.

In 1968, in his walking classic *Journey through Britain*, John Hillaby describes Kington as 'a little, squashed-up, narrow-streeted market town on the Welsh frontier where they sell cartridges and sheep dip, fertilizer and men's flannel underwear', and little seems to have changed much since. It was reading that description ten years ago, sitting in one of the town's fabulously lowfalutin pubs, that the idea for this book was born. Frontier! That was the word that lit the spark. The line that I'd crissed and crossed all my life, a thing of eternally quirky intrigue, suddenly took on a whole new depth and darkness. A frontier is no mere scratch in the sand, some postcard oddity, but an entire state of mind with all its own rules. We think of a frontier's tension, the bow pulled taut and poised, but forget its flip side, the trading and the tippling, the coming together in hot, flyblown days and wild, lawless nights. Nowhere do they feel so close to the surface as in Kington.

On my first night in town, I'm sat supping a pint in an old coaching inn, eavesdropping. Some lads playing pool are talking about heifers and football, while an old lady behind me suddenly announces to her companion, in a borderland burr as rich as butter, 'Didn't I ever tell you I can turn my eyelids inside out?' It takes every ounce of self-control not to turn around and demand proof. On my second night, I pass a small gallery, gleaming new on the dusty main street, and glimpse an overlit crowd of folk within, clutching glasses of fizz and talking fortissimo, though not loud enough to drown out the turbo exhausts of the mud-spattered jalopies and souped-up Fiestas roaring past, their solitary working brake lights glowing brazen as they take the corners. On my third – and sadly final – night, I walk back to my B&B along the same street, and have to go right through the middle of a cluster of police cars, their blue lights lashing the fine buildings, their officers chatting contentedly with a small gaggle of bystanders. No one seems hurried, or much bothered. I have no idea what is going on, and neither it appears do they.

My landlady is a blow-in, and tells me that Kington remains a very agricultural town, and that the old local families still run the show. This is not done aggressively, she is at pains to assure me, but quietly, firmly, and has so far kept the tide of Hay at bay. Other people echo the same idea, with varying degrees of enthusiasm. Most though see the value of the town's deep old roots, and are fully aware that tinkering too much with the formula might kill the very thing that makes the place so appealing. People in Presteigne and Hay, however, are far less sanguine about their neighbour, which they see as a clodhopping throwback, still loitering in the sixties.

In the Kington museum, a real cabinet of curiosities, the volunteer curator is adamant that change should only be gradual, perhaps even glacial. When forced upon them, things go badly wrong. The biggest blow of recent times, he says, was the closure of all the banks within just a couple of years: 'everyone has to go to Leominster now, and they bypass us'. The same has happened to Presteigne, all small towns, even Hay, and he's right. The bank stop was an important hook for the weekly trip to town for many farmers, small businesses and outlying inhabitants, but there's a more nebulous point too, of status. A regular definition of a town, as opposed to a village, was that it had a bank.

Their passing from rural life is more than just a pragmatic loss. To those of a certain age or inclination, the bank was an anchor in the town centre, steadfast and austere, and its manager an exalted member of the civic hierarchy. As Walmington-on-Sea's bank manager in the sitcom *Dad's Army*, the priggish Mr Mainwaring, though little suited to the role, was always the only real candidate for captain of the platoon. The banks have gone, and their florid buildings are now wine bars and charity shops. *Their* managers would never make the grade.

The curator tells me of another recent outbreak of change, though this one was rebuffed, at least for now. After the first few months of the pandemic, the murder by police of George Floyd in Minneapolis ignited worldwide revulsion over racism, and fuelled the rise of the Black Lives Matter movement. In Britain, its most tangible result came two weeks after Floyd's murder, when the statue of Bristol slave trader Edward Colston was pulled down by protestors and dumped in the city's harbour. In its wake, gravestones and statues all over the country were re-examined, and many removed by the authorities.

Names too were challenged, and changed. In Kington, the 400-year-old high school is named after Lady Margaret Hawkins, its original benefactress and widow of pioneer slave trader Sir John Hawkins. As the protests escalated, some people – incomers, says the curator – demanded a new school name, but this was resisted. 'It was her money that founded it, not his,' he insists, and this was the line, the perilously thin line, to which everyone stuck. In the *Hereford Times*, the school's Director of Humanities called the links to slavery 'tenuous', and said, 'As tempting as it is to make suppositions, there is no evidence to support the claim that money made from the slave trade was the foundation of the school.' Seventeen years earlier, though, the same teacher had written a slender book about Sir John, saying that his widow's 1632 bequest 'almost certainly was made possible through the fortune her husband made in slave trading'. He also ran a project with some students to explore the issue in a short film, which was given the unambiguous title of *The Slave Trade Built Our School*.

It's all frontier talk: national borders, class and racial divides, culture wars. Lines are drawn, and the no-man's-land in between might be a dustbowl, or it could be a minefield. Only when we inch across it do we find out which. Everyone I speak to about the school name controversy sighs and looks away; many try to steer the conversation elsewhere. In the museum, the curator rounds me up with the efficiency of a sheepdog and herds me into a side room, where the military memorabilia lives. It's quickly clear why, for it includes a display about the thousands of American GIs posted to the area in the Second World War. At first, black and white soldiers mixed in town of an evening, but the white boys didn't like it, especially with some beers inside them. A displayed letter from General Eisenhower sets the scene: 'white soldiers, seeing a girl walk down the street with a negro, frequently see themselves as protecting the fairer sex and believe it necessary to intervene even to the extent of using force'. The image that his words conjure up is horrific.

The problem was repeated all across Britain, resulting in the USA's Visiting Forces Act of 1942, stipulating that soldiers abroad had to maintain the same rules of segregation as at home. The British government, desperate not to offend the Americans, meekly capitulated, so that in Kington and many other British towns, on some nights of the week there were only white GIs in the pubs, and on some only black. The museum display assures us how alien this idea of segregation was to local people, and illustrates it with a folksy tale of a young black American soldier doing some gardening work for a local family, and then refusing to go indoors for tea and cake, because 'I'm not allowed to sit at a white man's table', something the family find 'terrible'. The display continues: 'Contemporary reports, as with those from Kington, showed that most people in Britain believed that all who were fighting for freedom in Europe should be considered equal, regardless of colour.'

Perhaps. But I also see and wince at the comments under the *Hereford Times* pieces about the school name controversy, hear of a parish councillor a few years ago who didn't want to signpost footpaths because it might 'attract blacks from Birmingham', and meet a man who hails from the same part of the world as me, but says that he moved because 'we've lost Worcestershire, so I had to come here'. He

tells me this at the gate of a quiet Norman church, with rooks in the distant trees and imaginary hordes just over the brow of a hill, pressing down on him.

There are more frontiers, always more frontiers, and we will follow them across lands of growing wealth and ballooning inequality, all along the serpentine Wye, and all the way to the southern sea.

*   *   *

Lovely though the towns are, the real pleasure of this part of the border comes in losing yourself in the lanes and tracks between them. On these May days, they are at their very best, high-banked and bursting with buttercups, bluebells, campion and cowslip, and wafts of cow parsley that sway in my wake, but I've explored them in all seasons, and there is no down time. In summer, the contrast between green fields and ploughed red earth plays you like a sorcerer, making your eyesight dance. Autumn's fiery palette shimmers through the woods, and shines colder, sharper across the wiry moorland above them.

In winter, the pot-bellied hills are stripped back to their bones, and a thin, low light floods ancient stone and timber, catching every scar.

There is no mistaking that this is contested territory, torn between masters, yet servant to none. Lumps and bumps of old forts and fortresses appear round every corner. Castles have crumbled into farms, while farms (and barns and churches) look like castles; thickset, squat but sly, liable to switch from domestic to military at the merest whisper from across the plains in front, or the mountains behind. On occasion, all uses slide into one. At Michaelchurch-on-Arrow, the last of Radnorshire lost in the hazy lanes, the massively outsized tower of the church, punctured only by the thinnest of arrow-slits, clearly identifies as a fortress, but also makes do as a farm. All but the most recent parts of the churchyard have been fenced off for sheep, and there they graze, unperturbed, among long-gone Prices and Lloyds.

From the vantage point of today, one of the finest features of this muddle of lanes is how often you pass a half-timbered building, hundreds of years old and quite content to show it. For all but the last few decades, this was the normal appearance of Tudor or Jacobean houses: patched up and sagging, rotten in places, faded and unkempt but quite literally pulsing with breath, the orchestra of wildlife that called them home. It is strangely moving to see these houses girdled by cobbles and courtyards, sprung with dandelion and valerian, rather than an even coating of gravel and a thick cloak of silence.

Fifty years ago, the dereliction of sixteenth-century Penrhos Court, a mile east of Kington, was almost terminal. It was on the point of being demolished when it was spotted by Martin Griffiths, fresh off the plane from a few years of living in Africa. While there, he'd 'dreamed of England', he later said, or at least the version of it that he saw in Penrhos and, having bought the near ruin for £5,000, spent the next two decades painstakingly recreating that dream. Cod-medievalism was all the rage in 1970s Britain, an antidote to the age of beige. Penrhos became a cult hangout for the likes of Queen, Led Zeppelin, and Monty Python's Terry Jones. In 1977, as Richard Booth was launching his tiny kingdom up the road in Hay, Jones and Griffiths founded at Penrhos Britain's first microbrewery, a landmark in the campaign for real ale. In the Eighties and Nineties, it became the home of an influential organic cookery school and *pied-à-terre* for some of the biggest names at the Hay festival. Griffiths sold up in 2012, and Penrhos is now fully spruced and sanitised, marketed as a wedding venue and luxury holiday cottages. The gravel is smooth yet exceedingly crunchy.

Of all the hairy rockers associated with the place, none struck a more plaintive tune than Mike Oldfield. After the massive, unexpected success of his 1973 instrumental album *Tubular Bells*, the reclusive Oldfield ran away from London, and on a whim bought The Beacon, a ramshackle house overlooking Kington. 'I wasn't exactly happy there,' he wrote in his autobiography, 'but for some reason I felt secure.' Security was huge for Oldfield. His Home Counties upbringing had been deeply troubled, and a terrible acid trip had left him with a residue of crippling panic attacks. Once again, the borderland became balm. He soon found Penrhos Court and Martin Griffiths ('a bit like your favourite barman, you could really talk to him'). Griffiths persuaded Oldfield to become Penrhos's resident minstrel, turning out a few folk tunes for the diners by the massive log fire in the main hall, and being paid in wine, and lots of it. It was, he writes, 'the safest I'd ever felt'.

Opposite The Beacon is the great whaleback of Hergest Ridge, one of the most singular hills on the border. Walking up it from Kington town is like riding a rolling wave, a tremendous sensation of forward propulsion pushing you on to the summit, and over, breaking, falling into Wales. Even were it not crowned by a mysterious boulder, the Whetstone, and an unexpected glade of monkey-puzzle trees, Hergest is exhilarating, and unforgettable. It bewitched Mike Oldfield, who flew his model planes and walked his Afghan hounds on its flanks, and named his follow-up album in its honour. *Hergest Ridge* fulfilled all of the clichés of the difficult second album, being – in his words – 'cobbled together'. The critics and audiences, desperate for another *Tubular Bells*, were not shy to point that out, making Oldfield turn only further inwards. Wanting not to travel at all ('I had difficulty enough just going down to Kington, let alone getting on a plane'), he built a studio at The Beacon, where his third album *Ommadawn*, said to be his masterpiece, was recorded through 1975.

Though I've never been an especial fan of Mike Oldfield's music, there was something in it that I recognised on an instinctive level: the sound of Middle England, and its young men in particular. He was huge in my Worcestershire school among the willowy boys who thought they were probably poets, but who ended up in corporate law. His biggest chart hit, a rendition of the traditional hornpipe air 'Portsmouth', was played on a loop in my childhood home, accompanied by my dad and a troupe of his mates from Round Table who loved to Morris dance to it. Though turbocharged by electronica and amplification, Oldfield's was still a hurdy-gurdy Albion of real ale and medieval ruins, flutes and pixies and comely young maidens, 'this blessed plot, this earth, this realm, this England'.

In this century, there has been no moment more inclined to evoke that 'sceptre'd isle' of William Shakespeare than the opening ceremony of the 2012 London Olympics – and there, centre stage, was Mike Oldfield. Only a decade on, the occasion already looks like a relic from a lost world. The exuberant England portrayed by a cast of thousands was so appealing, and on that warm, sentimental evening it was easy to hope that it was the version that might prevail. It didn't, of course. When a Conservative MP tweeted during the ceremony that it was 'leftie multicultural crap', he was ridiculed and condemned in equal measure. Now, all he would need to add would be the word 'woke' and he'd have numerous newspapers, websites, columnists and influencers chanting his name, and a guaranteed hotseat on the news channels.

This rapid polarisation, the scraping away of layers and context to expose only the bleeding stumps of discourse, has come from all directions. As Mike Oldfield played, up popped author J. K. Rowling to read an extract from *Peter Pan*; a decade on, both reader and text would provoke howls of rage. The short videos of singing children to represent the other UK nations already felt a little tokenistic in 2012; now there would be red-hot indignation and ministerial statements in devolved parliaments (that the children representing Wales sang the mighty 'Cwm Rhondda' in English would alone keep the Cardiff news cycle whirring for days). Two Welsh footballers in the all-British team declined to sing 'God Save the Queen' before the opening match; only the *Daily Mail* made anything of it, but today it'd be a rolling Twitterstorm and ubiquitous prime time. And Oldfield himself, soon to be an enthusiastic Brexiteer, had already quit Britain, denouncing it as 'a nanny state'. He'd moved, for the second time, to Spain, where, he said, 'I haven't seen any cameras … and you can smoke where you like.'

In 2022, asked in an opinion poll to list the five best things about Britain, almost a quarter of respondents plumped for 'being an island'. An inalienable fact of geography, it nonetheless scored the same as the BBC and the arts, and higher than our history of innovation, welfare provision or sense of community. The sentiment was greater among older people, Conservative voters, Midlanders and men, and dramatically higher among those who voted to leave the EU over those who wanted to remain within it. Their guiding star is more Mike Oldfield than Shakespeare, but most of all it's the likes of Sir Ian Botham, the combative former cricketer who pledged allegiance to the Leave campaign in a 2016 television interview with the words: 'Personally, I think that England is an island. And I think that we should keep that.' On the arrival of Boris Johnson in Downing Street, such insight was clearly needed on the frontline, and Botham was elevated to the House of Lords, and given the job of trade envoy to Australia.

Whether it's 'this sceptr'd isle … this precious stone set in the silver sea', or Botham's very much lumpier version, we are bewitched by our own insularity, and constantly conjure it. The Germans call us *inselaffen* ('island apes'), a badge of thundering disdain that we wear with pride. Britannia, we sing, 'arose from out the azure main', and our cultural horizons are never happier than when bounded by it: from *The Tempest* to *Treasure Island*, via *Robinson Crusoe* and *Gulliver's Travels*, Avalon, Atlantis and Utopia. We love the stories that use a tiny isle as a mirror in which we can gaze at ourselves: *Lord of the Flies*, *The Admirable Crichton* or *The Wicker Man*, and for our youngsters, there are the starter islands of Neverland, Sodor, Kirrin or Azkaban.

Islands, as both fact and fiction, play into a very particular nation-alist discourse, one that the British are suckled on. Even the name is appropriated to the cause. Great Britain is a geographic term, a way of differentiating the larger Britain from its smaller cousin, Brittany, but we will hear none of that, and take the name instead as a divine state-ment of supremacy. Woven into that is the notion of the island as the epicentre, of Empire and of civilisation itself. The Irish, inhabitants of the world's twentieth largest island, were encouraged to think of the eighth largest as 'the mainland', a deeply revealing term still tragically common among Ulster unionists, while an actual mainland, Eurasia, the biggest landmass on earth and only 20 miles off the coast of Kent, is held delicately at arm's length as 'the continent'. To muddy it further, despite England accounting for only 60 per cent of its area, most people hold Great Britain's island identity as an almost exclu-sively English force, the ultimate in the long-standing conflation of the two. Baron Botham is far from alone.

Though the big prizes were India, Canada and South Africa, it was the islands of the British Empire that generated especial sentiment, even their names an incantation: Ceylon and Singapore, Malta and the Maldives, Jamaica, Trinidad, Hong Kong, Zanzibar. It was always the smaller nuggets of the Caribbean, the Indian and Pacific oceans that provided the most syrupy television footage of royal tours: their arrival at tin shack airports, or sleepy little harbours suddenly overwhelmed by the heft and majesty of the royal yacht. Then we saw them garlanded with flowers, carried aloft through the streets, serenaded with song and dance and even worshipped as gods, in the case of one Micronesian tribe regularly twinned with a condescending smile at the end of the news bulletin. The symbolism of supremacy was never subtle.

Neither is it a relic of distant history. Even in the third decade of the twenty-first century, the tiny islands of Empire still prop up the big one, not so much with televised opportunities for royal tours, which don't tend to go so well these days, but as an essential lubricant for the machinery of Western power. We want to imagine, as we did on that halcyon evening in the Olympic Stadium, that our elevated place in the world is thanks to literature, music and a universally admired sense of humour, but the truth is far grubbier, and found on the last few islands still flying the flag.

In the latest Tax Justice Network's biannual index of corporate tax havens, where every territory is assessed for its levels of financial secrecy, tax evasion and prevalence of offshore accounts, the top three in the world, all given an absolute maximum score for how much abuse their financial systems allow, were the British Virgin Islands, the Cayman Islands and Bermuda. Jersey was eighth, the UK itself thirteenth, and also in the top twenty were Guernsey, the Isle of Man, the Bahamas and Mauritius (the last two Commonwealth territories whose final court of appeal is in London). On our tiny lumps of rock sits an entire financial ecosystem of oligarchy and global corruption.

In the years running up to Russia's invasion of Ukraine, long after Putin's intentions had become horribly clear, many called for the UK to hit his regime where we so easily could and where it would hurt the most: in the luxury properties and myriad investments, from private schools to football clubs, lawyers and accountants to journalists and politicians, into which so much of the dirtiest Russian money had long flowed. Such calls were batted away, even as other countries took action and even after the nerve agent attacks in England on Alexander Litvinenko and Sergei Skripal. Only finally on the invasion of Ukraine in February 2022 did action become politically unavoidable. Among the sanctions was a six-storey superyacht, the *Scheherazade*, seized in a Tuscan port. Containing a gym, gold-plated bathrooms, a spa, a cryotherapy chamber, two helipads and an indoor swimming pool that converts into a dancefloor, its ownership is opaque, but – according to Italian police – lies within 'prominent elements of the Russian government', likely Putin himself. We do know for sure though that the *Scheherazade* is registered in the Cayman Islands, the British Overseas Territory half the size of the Isle of Wight.

If Hay-on-Wye is a British Liechtenstein, as decreed by its late king, then we also have our own Vatican: the City of London. Virtual islands exist far inland too, and there is none more insular than the square mile, with its liveries and guilds, aldermen and sheriffs, run by a Corporation entirely outside of any other local or regional government jurisdiction, and elected by an opaque system abolished for the rest of the UK in 1835. The votes of the City's 9,000 inhabitants are far outweighed by those of the banks and corporations based there. It is a stand-alone county, has its own police force and port authority, runs the Old Bailey, Epping Forest and Hampstead Heath, and its Lord Mayor is outranked only by the monarch. Just as the Vatican holds the dark and furtive essence of the city and the state that surround it, so too in the City of London is the full DNA of the United Kingdom in miniature, the secrecy and splendour, pomp and circumlocution alike.

The England–Wales border is also riddled with isles literal and allegoric. Hay – *The* Hay – is an island between them, a rocky Ruritanian castaway in the middle of a swollen green sea. My journey along the border started in its middle, at the 'jigsaw tab', the peninsulas or *presque-îles*, 'nearly-islands', that hook the two countries together. We have been to the Maelor and the Clun Forest, islands of one side washed up on the shore of the other, and will soon encounter Monmouthshire, the county that hovered between the two countries for 400 years and was only finally nailed down as Welsh in 1974. And tucked away next door to Monmouthshire is the Forest of Dean, a long wooded wedge between the English bank of the Wye and the Welsh bank of the Severn, an isle full of noises and fierce intrigue.

Buried deep in the map is an invisible island, a British Mesopotamia (literally, 'land between rivers'). Instead of the Tigris and the Euphrates, we have the rivers Severn and Wye, our longest and our loveliest, which rise only a mile apart on the boggy slopes of Pumlumon, go their separate ways for hundreds of miles, and then meet again at the last at Chepstow. Between them is an island the size of Devon, edged by its frontier towns of Gloucester, Worcester, Hereford and Shrewsbury, Hay, Monmouth and Welshpool. Despite being spliced by the national boundary, and containing such a variety of landscapes, architectures and accents, the island unquestionably holds some sort of unified identity, a secret sense that the towns and villages within know each other as family, with all of the affection and respect that that suggests – but so too all the feuds and grudges.

In early medieval Wales, *Rhwng Gwy a Hafren*, 'Between Wye and Severn', was a distinct province, so the concept is not new. Though long dead as a polity, its ghost endures. Andy Johnson, the founder of Herefordshire's excellent Logaston Press, tells me that when they held a book launch in Radnorshire during the Welsh devolution referendum campaign, the people there 'didn't really want a Welsh Assembly but one for Radnorshire, Montgomeryshire, Breconshire, Shropshire and Herefordshire, for that's the unit they feel a part of'. Intermingling, he says, has always happened, 'whatever warfare was going on. I like the very porous feeling to the border. It's pleasingly complicated and slightly mysterious.'

Radnorshire and Herefordshire are the heart of this mystery and the oddest but most endearing of twins. First-born sons of Herefordshire farmers were sent as apprentices to learn on the harsher, heavier soils across the border, while an old Radnorshire saying has it that a farmer should go 'up country for a wife, down country for land'. They also both hold arcane island qualities, each being their respective nation at its most endearingly rudimentary. Radnor was by far the least populated county south of the Highlands, where buzzards mewl in dark skies and sheep outnumber people by fifty to one. From England, it is barely known at all, but even within Wales it is an enigma, often regarded as suspiciously anglicised, *hen Saesnes rhonc* ('a right old Englishwoman') as a piece of Edwardian doggerel had it. Yet it was in Radnorshire that the body of the last native Prince of Wales was buried, at Abbeycwmhir; where Owain Glyndŵr won his final battle, at Pilleth; and where originates the most important foundational text of the early Welsh chronicles and source of the global Arthurian industry, the *Red Book of Hergest*. According to Peter J. Conradi in his elegant love letter to the county *At the Bright Hem of God*, 'Radnorshire is Wales's true forgotten centre.'

The 1536 Act of Union created the county, along with the others carved out of the holdings of the Marcher lords. This attempt to impose the English shire system onto Wales was here only ever semi-successful. A wiry hillscape of isolated farms and hamlets was never going to be a Dorset or a Durham, not even a Rutland, as the shifting search for a suitable county town demonstrated. Rhayader had a brief go, but a judge was murdered on his way to court there, and the imperial circus swiftly moved east. The planted settlement at New Radnor never quite took off (and has a keening, unfulfilled atmosphere even today), so the apparatus of county administration ended up at Presteigne, so close to England that the border bisects the bottom of its main street. The old Shire Hall and court building is civic bravado in perfect miniature, stentorian and sweet in equal measure.

Next to Radnor, Herefordshire is a giant, but look the other way, towards its English siblings, and it shrinks like Alice in Wonderland on the 'Drink Me!' potion. Through the tiny door we go, and there we are in the Queen of Hearts' garden, now a rosy-red orchard. In the 1970s, the county was forced into a shotgun marriage with Worcestershire. After contemplating the name Wyvern, an English update of *Rhwng Gwy a Hafren*, the new authority was called Hereford and Worcester, and despised from the outset by Herefordians, who rightly saw it as a takeover by their larger, louder neighbour. They preferred to look west, at their little buddy over the border. Andy Johnson perfectly illustrates the difference between the three counties: 'if we did the same subject matter in a book on Radnorshire (population 26,000), on Herefordshire (194,000) and on Worcestershire (596,000), we would print the same number of copies of each of the three. I always used to joke that the sheep in Radnorshire must read, every family in Herefordshire probably reads, and that someone in a street in Worcestershire reads.'

Hereford and Worcester was soon buried in the same municipal grave as Avon and Humberside, and 'The Shire', as locals like to call it, is proudly back on the map. Ruritania or Hobbiton, Herefordshire is 'God's Eden-land unknown', as Elizabeth Barrett Browning had it in 'The Lost Bower'; 'a fine land, the west land, for hearts as tired as mine', according to its native son John Masefield, the longest serving – yet strangely forgotten – Poet Laureate of modern times. He's right. A couple of days walking and church-crawling in the beefy red shire, and its thin twin over the border, is the finest answer I know to a multitude of malaises.

Mike Oldfield's brief stay in the county, high up on the windswept border, eased his tired heart, but the Avalon didn't last. It rarely does. He fell out with the local farmers when his Afghan hounds killed their sheep, and everyone else after a drummer friend spent a day practising his timpani playing on the common. 'A delegation of the neighbours came en masse to tell me to shut up,' he wrote, and 'that was it, really.' It was coming, anyway. He was tired of the remoteness, and tired especially of being so far from an airport. Over the coming decades, he moved to the Cotswolds, the Chilterns, Switzerland, Ibiza, Somerset and Spain. For the past few years he has been living in the Bahamas. Like so many public school rock gods, his natural habitat proved to be not a Celtic hermitage, but a tropical tax haven.

10.

WAY-ON-HIGH

/// majoring.rainy.limbs

Only when the path takes a definite dip down towards the horizon do I finally give up. I'm on the Hatterall ridge south of Hay Bluff, and somewhere behind me is the highest point on the entire border, at 2,306 feet, 703 metres. If that fact wasn't deemed worth marking, it is also the summit of the Offa's Dyke path, which would surely merit at least a little cairn of stones, perhaps a post or plaque. People who do long-distance paths like that sort of photo opportunity, and I cannot believe that no one has bothered. I'm sure too that I'm not the only one to have felt surprised – and quite cheated – by the wide expanse of nothing. Later, I look at some walkers' blogs, and find that I was far from alone. 'Is the highest point on the path that tussock – or that one?' reads one photo caption.

My disquiet is only heightened by the knowledge that this is a spot I've anticipated for almost half a century. When Hereford and Worcester were shunted together in the 1970s, I was seven years old, and overjoyed at the prospect of the new county, for it suddenly made my humdrum hometown of Kidderminster infinitely more exotic. I even announced to my bemused family how our county's highest point had now almost doubled in stature from the fair-to-middling Malvern Hills to this ridge on the edge of the Black Mountains, half in Wales. That it appeared to have no especial name should perhaps have alerted me to its inconsequence. I cannot believe that it's taken me so long to get here, nor that it should leave me so underwhelmed.

Other factors compound the unexpected gloom. It's not quite summer, but the peat hags are already baked dry, the air listless. Yet again, it has been such a parched spring. Even in my fold of the Welsh hills, our well was reduced to a trickle months ago and the streams are as thin as they'd be at the end of an August drought. Things are unquestionably changing. And here on the border, near the very heavens, even the skylarks ascending sound anxious.

As well as the mountain ponies, soft-eyed and imperturbable, there is a steady trudge of walkers along the paving slabs that snake across the high moor. Many slow down for a chat, especially those (and it's the majority) that are walking alone. As always on a long-distance footpath, the conversation starts by comparing notes: how much of the path you're walking, how quickly, where you've stayed and so on. Sometimes, aided by the curious security of a fleeting encounter in limbo, the talk turns intimate remarkably fast.

Most confess how profoundly happy they are to be alone, how much they needed it, and how guilty they'd felt about needing it. With every mile ticked off, that guilt fades a little further, breathing comes a little deeper, and horizons imperceptibly widen. Everyone's lives have been transformed by the ructions of the last few years, in ways that are only slowly, and often painfully, making themselves known. Our skins have been rendered thinner, and our inner wells too have run dry. There is a collective sense that we all need to recoup and regroup, to replenish meagre stocks for almost certain shocks ahead. Times of schismatic change are both terrifying and exciting, but most of all right now they are exhausting. I can see that in their faces, and they too in mine.

Even outwith the pandemic, this section of the Offa's Dyke path undergoes its own annual mini-lockdown, an enforced fortnight's hiatus from which it is only this week emerging. Hay is a much-prized stop on the trail, but the literature festival eats up all the available accommodation and so takes out a whole 40-mile chunk of path, much to the dismay of the B&B owners a little further up and down the line. There's a metaphor in there somewhere, but I cannot nail it, as I'm hot, bothered and eager to descend.

Really eager, in fact. I'm not sure if this is middle age, or a reaction to the ravaged moors and mountain tops, but for most walks these days I'm finding myself far more drawn towards slipping through valleys and woods, along animal tracks and riverbanks, than striding to 'conquer' craggy or boggy heights. Though this climb up to the border was staggering, a sharp ascent of the iconic Cat's Back ridge, it's the valleys below, the Olchon in particular, that are calling me the loudest.

To understand the Black Mountains, there's no better guide than their brilliant son, Raymond Williams. In his final work, an experimental novel *The People of the Black Mountains*, he introduces the geography of the massif: 'See this layered sandstone in the short mountain grass. Place your right hand on it, palm downward.' After spreading your fingers – 'not widely' – you have a map: the bony fingers the five ridges, the gaps in between the rivers and their valleys. The Cat's Back (a.k.a. the Black Hill; yes, another one) is the thumb, the easternmost digit and the only one wholly in England. The border with Wales runs the length of the Hatterall ridge, the forefinger, and in the gap between them is the great glacial scoop of the Olchon valley, opening out to the sunlit south. 'You now hold this place in your hand,' says Williams, and I truly did. The old bridleway down into the valley was to be my ultimate return route, something I was looking forward to immensely. Years earlier, I'd walked the lower reaches of the track, along a deep sandstone holloway, and been bewitched by it.

If anything, it was even better than I'd hoped. Though the Olchon brook was reduced to a dribble and the waterfalls marked on the map silenced, the bridleway scampered down into the wide, green smile of the valley, over rocks and turf, past twisted hawthorns and rowans, through clouds of whinberries and flocks of fat lambs. The walls of the valley – the Black Hill on one side, Hatterall ridge on the other – rise sharp and sheer, raw with landslips and rock striations, like the claw marks of a giant cat. They fade into a wooded patchwork of fields and farms, 'more secluded, more secretive than other valleys', writes Owen Sheers in his wartime novel *Resistance*, set here. 'No one ever came into the valley by accident.' Its remoteness, the last valley in England, a dead end with a single rough lane in and around it, has also been its curse. On the map, the farms sing their splendid mishmash of names: Boskyn, Blaen, Pencelley, Rhyd-lâs, The Townhouse, The Place, Silver Tump and Aubreys, but on the ground they are either roofless mounds of stone, shrouded in nettles and elder, or holiday lets, all tell-tale tastefulness and low-maintenance gardens.

When I'd arrived the previous evening in Longtown, a few miles south at the far end of the Olchon, the sun had long gone off the east-facing ridge at its rear. The line between Wales and England was deep in shadow, an impenetrable black wall rearing up, locking us in. The following morning, washed gold by sunrise and serenaded by the dawn chorus, it was a different beast altogether, infinitely softer and sweeter. So too the border itself. A 10-mile ridge, a couple of thousand feet high, is such a clear and palpable divide that there is no need for debate. God has decided; we don't have to.

Consequently (and most unexpectedly) this feels like the least conflicted part of the frontier that I've yet encountered. At first light, I walk from Longtown down the valley to the neighbouring village of Clodock. It is not yet six o'clock and I have the world to myself: cack-crusted lanes hedged with dog-rose, and the sweetest of field tracks tiptoeing alongside a river that glows amber in the rising sun. The path disgorges into the grounds of St Clydawg's church, over a Georgian gravestone redeployed as a stile. Though I feel faintly sorry for John Price of Lower Cwm and his 'relict' Elizabeth, I soon see the reason for their eternal indignity, for the churchyard is stuffed with tombs, 850 of them in lop-sided ranks, jostling for position and a warm place to doze.

The early sun is washing the graves and their cushions of grass, but most dazzling of all it is spotlighting the brand-new Union Jack flying huge and high over the church tower. For the best part of an hour, I walk the lanes and paths around the village, and that flag dominates every view, its paintbox primary colours and angular design such a sharp contrast to the soft green curves and weathered stone around it. The Queen's diamond jubilee is next week, and I've seen more Union Jacks out in the wild this last fortnight than I have in years. It's been fascinating clocking the geography of them, tabulating the symphony of Britishness as it rises and falls across the land. Driving from the mid-Wales coast to south Birmingham the other day, I didn't see my first flag until Rhayader, from where the number grew slowly but steadily as I neared the border. Crossing into Shropshire they instantly multiplied fivefold, and then further still through the villages of Worcestershire and Warwickshire, where they adorned everything: houses, shops and pubs of course, but also churchyards and car parks, mobility scooters, bus stops and bins. And then, coming into Birmingham, they died away immediately, like a half-remembered dream.

As a ten-year-old at the time of the 1977 silver jubilee, I was fiercely proud to hoist a Union Jack up the lamppost in front of our house, and bereft when it was stolen one night. Things have changed since then. While I don't have the instant meltdown of some at the sight of the flag on a bag of supermarket carrots, its growing ubiquity in such settings, or as decoration in pubs and TV studios, makes me very scratchy. Worse, to have as the now obligatory backdrop to every inane political posture a serried rank of flags, pressed and creased in hypnotic uniformity, makes me furious, and not a little frightened. Here though, on a Clodock morning, wood pigeons cooing and an aeroplane vapour trail stitching across a pure blue sky, I cannot find the fire to feel offended. If there was one place where it could perhaps be forged with a new meaning, it might just be here, in the tricksy between-world of not-quite-Wales, not-yet-England.

Trying the church door, I'm amazed that even at this early hour it creaks wide open. Through it pours such a sweet old smell, a rush of the centuries: hints of spice and gunpowder, pollen and earth, ripe old oak and love and treachery. I sit in the seventeenth-century minstrels' gallery and breathe it all in, watching the early morning sun dance across the wall paintings and marble memorials.

Despite his atheism, Raymond Williams chose to be buried here, because – according to his son Gwydion – 'it preserved a connection with both place and people': his place, his people. Though Williams became an internationally celebrated cultural theorist, author and academic in both Oxford and Cambridge, his attachment to the Black Mountains was steadfast, and not just sentimental. In the borderland's values, in its bony embrace, he saw 'the end of exile', a condition he fought all his life to win for all. I feel it too, sat in this ancient stone sanctum of light, lodged deep in its Eden, and so have others. In a heartbreaking 2021 Radio 4 programme (*Black Hill, Bleak Summer*) about the 2001 Foot and Mouth outbreak, they tracked down the young Norwegian vet sent here to oversee the horror of mass culls and burning pyres of carcasses, and to break the worst possible news to the farmers. Now living and working in Israel, she says of that time, in tones approaching the most unexpected reverence, 'Twenty years after, there's not one day that I don't think about the people down there, in that valley. Incredible, resilient, generous, these people have inspired me for the last twenty years.'

In being buried at Clodock, Raymond Williams achieved the end of exile in a most literal way, 3 miles from his childhood home at Pandy, the village that he so vividly evoked in *Border Country*. Between the two villages runs the border, as set down in the 1536 Act of Union, but 500 years is clearly a mere heartbeat here.

'The folk who move in here are generally English,' says the landlady of the pub in Longtown, before remembering something. 'I suppose we are too, technically anyway, but everyone local is at least descended from Welsh farm stock. We're all from the land.' The pub is 'mad lively' on international days, she says, happily split down the middle and roaring with laughter. Intriguingly, she also tells me that the border was moved only fifty or sixty years ago ('when we used to be in Wales'), placing them administratively in England.

Others tell me versions of the same thing, that the border was moved relatively recently. Everyone seems to pin the date to some time just before they themselves were born, in that mythical and moveable yesterday that snares us all one way or another. To people here, a sense of Wales comes from the same place as the memory of warmth in their grandparents' kitchen, a forgotten tune or the smell of a baking cake. Unlike most concepts of Welshness in retreat – and there are so many – it appears to have no sharp edges, nor hold any anguish or compromise. It's fascinating, for the folk memory, while technically wrong, is so very strong.

The veneer of England is wafer thin in this corner of Herefordshire. Clodock, its name rolling round the tongue like an old-fashioned toffee, is really Llan y Merthyr Clydawg, named after one of the many saints spawned by Brychan, the legendary fifth-century king of Brycheiniog (Breconshire). Longtown's original name of Ewyas Lacy is an echo of the small Welsh kingdom of Ewyas, later a Marcher lordship until the Act of Union tidied it into England.

Ewyas Lacy has melted from the map, but the kingdom's name lives on in the village of Ewyas Harold, 5 miles and many contours deeper into England, the gateway to the Golden Valley. There it buffered the post-Roman Welsh kingdom of Ergyng, essentially all of western Herefordshire to the south of the Wye. When it was subsequently anglicised as Archenfield, the area maintained a distinctively Welsh character, in custom, law and language, even in its currency and measurements. Offa saw no need to build his dyke through its territory, as the Wye sufficed as a relatively peaceful and porous border, and in the Domesday Book, Archenfield was accorded a separate section from the rest of Herefordshire, wherein its special privileges and responsibilities were detailed. Its priests were tasked as go-betweens, including as translators, for the Normans' passage into Wales. The Welsh language was widely spoken in Archenfield into the nineteenth century, and lingers still in names of fields, lanes and villages like Llanwarne, Llandinabo and Llancloudy, Much and Little Dew(i) church, Moccas and Pencoyd.

To Owain Glyndŵr, this was all still Wales. From 1409, when his last stronghold of Harlech fell, the insurrection that had so briefly united and electrified his people faded fast. His last known appearance was in 1412, whereupon he vanished, almost certainly to the home of one or more of his four daughters in Herefordshire. Despite living for at least another four years, and despite the huge price on his head, his whereabouts were never revealed. Gossip in the alehouses and farms would have been ferocious, and plenty must have known where he was, but no one snitched. It is a remarkable testament to the loyalty that he still conjured in a region that was soon to become officially and forever English.

Even today, we don't know for sure where he was buried. In vanishing like morning mist, leaving only the faintest of clues, Glyndŵr became eternal, a new King Arthur biding his time, sleeping with the dragons in the dark heart of a mountain. There could be no better Welsh symbol, for his name, even the very *notion* of him, shape-shifts into the force most needed at any given moment. Such mutability, its fierce intent spliced with heady romance, is anathema to English rationalism, standing there a little awkwardly, with its compasses and rulers, charts and theses. That it is so alien to the neighbours only makes it doubly effective to Welsh eyes.

The capital of Archenfield was the suitably spectral community of Kilpeck, a few miles south-west of Hereford. The name and original settlement is Welsh, the re-foundation Saxon, the castle Norman, and its heyday the Middle Ages, after which the population began to fall. It never recovered. The evidence is there today in the widely dispersed settlement, the ridges and bumps spotted in low sunlight in the surrounding fields, but most of all in the breathtaking church of St Mary and St David. Had it been in a more prominent location, it's hard to imagine that the finest example of Herefordshire Romanesque would have survived intact.

The Herefordshire Romanesque is exuberant proof that the borderland was far from a backwater. A thrilling twelfth-century school of architecture and stonemasonry, in its riot of carvings, on columns and corbels, archways and friezes, in its shapes and symbolism, it bridges not just Wales and England, but animal and human, Christian and pagan, heaven and earth, life and death, spiritual and secular. Its geography is equally catholic, for in this seemingly remote part of the world we see in its few dozen churches clear influences from the Norse lands, Spain, France, the Holy Roman Empire, Scotland and Ireland; some seem tinged even with hints of the Aztecs or Africa. The school is one of the greatest glories of British ecclesiology, yet is little

celebrated much beyond the local – and sometimes not even there. Growing up in Worcestershire, a handful of miles from many superb examples of the school's output, I was utterly ignorant of it, just as I was of the many Welsh connections in the area. We were not told or taught any of it.

At Kilpeck, 'all the life of a busy and bawdy Herefordshire village is depicted on its church', writes Simon Jenkins in *England's Thousand Best Churches*, and it is the bawdy that has contributed most to the suppression of the Hereford school's profile. The carvings of basilisks, dragons, phoenixes and serpents were suspect enough, laced with heathen beliefs straight from the greenwood, but the unblinking fertility images put them beyond the pale. Of Kilpeck's eighty-nine carvings around the roof line of the building, six have been chiselled off entirely, and a few severely edited by mutilation. Looking at the most famous, the classic sheela-na-gig pulling open her vulva, it is remarkable that it survived intact, and begs the question: what on earth were the images deemed unacceptable?

We get clues from the first detailed catalogue of Kilpeck's treasures. In 1842, London artist George Robert Lewis noted the church's 'present disreputable appearance', and begged that it be 'taken in hand by the highly educated, for to expect parishioners of an obscure village to be aware of beauties and intelligence that are in works of imagination is more than we have any reason to do'. The metropolitan snobbery continues. He dislikes the church porch, which reminds him of a pub, as does the belfry ('a beer-house chimney') on the gable end above it, so in many of his illustrations he just gets rid of them. He replaces the belfry with a large cross that he believes would have been there; 'pulled down as an offensive object (I suppose)', he conjectures wildly. It's nothing next to his tortuous explanations for each of the carvings, forcing them into biblical shapes and stories. The sheela-na-gig 'represents a fool', he writes, 'the cut in his chest, the way to his heart, denotes it is always open'. In his flagrant mis-drawing of the corbel, the sheela's arms are at her sides, her hands pointing outwards and nowhere near her (reduced) vulva.

Predictably, Lewis has little time for the historic Welshness of the kingdom of Ergyng / Archenfield. He declares that the documents in the twelfth-century *Book of Llandaff* have 'every appearance of being forgeries' that 'pretend that a church here was given about the seventh century to the see of Llandaff'. To him, nothing of note came before the Normans.

The conflicted relationship with Wales is a feature of many fine Herefordshire churches. Dragons are everywhere, usually being symbolically held at bay, or slaughtered. At Mordiford, where the Lugg joins the Wye just east of Hereford, a twelve-foot dragon was painted on the western gable end of the church for a century or more, until 1811 when the vicar declared it 'a sign of the devil' and had it painted over. There are numerous wall paintings, wooden carvings and stained-glass windows of St George slaying the dragon, including a particularly fierce window in Hereford cathedral, where the beast is howling shards of fire as the knight's lance pierces both its jaws. Just around the corner in All Saints church, an improbably blond and boyish figurine of St George skewers the dragon halfway up a pillar (eye-catching though he is, he's not the church's most notable carving. That accolade unquestionably belongs to the naked man, lying on his back, legs tucked behind his head and with absolutely everything akimbo, high up in a dark corner. Entirely unobserved for centuries, until the construction of an upper gallery and café twenty years ago, he has gone predictably viral since).

Another piece of propaganda that fast became the official story concerns Owain Glyndŵr and his scorched earth policy, when he was said to destroy – among much else – thirty Herefordshire churches and twenty-two in Shropshire. This depended on an immoderate report by the then Bishop of Hereford, and its subsequent further exaggeration, based on wilful mistranslation of his Latin. Recent research into other documents of the era has upended the idea. Much of the damage attributed to Glyndŵr was already done. The Black Death of 1348, twelve further outbreaks of plague over the next sixty years, and a chronic period of depopulation, particularly of the young men who would have been building or repairing churches, farms and houses, had a severe impact. Marcher men were particularly valued as archers, and many had been recruited to the military throughout the Hundred Years' War. Glyndŵr would have no reason to sack places full of his compatriots, and the area's loyalty to him in his final years suggests that the respect was mutual.

Just as Welsh vindictiveness was massively overstated, so was any sophistication repeatedly downgraded. Again, state religion played its ignoble part. On that golden morning in Clodock church, I find the burial stone dated from the eighth or ninth century, carved in a style common to the era in Wales, Cornwall, the Isle of Man and southern Scotland, *yr hen ogledd*. These memorials were traditionally seen as rough and simplistic, in bad and broken Latin, especially when compared with the earlier Roman examples always held up as the gold standard.

Recent scholars have found much more to them than was assumed, using not just the words themselves, but the way in which they were carved, using the elaborate structures and word patterns of biblical Latin, as taught in the monasteries. In an email exchange with me and Graham Murphy, author of *Land of Sacred Legends*, Dr David Howlett, Fellow of Oxford's Faculty of Classics, said that the best of these were undoubtedly 'composed in the highest literary register, with the lines ending in metrical *clausulae*, showing that the ancient system of rhetorical instruction survived in Britain'. He believes that St David himself was responsible for some: 'No dark age here,' he concludes. Graham Murphy fleshes it out further: 'Because the inhabitants of the Celtic kingdoms lived in simple conditions they are assumed – like the Chinese assume of the Tibetans – to be short of intellectual achievements. It fits with a narrative on the part of those English who like to think of themselves as guardians of civilisation for the whole of Britain.'

*　*　*

Clodock church is also where journalist Quentin Letts says he would send a stranger if they wanted to find the essence of Herefordshire, and had time to visit only one place. In a 2020 interview with the *Hereford Times*, he described an autumn night singing there as part of a choir: 'the road drops dramatically into that valley and you could be entering somewhere out of Tolkien'. 'The church's angled walls almost throb with history,' he continued, 'and on top of all that the service was taken by the … most bracing of preachers, one of those rare clergymen who actually seems to believe.'

Letts, a waspish populist known for his parliamentary sketches and books that rail against 'the elite' with titles such as *50 People Who Buggered Up Britain, Stop Bloody Bossing Me About* and *Patronising Bastards*, is one of Herefordshire's most ardent cheerleaders. Once a prep school boarder on the western flank of the Malverns, he returned to the area over twenty years ago. 'The county's churches are its greatest glory,' he says, though – as hinted in his assessment of the preacher at Clodock – he is swift to sniff out any hint of clerical trendiness. He won *Celebrity Mastermind* with Hereford cathedral as his specialist subject, and is active in his own parish, above a loop of the Wye between the city and Ross. There, as churchwarden, he's campaigned successfully for the reinstatement of traditional liturgy, and curates the church web pages, where he appears in videos and pictures of cheery communion, song and worship.

As a reliable controversialist, he is a staple of TV and radio. And thanks to an expensive education in a world carved in his own image, he has the training to sound cast-iron certain, even when palpably wrong. I know that training, just as I know Letts. Not personally, but as a tinny echo of the boys I was at school with, in the shadow of the cathedral just up the road in Worcester; the quick-witted lads whose withering sarcasm first deflected the bullies onto others, and then won them a place as their courtiers. When Letts declares a love for 'green and bosomy' Herefordshire because it is 'British to its core', I get it, even though his version of 'British' and mine, for all their common roots in the same churches and pubs, rivers and hills, are aeons apart.

There are many versions, and so many crossovers. One has Hereford as a parallel English capital, a western bulwark of the mythic nation. Alternative royal courts have often found their place here, including those of kings John, Stephen, Henry III and IV. Queen Isabella, Edward II's estranged wife, made the county a base with her lover, Roger Mortimer of Wigmore castle, the most powerful Marcher lord. In Orleton church, they are forever frozen: stone heads of Edward and Isabella glare at each other across the nave, while a corbel of Edward's lover Piers Gaveston appears above him like a coy dream. From the top of the chancel arch, Mortimer surveys the scene, clearly in control, biding his murderous moment.

Nell Gwynn, royal history's most famous courtesan, came from the city, and the son of the eldest boy that she bore to Charles II was Bishop of Hereford for over forty years. Most totemically, this was a major headquarters of Harold Godwinson, King Harold II, he of the arrow in the eye on the Bayeux tapestry. Though his reign as English king was short, his resistance to growing Norman influence under predecessor Edward the Confessor, while also beating back the resurgent Welsh, has garlanded his reputation, and that of his adopted city too. Even if he is buried far away in Waltham Abbey, Hereford feels very strongly that it is the natural – almost *inevitable* – home of the last Anglo-Saxon king.

Had former policeman Anthony Hall had his way in the 1930s, Hereford would have been the capital for real. On Saturday evenings, he often addressed boisterous crowds by the town hall, claiming to be the last of the Tudor line, descendant of a bastard son born to Henry VIII and Anne Boleyn when the king was still married to Catherine of Aragon. As the decade progressed and his infamy spread, having publicly challenged 'usurper and foreigner' King George V to a duel to the death, he addressed ever-larger meetings all over the Midlands and south Wales, outlining policies that included stronger beer and full employment, and selling for a penny a time a genealogical chart that he promised would be the pound notes of his forthcoming kingdom. It's very Hereford. His Saturday-night orations sometimes attracted a thousand spectators, and brought the city centre to a standstill.

As with Chester, proximity to Wales and the convoluted history of a frontier town has sharpened its Englishness to a fine point. Some of the most celebrated national icons are abundantly Herefordian: apples and cider, oak trees and mistletoe, red earth and rosy cheeks, beef and belligerence. They're proud in these parts of their contrarian instincts, honed keener by a military sensibility that runs long and deep. The SAS have been based in Hereford since 1960, and on both my last couple of visits to the city, army squadrons were parked up in High Town, the central square, handing out leaflets and encouraging kids to play on their tanks. Over the way, the life-size statue of a Hereford bull looked on in stalwart approval, as giggling teenagers copped a selfie tickling his great bronze balls.

A week short of Christmas 2020, as the country was plunged into ill-tempered chaos by a surging new strain of the coronavirus, the Health Secretary reluctantly announced new restrictions over much of England. Most places were bumped up a tier or even two, and every-one had to scale back their festive plans – except in Herefordshire. It was the sole authority to be dropped down to the lowest rung of all, joining only Cornwall and the Isles of Wight and Scilly. In *The Times*, where he'd recently landed after decades on the *Daily Mail*, Quentin Letts said that the news had made him whoop, and that it should be remembered with the same joy as non-league Hereford United's legendary FA Cup giant-killing of Newcastle in 1972. People poured into the county from neighbouring regions – south Wales especially – just to be able to sit in a pub or a restaurant, but by New Year's Eve infections had soared, and Herefordshire was placed two tiers up, shortly before the whole country was put back in lockdown for three months.

The county's brief festive fortnight in the sun is recalled still as a bizarre badge of pride, a shibboleth of its status as the chosen one. Less well remembered is Herefordshire's other moment in the pandemic headlines, right in the early days, when the virus ripped through temporary agricultural workers, mainly from eastern Europe. The outbreaks shone an unwelcome light on the rudimentary conditions of housing and hygiene on too many farms, and showed all too clearly that lurking in the county's rural shadows, behind its blowsy hedges and folksy marketing, are a host of questions that we prefer not to ask.

If we don't ask them, we leave the field open to the likes of Mr Letts' alma mater. In 2012, someone spray-painted the word POLAND over the 'Welcome to HEREFORD' sign coming in on the Ledbury road, and the *Daily Mail* made such a meal of it. Their language was as blunt as a rusty saw: 'People living in one English city are so fed up with eastern European migrants flooding into the area they have renamed the place Poland,' it began, going on to hit all the clichés, about 'the pressure the migrants and their children are putting on schools', 'the Poles taking over the area' and 'signs in Polish'. One photo of four men in a shopping street was captioned 'Milling around: People have complained about Eastern European migrant workers walking around Leominster, Herefordshire.' They succeeded in finding a local resident – by the name of John Bull, no less – who huffed on cue that 'the town now feels more like Krakow than a traditional market town'. Four years and thousands of incendiary front pages later, Herefordshire voted 60–40 for Brexit.

This is, you'd assume from all that, or indeed from a tour of its lanes and villages, traditional Tory England, and in many ways you'd be right. Both of the county seats have returned Conservative MPs for almost all of the last century, but it's far from the glacial true blue of Hampshire or Surrey. Herefordshire, Powys and Shropshire – the natural unit that Andy Johnson of Logaston Press talked of – share a politics as blurry as the border, in a stubborn liberalism and patrician Toryism that collide as old opponents, but with a deep sense of duty and morality in common. Forged where the tectonic plates of nationality nuzzle up against each other, marinated in nonconformity and rural radicalism, and largely out of metropolitan earshot, this western borderland has produced some of our most distinct and morally impressive political voices.

This was the slumbering force awoken by the Liberal Democrats in the Shropshire by-election just before Christmas 2021, the first big stake through the heart of Boris Johnson's premiership. Six months later came another shot when Hereford MP Jesse Norman, hitherto a loyalist, put out an excoriating statement, the strongest yet by any Conservative, telling Johnson to go. It nudged open the dam gate to others and finally triggered a vote of no confidence; although the PM won, it was not by a sufficiently conclusive margin to staunch the wound.

Norman has some interesting predecessors as Hereford MP, none more so than Frank Owen, son of a city innkeeper of Welsh stock, who nicked the seat for the Liberals in the 1929 general election when he was just twenty-three. Though his time in parliament was brief, he made quite an impact. Even before Oswald Mosley had left Labour to form the first of his fascist parties, young Owen had the measure of him. 'He preaches the crudity of economic nationalism,' he levelled at Mosley in the Commons, calling him 'the Napoleon of the new empire' whose jingoism would take us 'more than half-way to a new and a more frightful world conflict'.

After losing the seat in 1931, Owen went back into journalism. Before parliament, he'd trained on the *South Wales Argus* amid the growing despair of the mining valleys during the Depression. It gave him a lifelong hunger for social justice and a fine-tuned nose for fascist apologism. Through the 1930s, he watched with growing horror the British appeasement of Hitler and Mussolini by the politicians he'd so recently sat alongside. As the new editor of the *Evening Standard*, when Chamberlain returned from Munich in 1938 with the 'peace in our time' pledge, Owen resisted the avalanche of fawning and instead published for a whole month daily extracts from Hitler's *Mein Kampf*, carefully contextualising them and showing exactly the measure of the man.

Inevitably, war came, and in its early months he and two journalist colleagues, Michael Foot and Peter Howard, decided to name and shame. In four days flat, they wrote *Guilty Men*, a searing polemic that was published weeks later, and within a couple of months had run to eighteen reprints and sold over 200,000 copies. The book opened with its cast of fifteen and a slogan 'Let the Guilty Men Retire'. Paramount among them were the three most recent Prime Ministers: Labour's Ramsay MacDonald, and the Tories' Stanley Baldwin and Neville Chamberlain. Their self-satisfied preening and 'policy of ostrichism' to the terrible evidence that had been mounting for years is catalogued mercilessly, but the authors, writing pseudonymously as 'Cato', make quite clear that the problem is systemic, not individual. The blame lies with a political morass 'of little men' full of their own self-importance, with a House of Commons where 'a huge and docile majority yessed the Government through every situation', and with the 'miasma of acquiescence', throttling both parliament and press. Though the speed with which it was written produced some glitches, it also gave *Guilty Men* an astonishing vitality that sizzles still. So too do many of its conclusions, as button bright in today's Britain as they were then.

Guilty Men is polemic as fine Herefordshire cider: fragrant but sharp, dry and profoundly refreshing, a heady, golden brew through which the world becomes so much clearer. By contrast, its grandson, Quentin Letts's *50 People Who Buggered Up Britain*, is the raw cider apple: hard, bitter and indigestible, likely to repeat biliously on you for days. Some of his targets are woefully limp: a weather presenter for being a 'northern-accented show-off', or the children's TV characters

Topsy and Tim who 'live in a town and lead lives of blameless, centre-Left orthodoxy'. Others fall at the first hurdle: Rupert Murdoch is there, but only because *The Times* letters' page is not what it once was. Tradition, entirely unto itself, is very important to Letts. Former Prime Minister James Callaghan is listed, for the crime of initiating decimalisation: 'a victory for the "make it simple" brigade', Letts thunders, an extraordinarily obtuse fight to pick.

And then, in the middle of the peppery prep school wise-cracking come the lines that make it clear why we're really here: Edward Heath makes it into his rogue's gallery for one particular action: the sacking of Enoch Powell after his 'rivers of blood' speech, which Letts has as 'the moment our country yielded to the sorry creed of multiculturalism'. Pull up the rocks of Britishness, the solid great slabs on which we're told the civilised world was built, and that is what you always find scurrying around underneath, blinking furiously in the unbidden daylight.

* * *

November 1999. We're told that this year western Europe will get the best of the annual Leonid meteor shower, and that in the wake of a passing comet this could be the finest show for thirty-three years. Hearing that, I know immediately where I want to be. I want to witness it in the velvet black of the Vale of Ewyas, the space between the fore- and middle fingers of Raymond Williams's hand map of the Black Mountains, the first valley in Wales.

So, when I mention it, do a few of my friends in Birmingham, and before long I've crammed as many as I can into my camper van, and followed by a couple of cars we scrape our way out of the suburbs and head west. There was a full solar eclipse a couple of months earlier in Cornwall, and the new millennium is only weeks away. Everything seems pregnant with portent and the possibility of change.

I'd first encountered the Vale of Ewyas six years earlier, driving the thin ribbon of tarmac that climbs out of Hay, across the sheep-straggled shoulder of the Black Mountains, before descending into the folds of the valley of the infant Afon Honddu. 'Something in the air of the place seems to have a profound spiritual effect,' said the 1969 *Shell Guide to Wales*, words I could only whisper in awestruck echo. It felt like processing down the nave of a great green cathedral, buttressed by mountains and baptised by the scampering waters. The roll-call of pilgrims, hermits and oddballs who have found solace here is long, and I yearned to join them.

Spirits are high and skies clear as we cross Herefordshire in the gathering depths of that November night. We stop at a pub by a quiet crossroads, and mutiny festers. This is the middle of nowhere, someone says. The night sky here will be terrific, here by the cosy pub fire with a cat snoozing happily on a bar stool; why don't we just stop? Perhaps some people stay, I can't really remember, but I am hell-bent on getting across the border, and those relying on me for a lift have little choice. 'There'll be other pubs,' I promise.

There aren't. Passing the *Croeso i Gymru* sign, and then pulling off the main road and heading into the hush of the long valley, we go by the Queen's Head, where I'd often camped, but now dark, locked and silent. So too the underground bar carved out of the gaunt ruins of Llanthony Priory, and the Half Moon just beyond. It hadn't occurred to me that the places I knew from happy bank holidays would not be open on a cold midweek night in November. Having never lived anywhere dependent on tourism, I had no sense of how much it skews everything. Fortunately, supplies have been brought; cans are cracked open, Rizla papers gummed into shape.

A gang of us head off for a walk, giggling expectantly. Though we are still hours away from the predicted peak of the meteor shower, a few stars break loose and skitter across the sky as an appetiser. As we whoop, my dog Patsy, who I'd scooped off the streets of Sparkhill a couple of years earlier, can barely contain her excitement at the black infinity around us. Me neither. Against a heaven of hard jet, glittering with stars and a low, waxing moon, the mountain shapes loom, inked in and indelible. Our breath pools in crisp air that smells of turf and damp wool. I gulp it down greedily, holding it in for as long as I can.

Back in the van, the party's in full swing. Someone's cracked open a bottle of brandy, the air is thick with smoke, the CD player pumping, and I'm trying not to worry about the possibility of a flat battery. I've already made it clear that I shan't be driving back before daylight, so take a slug and a toke and dive right in. Truth is, I bellyflop. What seemed like such a great idea in the pub last night is already feeling like a chore too far. No one seems much interested in star-gazing, or even leaving the stale fug of the van. It's too cold, I'm told, so I brew up a pot of tea for everyone and head back outside. By the time I get back, the hob has been re-lit for warmth, and the reek of gas is scrapping with the dope and the sour stench of unwashed crusties.

The dog and I head off once again into the night, and find a grassy hillock to settle on. Ice is beginning to rime the fronds of dying bracken, and when I shine my torch into the black, the beam of light catches the steamy breath of sheep and makes their eyes gleam alien green. I snap it off, and revel in the nothingness. A meteor scorches across the sky, then another, and I'm watching rapt, and wanting more. The pace is definitely picking up now.

The millennium, this vertiginous block of time, is the one in the frame right now, and as Patsy and I sit there, her nuzzled into my side, I wonder what this valley was like 1,000 years ago. Far more wooded, but otherwise I think physically little different. The abbey, whose ruins rule its landscape with such poise, was imminent, built after the Marcher lord of Hereford rode in and was overwhelmed by the peace and sanctity of the place. In 1188, Gerald of Wales described it as a 'happy, delightful spot, most suited to the life of contemplation', though he also details splits, spats and brutal border warfare that had erupted in the abbey's first eighty years, rather undermining the assertion. I think too of the city we left this afternoon, the clanking great machine of light and life, boisterous noise and insatiable youth. In the Domesday Book, Birmingham comprised nine households, and was valued at £1.

Far below, someone has put the lights on in the van, and I can see the windows dripping with condensation. The side door opens, and a burst of techno tumbles out into the icy air, followed by a couple of swaying silhouettes. I hear my name being called, and stand up to shout back, at just the moment that a meteor blazes across the black sky, so vivid that it leaves a watermark on my retina that's still there several seconds later. That would be the one to wish on, and though I don't consciously do so, something clearly gets through. When we head back tomorrow, it will be for the last winter of the millennium, and though I don't yet consciously know it, it will also be my last winter in England.

11.

TRESPASS

/// brilliant.pleasing.chatting

The teacher looks haunted. You would be. She's sending a pack of inner-city teenagers rampaging off into the forest, and this is no fairy tale. They've only gone a few yards, and already a couple of them are shrieking. In fairness, if you're so disposed, the Biblins bridge is easily enough to bring on the terrors. A rope suspension footbridge slung between two countries over the wide brown Wye, it doesn't so much wobble as vibrate threateningly, a deep bass throb that rises up through the feet to engulf your whole body.

As they land on the Welsh bank, where I'm waiting to cross, I see in the faces of a few of them a look that I know instantly. Eyes are alight with the scope and scale of it all, at the palette of new colours, shapes, sounds and smells, ones that they may never have encountered before. In a few days camped by the river, seeds have been planted, and as I wish them a good morning, a truly great morning, I pray that those seeds might get the chance to flower. At that age, it can take just one single day of fierce wonder to swivel your life in a new direction, to point you to where you most need to be, but it requires encouragement, investment and equality of opportunity, and they are all in perilously short supply right now. The teacher gathers them all to issue their final instructions, and as I take my leave and head over the bridge I grin at the yelps and squeals as they plunge into the woods, into another country.

Other groups are gathering on the northern bank for their day's activities. The Biblins Youth Campsite is huge, snaking along the Wye's edge for over half a mile as the river swings round in a large, lazy loop. Describing itself as 'a back-to-basics camping experience', so no electricity or wifi, and only the most sporadic phone signal, it is run by the Woodcraft Folk, the youth organisation set up in 1925 as a pacifist (and pagan) alternative to the boy scouts. On this quiet midsummer morning there are tantalising breakfast smells wafting on the breeze, people cycling and walking under the wooded cliffs, and an air of effortless sweet contentment.

Three counties meet here: Herefordshire on the northern bank, Gloucestershire and Monmouthshire on the southern. The latter's deepest incursion into England, a few hundred yards from the foot-bridge, is the easternmost point of Wales. I assumed that the title would belong to the furthest tip of the Maelor, poking deep into the plains of Cheshire and Shropshire, but thanks to the broad-bottomed nature of the map of Wales, this is it. It's further east than Hereford or Shrewsbury, Preston, Carlisle and even Edinburgh. A pink sandstone boulder marks the spot, at a junction of forest paths.

Wales's first few acres are strangely symbolic. Lady Park Wood is its name, the most secretive part of this massive cross-border forest, untouched ancient woodland that was set aside as an ecological reserve in 1944, to study what happens when the trees and the wildlife are left to their own devices. After forty years, it was agreed to tweak the rules, as wild deer were causing havoc; fences were erected to keep them out, and us too. Paradise lost; abandoned nature; ring-fenced playground; bastion against modernity; place of No Admittance – take your pick which Welsh metaphor fits.

The path that hugs the river's edge is the track bed of the Ross to Monmouth railway, closed in 1959. It must have been a spectacular journey, funnelling under limestone cliffs and vertical forests, through tunnels and over bridges as it wove a dance with the Wye. When the river was in flood, the train would go at snail's pace, inching slowly through the water, with the fireman on the bottom step of the foot-plate, checking the depth. Perhaps as well that the railway is gone, for the floods are getting worse. Everywhere I go I see mementoes of the terrible inundations of February 2020, the gravest yet. More than two years on, dehumidifiers still whirr in riverside churches, and tidemarks on their ancient stone pillars show that the phenomenon is becoming ever more regular.

The old railway line is the route that I walked early this morning from Symonds Yat, and it was magical. I saw no one else until the Biblins campers, but was accompanied by blackbirds and chiffchaffs, robins, thrushes and warblers. Herons were poised greedily on rocks in the river, and above us all, jackdaws wheeled on the breeze, calling into the morning from high up in their clifftop kingdoms. At Symonds Yat, the houses themselves look like birds' nests, a haphazard scatter of hovels and summerhouses that have grown into full-time dwellings, clambering inelegantly up the rocky slopes and pointing where they please for an optimum view, or to snatch a sliver more sunlight. The surrounding miles are a sturdy rural landscape of farms, fields and castles; the Wye gorge slices through, spreading a kind of anarchy in its sinuous curves and sweeping cliffs. Symonds Yat is the greatest surprise: an unexpected hill-station from the Raj, a confection of nature, a great fancy.

Since the eighteenth century it has been one of the big stops on the Wye Tour, the first flourish of modern tourism, in all its brass neck and buccaneering. Early visitors came down from Ross by boat, past the cliffs and crags, limekilns and furnaces, and now they squeeze ever-larger vehicles down clogged lanes, but really, nothing much has fundamentally changed. Everything has its price. In the case of The Chalet, an Edwardian prefab that grew into a fishing lodge and then a holiday home, that price now starts at over £1,000 a night. The distinctive red-and-white villa, peering through the trees and gazing imperiously down the river, is instantly recognisable as the highly desirable home of the main characters in Netflix's global hit *Sex Education*. To fans of the show – or rather, to their parents – it is a small price to pay for a precious slice of reflected glory. I doubt that there's much of a crossover between the teenagers that get to stay at The Chalet, and those camping a mile away at the Biblins.

Sex Education has a coy rootlessness at its heart, a mischievous sense of both place and time that keeps us guessing. Though filmed almost entirely in Monmouthshire and Gloucestershire, the show is not explicitly Welsh, English or even British, but saturated in a mid-Atlantic half-light, and burnished with retro touches that make the 'when' as tricky to pin down as the 'where'. It perfectly fits Symonds Yat which, like many places given over to tourism, has a nomadic quality – as if it doesn't quite belong anywhere. That it sits on the lip of England, divided between two of its counties, and just an eagle's wing away from Wales, only compounds the unreality. And as with many tourist honeypots, locals live with it in an odd and sometimes conflicted relationship.

I get chatting to a woman working at one of the riverside hotels. She's been there years, loves it, but is always happy to get away at the end of a shift. Shortly before her husband died seven years ago, they climbed up to the viewpoint on Symonds Yat rock, a pinnacle on the narrow neck of a huge loop of the Wye, and the single biggest reason that the place has been pulling in crowds for centuries. 'We were so blown away by it,' she says in a fine Forest of Dean accent, unmistakably west but harder, flatter. '"Why haven't we been here before?" we said to each other.' Her late husband was a fisherman from Monmouth, 'lived for the river', so between them they spanned the border, not that they ever considered it as such. Monmouth is only homeopathically Welsh, and Dean is an entire world of its own, one that she loves with a passion. 'I'm Forest through and through,' she says, and grins.

Foresters talk of the place as a life force all of its own, a character in their lives as real and influential as any favourite uncle or long-lost mam. Of all the many islands along the England–Wales border, the Forest of Dean is the most fiercely autarkic, with every sense that you have drifted free of both countries, and all the better for doing so. Such insularity comes first from the Forest's unusual geography, as a triangle of land, wooded, hilly and rich with minerals, bounded by the Wye on one long side and the Severn on another. Historically, it's also a place apart. Like all Royal Forests, it was an ancient estate of the

Crown, and on the arrival of the Normans a much-favoured hunting ground. Governed by Forest Law, so based 'not on the Common Law of the realm, but on the arbitrary legislation of the King', as a twelfth-century bishop defined it, Dean was also extra-parochial, outside of the church system. Forest Law was administered locally by the Constable of St Briavels, based at his castle together with his splendidly named officers: Gavellers, Verderers, Regarders and Foresters of Fee.

Perhaps the most significant difference, one that still underpins the Forest's sense of self today, is the tradition of the Dean freeminer. Men over twenty-one – and since a legal challenge in 2010, women too – who were born in the forest, and who have been a miner for a year and a day, are eligible for the status. That gives them the right to dig for coal, iron ore and stone within a small patch, known as a gale, as agreed with the forest's Gaveller. This unique concession was granted to Dean miners in the late thirteenth century as thanks from Edward I for their help in digging beneath and so critically undermining the castle at Berwick-on-Tweed, far away but on an equally fractious and strangely familiar border.

The fruity titles and language, even the pantomime timespan of a year and a day, make it all sound archaic, but hell will freeze over (or more likely, heaven burn to a crisp) before the Forest of Dean gives up its freemining. Extracting coal may be frowned upon, but the dwindling band of miners have turned instead to stone and the variety of coloured ochres to be found underground, popular with artists and useful in cosmetics. Since the closure of the local maternity unit in the 1980s, the biggest threat to the future of mining is the stipulation of being born in the Forest. A new community hospital is under construction in Cinderford, the largest town; the district council voted unanimously for some kind of birthing facility there ('to give local women the chance to give birth to their own little Foresters,' said a councillor), but the health board has refused, 'on the basis that a clinically safe and sustainable service could not be provided'. They do however promise to 'promote home births for women', and that will have to do for putative freeminers.

That twenty-first-century maternity services might be tailored to a thirteenth-century rule about people having the right to burrow under oak trees with a pick and shovel is about as Forest of Dean as it gets, and only makes me love it more. No attempt to smooth its creases or comb down its hair is ever going to convince. Visitors are welcome, overwhelmingly welcome in fact, but entirely on Forest terms. Barrelling down its tracks and roads, the miles of wood either side skipping by puckishly, you cannot dodge the sense of things seductively dark sucking you deeper into the green. Its glades are lovely, but studded with rust and remnants of pits, pools and railways, cars and fridges – and long-lost innocence. Villages are trim, though half-eaten flowers and scuffed-up roadsides reveal Britain's largest wild boar population, rampaging through in the small hours. Most of the pubs are gloriously un-gastro and full of dogs, kids and raucous bands. The Forest is stuffed with the unexpected and contradictory, simultaneously hard as coal and soft as a bed of woodland moss. It has many of the qualities of the mining valleys further west, over the border, and indeed is just as stippled with scrap and chapels, and just as proud of its rugby, silver bands and even *eisteddfodau* as anywhere in Wales. Make no mistake, though: this is England. This is Gloucestershire, but banish all thoughts of Cheltenham or the Cotswolds.

Coming down into Coleford, the Forest's handsome old charmer of a second town, eyes still twinkling but his grin full of gaps, I'm brought to a skidding halt by a massive gable-end mural of three faces in forensic close-up. More west Belfast than west Gloucestershire, it is a memorial to three favourite local writers, each of whose work is soaked in the spells of the Forest. There's poet and memoirist Joyce Latham, an illegitimate child of the 1930s brought up in an extended Forest family, who absorbed many of its vernacular rhythms working behind the bar of various local pubs, including the now closed Mason's Arms on which the mural is painted. Alongside her is F. W. (Will) Harvey, a First World War comrade and poetic compatriot of Gloucestershire's great Ivor Gurney.

Although painted the same size as his Forest stablemates, Dennis Potter looms over them both. In his work as one of the first

playwrights to really understand the power of television, he made the genre his own, from the 1960s to his swift death from pancreatic cancer, aged only fifty-nine, in 1994. Born and raised in Berry Hill, between Coleford and Symonds Yat, Potter never fully left the Forest of Dean, even when he was living and working far, far away. In his first book, *The Glittering Coffin* (1960), he called it 'the heart-shaped place between two rivers', and it was in everything he wrote, sometimes euphoric, sometimes hellish, but its blood always flowing warm and red with borderland *hiraeth*. Potter was all borders: England–Wales of course, the Forest and not-Forest another, and boundaries too of class, politics, genre, time and taste. Straddling so many identities cut him the freedom that he needed to remain an inveterate outsider.

For all that it informed so much of his work, he kept even the Forest at arm's length, settling in Ross-on-Wye, only 8 miles from his childhood home, but firmly over the county line in Herefordshire. It was, said one of his old neighbours, 'about as near as you could get without being in the Forest'. In his famous final interview with Melvyn Bragg, a month after his cancer diagnosis and with only a couple more months to live, he talked of the two co-existing Forests: 'the real one, with the same signs and stresses as anywhere', and the other one, 'a strange and beautiful place, with a people who were as warm as anywhere else, but they seemed warmer to me'. As a child, it had been his Holy Land: 'I knew Cannop Ponds by the pit where Dad worked, I knew that was where Jesus walked on the water; I knew where the Valley of the Shadow of Death was, that lane where the overhanging trees were.'

In rhapsodising a place and time to which he could never return, Potter echoes so many other border voices, most clearly A. E. Housman. In naming his most enduring Forest play *Blue Remembered Hills*, he made the connection explicit. The 1979 television production was Potter's take on his own wartime childhood, and featured a cast of seven children playing in the woods, waiting for teatime and home. Shot on location, it was soaked in distant summer sunshine and youth's infinite horizons. Over the final scenes, Potter himself voices the Housman poem that gave him his title.

This though is no sentimental 'land of lost content', for the rear view is brilliant, but unflinchingly brutal. The children whoop and run, but they also wheedle and bully each other, gang up on the weakest and shift allegiances on the breeze. It is a story of absences, of their fathers especially, away in the war, and of tiny cruelties amplified into terrible human truths. The final violence swells with shocking speed into a fatality, and whatever Eden we might have hoped for is annihilated. As the children freak out at the tragic outcome and their complicity in it, and the distant adults come closer, and with them an awful reckoning, in float those honeyed words of Housman, suddenly repurposed with a sting that had been sapped from them by decades of soft-soaping.

Though initially a shock, it takes only a couple of minutes to become assimilated to Potter's schtick of having adult actors play the children. A technique he'd deployed in earlier plays, it is devastatingly effective in *Blue Remembered Hills*. 'I used adult actors to play children in order to make them like a magnifying glass,' he explained. The lenses of artifice intensify our gaze: the supersized children are trying so hard to be 'grown-up' as they mimic the world around them and parrot its conventions without any real comprehension. In them, all human caprice exists already, but unfiltered by the orthodoxies and etiquette that we learn with age. As such, it's not just a magnifying glass, but a mirror too, for the approach reflects back on us, the viewers, caught in a light so bright that we dare not blink.

'I was trying to show childhood not at one remove but straight on,' he said to Melvyn Bragg, so as to focus on the 'constant present-tense preoccupations' of children. 'The nowness of everything' had long been one of his shibboleths, partly to check his own potential for nostalgia. Unsurprisingly, the intensity of now was much at the forefront of that final interview: 'The only thing you know for sure is the present tense, and that nowness becomes so vivid that, in a perverse sort of way, I'm almost serene.' He vividly illustrated the point with words that became the most celebrated of the interview, talking about the plum blossom that was flowering at the time on the tree beneath his study window in Ross: 'instead of saying "Oh that's nice blossom" ... I see it is the whitest, frothiest, blossomest blossom that there ever could be, and I can see it.' He fills those last four words with such wonder and urgent truth that they momentarily stop your breath.

Other truths, so very many other truths, tumble out in that electric fifty minutes, one of the most lucid and brilliant swansongs ever committed to film. Imminent death had heightened all his nows, including a sense of national identity: 'I feel the pull of tradition and I love my land. I love England. When I'm abroad, I genuinely feel homesick, for an ideal almost. I've always loved my country, but not of flags and drums and trumpets and billowing Union Jacks and busbied soldiers and the monarchy and the pomp and circumstance and all of that, but the real … something about our people.' That selfhood, of 'a brave and a steadfast people' he says, has been hijacked by dark forces, 'subsumed in this false imperial identity'. In the names themselves, Potter finds a gulf that grows only wider: 'I find the word "British" harder and harder to use as time passes … *English*. We English.'

*   *   *

The man-boys are creating, and everyone is looking. At first glance, they could easily be Dennis Potter's adults make-believing as children, but it's quickly obvious that they are just drunken public school boys, kids as grown-ups. Like a herd of jumpy bullocks, they swagger around the pub, faces flushed and smooth, hair lustrous and lips thick, voices loud and used to being heard. Egged on by his chorus, their leader edges out of the pack to throw some wisecrack at a young woman in the corner. She looks up, scowls and unleashes a verbal flamethrower at them, words to make you wince, hollering them out of her sight, and before long, out of the pub too. They rampage up and down the street outside, riding each other like ponies as they catcall and bellow. The landlord draws the curtains. 'Welcome to Monmouth,' grins Jon.

I've been trespassing all afternoon with Jon Moses, one of the leading lights of the Right to Roam campaign. He gained considerable traction with a social media photo essay in 2021 when he trekked along the River Monnow, plotting its miserable lack of public access. Monmouth has long struck me as somewhere that desperately needs its waterfront back, though I'd never much thought beyond the most egregious culprit, the A40 dual carriageway, which sliced the town off from the River Wye and its meadows in the mid-1960s. It's a thug of a road all the way through the Wye valley, ripping up villages and roaring through day and night, but nothing comes close to the damage it has wreaked on Monmouth. According to Jon, though, 'the Wye is lost', at least for now, but there is a far more winnable battle for the Monnow. The town grew up tucked into the crook of the two rivers' confluence, a literal bridging point and a strategic one too, the convergence of the axes of power between south (and west) Wales and the south of England, and all the way up the line of the border. Control Monmouth, and you have vast swathes of good land at your disposal.

We meet at the thirteenth-century Monnow Gate, the only remaining fortified bridge gatehouse in Britain, a memento of troubled border times, but more so a long local history of extracting tolls. Beneath us on this sultry summer afternoon, kids are splashing in the river, below a sewage outfall, Jon tells me with a grimace. I ask him to show me where the two rivers meet, half a mile away, across meadows that were once well used for promenades and picnics, balls, assemblies, fairs and the town's first racecourse, 'skirted by gentle eminences feathered with underwood or clothed with hanging groves of oak and elm', wrote William Coxe in 1801; today thundered over by a trunk road.

After that, Jon takes me on the walk that he catalogued in his online essay, up the final few miles of the Monnow. It was the River Monnow that I walked alongside that golden morning to Clodock church, and I've met it repeatedly since, every time a real pleasure. Rising up in the knuckle of Hay Bluff, its very first encounter is with the old priory of Craswall, the loftiest in England, where it is clearly abundantly blessed. For more than half of its 42-mile length, the river forms the national divide, watering some of the most haunting border landscapes of all, washing isolated churches and farms, and gaunt frontier castles ruled by vigilant crows. Here are the lugubriously dark whispers between England and Wales.

It is hard though to count the river's blessings in the town that takes its name: Monnowmouth, Monmouth (Monnow from the Welsh name Mynwy). To reach it, Jon steers me down an alley, round the back of the bins of a frozen food supermarket and into a dispiriting yard of razor wire and graffiti. From there, a filthy footbridge leads over the river, and signs make it abundantly clear that this cheerless experience is a privilege, not a right. The bridge and the path belong to the army, and they can – and do – close them 'at any time without prior notice'. Today, we're allowed to cross, but there are more signs, more razor wire and now – thanks to the landowner this time, not the Army – a tunnel of those metal fencing panels, the sort you see at festivals or demonstrations, to ensure that we don't leave the permitted path and partake instead of the riverside meadows. Once the panels end, Jon hops over the barbed-wire fence, steadying himself on the sign that reads

PRIVATE
PROPERTY
NO FOOTPATH
THROUGH
THIS LAND

I follow, considerably less gracefully. We're in.

The river curves generously around the edge of the fields, so jealously guarded but so little looked after. A few derelict huts – some military, some agricultural – moulder in the sunshine, and all along the riverbank are sturdy swathes of Himalayan balsam, an invasive weed that throttles all other plant life, and in winter, when it dies back, leaves riverbanks exposed to erosion. It's a sad husk of a place, yet its ghosts are glorious. This was the town's Vauxhall Gardens, its celebrated pleasure grounds and a much-loved stop on the Wye Tour. There were promenades, balls, music, a cascade, botanical wonders, scented groves and furtive corners. Even John Wesley came to visit. Though he had 'hardly seen such a place before', he found the gardens 'full as beautiful in their kind as even the hanging woods at Brecon'. Another eighteenth-century visitor found it all a 'Delightful prospect', especially the 'Ladies Dancing', another playing the 'Welch harp' and the 'fine View of the Town of Monmouth'. The view is all that we still have today, but it's no slouch. Spread along the cliff tops on the far bank of the river is a very elegant townscape, of grand gardens behind stout Georgian townhouses, gables, chimneys and shapely mature trees, the bulk of the castle and the heavenward spire of the priory church. Behind all that, the newer parts of town lie dotted over low hills.

There's no question: these meadows are Monmouth's centre stage, the breathing space that could bind the place back together again if they were given the chance. The town has turned away from the waters that made it, as they came trickling down from the stalwart mountains of the west, chattering excitedly in an old tongue. Locking that out of sight and out of mind, it has long preferred instead to look east, to parade grounds, public schools and royal palaces. If the quirks of Hay, Bishop's Castle, Knighton or Clun are Britain in miniature, the best of frontier cross-pollination, then Monmouth is the United Kingdom distilled, a very different beast. Its heyday was empire, and so too its pomp and ambition.

Monmouth likes to position itself as a county town on a par with the mightiest cathedral city, a Barchester of the border. Nelson came here briefly, and the connection has been exploited fulsomely ever since; much too is made of it as the hometown of Charles Stewart Rolls, the motoring and aviation pioneer, co-founder of Rolls-Royce. There he stands bestatued in the town centre, overlooked by the premier Monmothian of all, for this is, never forget (and you can't), the birthplace of an English king, Henry V. 'Has any town a market place more proudly named than Agincourt Square?' puffs the local volume of Arthur Mee's series *The King's England*, and the chorus cries *No!* as one. Shakespeare made him immortal, a wayward Prince Hal turned wisest of warlords as king. 'We few, we happy few, we band of brothers', outnumbered on the eve of battle, but with some very special weapons up his sleeve: a crack squad of Welsh archers and a God who was indisputably, devoutly English.

Neither quite one side nor the other, the same is true of the county to which it gave its name. Forged from assorted Marcher lordships, Monmouthshire was created by the first Act of Union in 1536, but in the second (1542) was made subject to the Oxford judicial circuit, not the Welsh Courts of Great Session. Thus was born the county's semi-detached status, the centuries of 'Wales and Monmouthshire', only finally done away with in 1974. Until then, and marked as such on Ordnance Survey maps, Newport, Pontypool, Ebbw Vale and Tredegar, even the Cardiff suburbs of Rumney and St Mellons, were all officially English.

Rivers play the long game, and perhaps the Monnow can wait. Jon, though, is a little more impatient. A real water baby, he steers us off to our next encounter with the forbidden river, at the weir to the north of town. He talks with fierce tenderness about the place, and how important it had been to him as a teenager; somewhere to come and find refuge, to tease out the world's strange ways in the green bosom of woods and water. Access then was straightforward, but a new salmon ladder was built nearly fifteen years ago, and suddenly there were gates, fences, padlocks, security cameras and very many signs. The mental health aspects of access are those that drive him most forcefully, and I share that entirely. The ugly paraphernalia of privatised landscapes and their occasional, grudging access burrow deep into our heads, keeps us fretful and disconnected, or as Jon put it in his viral essay, in an echo of John Clare: 'Fences are a spell propping up an illusion: that the world around us is a prison; that the beauty which surrounds us is not a collective inheritance; that we have no right to live free and rich with the natural world.'

He takes a dip at the weir, and then another one a few miles upstream, on a magical stretch of the river that we reach by wandering through a huge private estate. The sun is sliding into the evening, the shadows are lengthening, and when a kingfisher flashes by, unencumbered and electric blue, I have to plunge in too. We've seen no one on this last leg, no sign of life at all, but at the weir and around the old Vauxhall Gardens there had been a few other people quietly taking and enjoying their freedom. Things are changing, says Jon, and he tells me about the forthcoming open day trespass at the weir, and another one, with a focus on botany, that he's organising on the Badminton estate. At both, there will be speakers and activities, things designed to inspire, inform and help reconnect people to their land: 'Belonging is the first stage in the journey to protecting,' he says.

* * *

Even though I chose the three river basins of the border as the principal building blocks of this book, I still vastly underestimated them. Perhaps I saw them only as useful counterfoils to the political frontier, a cute way of both highlighting and challenging man-made division by juxtaposition with nature's. While that has been so, and has been useful, I hadn't really expected the river catchments also to bring something bespoke to the discussion, entirely on their own terms, and each so different.

The prosaic girth of the Severn basin gave by contrast a curious definition to the border, making it a focus and sudden flash of clarity, yet also bringing a kind of middle-of-the-road pragmatism to matters on both sides of the line. The short, sharp Dee sped everything up, magnified it, plucking an exorbitant *Cymreictod* out of the mountains and spilling it over the plumpest of English plains.

The Wye though, the Wye ... in this southern third of the border, the river and her bonny daughters steal every scene, and exert an extraordinary pull on their settlements, landscapes and people. 'To live with a river is to live with an alterity which expands consciousness as wide as its course, and as deep as its source,' wrote Jon Moses in his essay on the Monnow, and it's a truth I continually glimpse throughout the Wye catchment. The river is the primary identity of the region, its passion and privilege, and in its capricious curves and loops perhaps the single biggest reason that the political border here has always been so elastic and so porous. That the river's English name is a homophone for the biggest existential question of them all is a strangely canny fit.

In the spring, on the Wye's upper reaches, I'd been told that things were fair-to-middling with the river, but as I headed downstream and the season stretched into summer, a lack of rainfall saw the waters steadily drop and the colour leach from the fields, and it became glaringly obvious that this was far from true. I saw it walking from Symonds Yat: the Wye a thickening green soup, lapping at the banks with a dull slurp, algae blooms and a sulphurous yellow froth pooling by the rocks. The shortage of rain was only part of the problem. A 2022 House of Commons Environmental Audit select committee spelled it out plain: 'a chemical cocktail of sewage, agricultural waste, plastic and chemicals is polluting rivers', and it's impossible to know quite how badly, because 'outdated, underfunded, and inadequate monitoring regimes are getting in the way of getting a complete overview'.

All of those problems are found on the Wye, and in recent years they have worsened fast. Monitoring and enforcement budgets have been slashed over the last decade, and polluters – farmers, industry, individuals and, shamefully, the water companies themselves – know they can almost certainly get away with transgressions. In the *Guardian*, Hay-on-Wye's own Oliver Bullough wrote about the issue, and talked to a veteran Environment Agency inspector. 'The problem is that we don't have the resources or the legislative muscle to do what everyone knows we need to do,' he said. 'But you only have to look at some of the farms in Herefordshire – they are big businesses, they are not scared of loose legislation or penalty notices. They can ignore all that.'

Some on the right try to lay the blame on devolution itself, but obfuscation, buck-passing and threadbare infrastructure are ubiquitous and borderless. In his piece, Oliver Bullough wrote of how much the world of environmental enforcement reminded him of one with which he is far more familiar, namely kleptocracy and financial crime: 'On paper, the laws are perfectly acceptable and regularly updated. The problem is that they are rarely, if ever, enforced. The result is government by press release; Potemkin enforcement; regulatory theatre; decriminalisation by under-resourcing.'

Thankfully, the people are on it. Look at any village noticeboard and you will see fliers for public meetings, river campaign groups and citizens' monitoring schemes. The sense of responsibility that locals have for the Wye and its tributaries is phenomenal, far more in my experience than on any other river. It's a love and a commitment that crosses boundaries, not just of the many different interest groups, but often of wealth and class too. Nationality as well, of course; that the river straddles two countries is key. A synthesis of their best qualities, it is also beyond them both. The Wye is a republic of its own.

It is a republic with a legion of ambassadors. Angela Jones, dubbed 'the Wild Woman of the Wye', has spent hours on and in the river every day for the last thirty-five years, sleeping at its side at least a couple of times every week. 'This beautiful river is who I am, and what I do,' she says, a proximity that has let her monitor its declining health intimately: 'I started noticing gradual change roughly ten years ago – but about five years ago, things started getting significantly worse.' To highlight the problem, in the summer of 2021 she swam down the river towing a coffin, with DEATH OF THE WYE painted on its sides and accompanied by two Grim Reapers on paddleboards. The following summer, the churches followed suit, leading a four-foot-high wooden sculpture of Our Lady of the Waters downstream on a double canoe catamaran, church bells ringing all the way. Trumpets sounded as the convoy went under Bredwardine bridge, the monks of Belmont Abbey sang Georgian chants at Moccas, and the statue was processed into choral evensong at Hereford cathedral, an experience its sculptor described as 'sublime – totally medieval'.

The entire catchment is the church of Mark Jickells, proprietor of the inspirational Wye Explorer project. Reciting even the names of the rivers in his soft Hereford brogue, he makes them an incantation that sings of green spirits and cross-border communion: Lugg, Arrow, Dore and Frome; Monnow, Escley and Trothy; Loddon, Rudhall, Humber and Honddu; Olchon and Llynfi, Camddwr and Cammarch; Elan, Edw, Irfon and Ithon.

Mark is an unlikely evangelist: from an SAS family in Hereford, a former soldier himself who quit the army and with his twin brother Paul got stuck deep into partying, both as punter and organiser, spiralling deeper into drink, drugs and trouble. In 2010, their mum asked them where they wanted to go for a birthday trip, and – to Mark's surprise – Paul immediately said 'the source of the Lugg', the tributary that rises in Radnorshire and flows through northern Herefordshire, past their grandparents' old farm. 'We'd been banned from everywhere in town,' he says, 'stripped of community, so we turned to nature.' Going to the source of the Lugg inspired them to journey along the whole river, a six-day pilgrimage where they walked, swam and camped freely along its banks, all the way to its confluence with the Wye just downstream of the city. 'We were there two minutes,' Mark tells me, 'when two kingfishers come speeding down the Wye, side by side; one flies up the Lugg, and the other carries on down the Wye.' In that moment, the idea of walking the rivers, all the rivers, was born, and so too the Wye Explorer project, a kingfisher its emblem.

Since then, Mark has walked the major tributaries, 700 miles of them so far. It has completely altered his take on the area. 'You can put me anywhere and I can see all the arteries, I'll know exactly where I am in the Wye basin. From the rivers, this dialogue has emerged. They've given me such a strong sense of belonging that I'm almost not confused any more.' That is no small statement, because in 2016 his twin and soul-mate Paul suddenly died. The walks that they shared in his final few years were 'such a blessing, because those were the moments where the barriers fell away'. When Mark talks of entering 'a deep and meaningful dialogue' with the waters, it is no glib apho-rism, words to add to a sunset on Instagram, but something that I can see and hear has been very hard won.

He wants to show me a spring a few miles west of the city, and as we walk the Wye's bank we share our stories of water. It's my element too, one that has brought me back from many a brink, whether by hanging out with it, listening to its music, imbibing it or immersing myself in its infinite depths. We talk too of borders, and how man-made ones compare with those that rise up from the rock below, to find their own path of least resistance. Mark's main concern is the health of his beloved Wye, and he fears that the 'human ego' of differ-ent administrations and authorities is making that worse. All the same, he has always been drawn to the border, both for the sense of conflict and uncertainty that it holds, but also for its joys: 'Borders are the point at which hands are shaken, hugs are made. It's the crossing point, the bridge.'

We reach the spring. Mark has not oversold the place at all; it is magnificent. Deep in a wooded hollow, lit by sunlight flickering through ash and rowan, is a soft pink scar of sandstone. Out of the rockface bubbles a cascade of piping clear water, pooling into a small stream that flashes and sparkles like diamonds. On a warm, muggy day, the cold hit is bewitching, the taste that of the stars. I drink pints of it, and feel demonstrably brighter with every sip. Mark is thrilled by my enthusiasm, all utterly genuine, and we sit together by the water's edge, laughing, reborn.

A woman and child come gambolling down the path to join us. She looks as if she has been here a thousand times before, but we soon get talking, and it turns out that this is her first visit too. Like me, she is bowled over by the place, and so too her little boy. A tiny sprite, he jumps straight into the water, splashing, giggling and digging red mud pies. It's suddenly an afternoon of old confidences and fleeting horizons; sat like the ancients on rocks clustered around the babbling spring, we talk of water and hedge magic, plague and politics, death and rebirth, while the little lad scampers around clad only in sunshine.

He and his mam are heading back to their Radnorshire farm, in the family for generations. Her parents began to diversify over thirty years ago with a simple campsite, which has since grown into camping, the inevitable glamping, and activities from yoga to lake swimming, all alongside the working farm. She's passionate about doing tourism ethically, always conscious of the holistic importance of a good holiday in beautiful surroundings, something that she's seen become significantly more pressing during the last few difficult years. 'People have arrived absolutely ragged,' she says, 'and we try to give them the space and time to stitch themselves back together.' She's sceptical about the extra caution that has been the hallmark throughout of the Welsh government's Covid strategy, suspecting that it has come not so much from clinical need as a 'bitterness' that she has long identified towards visitors. 'It's hard to overcome,' she says, 'but we need to.'

This is a view regularly expressed, though rarely from within, and I admire her willingness to voice it. The pandemic brought much that was festering beneath up to the surface, including all of the worst cross-border attitudes on both sides. When Wales did anything even slightly different, the hullaballoo in some quarters of England was often deafening, and always swollen with a contempt that went far beyond the issue in question. And in Wales, as predictable as the cock's crow were the voices demanding stricter restrictions, even outright bans, on visitors as the answer to any and every question. That the overwhelming – and inevitable – majority of those visitors come from England was the fart left lingering in the room.

Our time at the spring is done, and we must re-enter the world, having put it to watery rights. On our return journeys, to Radnorshire, to Maldwyn and to Hereford, I know that we will all feel slightly improved by the unplanned hour that we shared, and the confidences and easy laughter that ricocheted so readily off the trees. As we leave, I turn back for one last look at the spring. The fresh water is pumping from the cleft of red rock, frothing and dancing in the lazy afternoon sun, before hurrying urgently towards the tired old river below.

12.

TIDE

/// signified.hosts.battle

Twenty-two meandering miles below the Biblins is what for centuries was the last border crossing of all, the old Chepstow bridge. Once the most notorious bottleneck into south Wales, semi-retirement has suited it well, allowing this most elegant of structures to parade its curves largely unhindered by traffic. The five-arch iron bridge, leaping from one country to the other with the grace of a gazelle, now makes for a wonderful promenade, a place to linger in comforting limbo.

There is no doubting where you cross the line. The entire middle of the bridge is homage to the fact, in an ornate cast-iron roundel, split into two by a carriage lamp: one side spelling out GLOUCESTER, the other MONMOUTH. The previous bridge, usurped by this one in 1816, was even blunter. In 1785, when the two sides disagreed on strengthening the antiquated wooden structure, only Monmouthshire pressed ahead and built new stone piers; the Gloucestershire half remained all rickety timbers. Though this strange arrangement lasted only three decades, they were the years in which the Wye Tour was becoming stratospherically popular, and enthusiastic amateurs were committing to canvas everything on the river's banks. Looking at prints of the half-and-half bridge, I swear I can hear the Georgian versions of my dad, muttering darkly about the better Welsh roads, and wondering who's paying.

In July 2016, 200 years to the day since the bridge's opening, a re-enactment brought thousands to celebrate. The town crier, his cheeks almost as scarlet as his frock coat, steered the parade from Chepstow town centre down to the Wye. There were speeches and songs, fancy dress and a cavalcade of vintage vehicles inching across the bridge. After three cheers, the crowds broke into an impromptu rendition of 'Happy Birthday' (*Happy Birthday dear Wye Bridge, Happy Birthday to yooooou!*), its sentiment so affectionate and its amplification by the cliffs so atmospheric that it was genuinely stirring to see. Once again, the umbilical link between the Wye and its people seems so unbreakably strong, and in Chepstow, perhaps more so than most.

You need only hang out by the bridge to appreciate that. The last town on the river has a unique connection with it, for the water rises and falls twice daily with such speed and force that it demands attention, respect and no little wonder. At the lowest tides, mud flats gleam deep and treacherous, and a brown stream, the colour of cheap chocolate, laps at the footings of the stone piers. At a top spring tide, the river up to fifty foot higher, the piers have been swallowed whole, and the bridge become an iron causeway skimming over the wide waters. The constant ebb and flow, the pull of the moon and stars, keep the town on its toes, yet anchored by its side.

It is impossible not to contrast Chepstow with Monmouth. Both have the handsome wide main street, remnants of Georgian swank, and both have the Wye. The old county town, though, has turned away from its waters, while its underling remains cheerfully entwined, and is all the more rooted as a result. In every regard: where Monmouth seems stiff and compromised in its nationality, Chepstow is in little doubt. Though it too is only inches from the border, the town is unambiguously Welsh, and like Hay, seems more so now than when I first visited thirty years ago. Even the famous Union Jack, painted regularly since 1935 on the limestone cliffs facing the town, is vanishing fast; on this latest visit, I had real trouble making it out. As poet Myrddin ap Dafydd puts it in the final words of his book *The Welsh Marches from the West*, 'In the heart of Wales our sorrow is that the country seems to be shrinking; here in the Marches it's as if the country is growing.'

On this keen edge, national stereotypes are literally cast in stone: on the Gloucestershire cliffs, the fading Union Jack is topped by a row of million-pound houses, while over the bridge in the rockface of Monmouthshire, a legendary cave, yet another place where King Arthur is said to be sleeping. Above him and his slumbering knights, the monster that is Chepstow castle. Even in its first landfall, Wales is already thick with belligerent ghosts, visibly manifesting among the turrets, towers, mullions and battlements that snake for 800 feet along cliffs they appear to have grown from. 'The most brutal castle is Chepstow,' wrote Jan Morris in her roll-call of Welsh castellar superlatives, 'like a huge fist of grey rock at the very gate of Wales.'

The middle knuckle of the fist is the great keep, the first stone castle in Britain, begun by the Normans within a year of the Battle of Hastings. That a distant muddy bank of the Wye, just short of its final confluence with the Severn, was fortified so swiftly and sturdily speaks volumes of the spot's strategic importance. It took the Normans barely four years to subjugate England, but they soon realised that Wales was trickier. Chepstow was the fist to smash a way into Glamorgan and beyond, though it was to prove a very long game. The creation of a buffer zone of Marcher lordships succeeded in semi-taming the borderlands, but what worked there was stoutly resisted in 'the Principality', the Welsh heartland of the west and north. Not until Edward I, over two centuries later, was that conquered.

In fortifying Chepstow, Monmouth, Goodrich and a sequence of castles up to Montgomery and Hawarden, and creating the autonomous earldoms at Chester, Shrewsbury and Hereford, the Normans scored ever deeper the line that had first been drawn 1,000 years earlier on the defeat of Caratacus. Though they were brutal warlords, there was some grudging respect towards the Welsh, and an unexpected kinship with those on the border, in the southern lands of the Wye especially. Culturally, there were many linguistic crossovers and similar traditions of community, hospitality, music and even rituals of warfare. Geographically, there was much to remind them of home,

Normandy being in the west of France and a borderland with Celtic Brittany. The fertile hills, fish-rich rivers and wild forests felt familiar, so too their salmon, trout, pork, veal and venison, their sweet orchards and plentiful cider. Even today, ambrosial hints of *la France profonde* caress us in the low, slow lanes, in the old villages, farms and great barns of Monmouth, Brecon and Hereford. It is the sweetest siren call, and there are plenty who hear it.

In Wales, house prices rose more during the pandemic than anywhere else. In Monmouthshire, long the most expensive area, they were already surging after tolls on the Severn bridges were abolished in 2018, ushering in a slew of excitable property puffs about 'the new Cotswolds', no less. Houses are going up everywhere. Whether the people who need them most, young locals and essential workers especially, will be able to afford them is another matter. On Chepstow's riverfront, an area that used to be warehouses and an oily boatyard is now sprouting complexes of chrome and blond wood apartments, each costing between ten and fifteen times the average local salary.

Covid was an obvious cause. When times are tough, the dream is sharper, of big skies and space to breathe, potent beyond measure for those cooped up under urban curfew in tiny homes already stretched to the limit, and suddenly required also to become two offices, a school and a leisure centre. To some, the Johnson government was also an effective recruiting sergeant for a life in Wales. Though the mortality rates for all four UK nations have pretty much evened out after more than two years of the pandemic, many noticed – and liked – the difference in tone and tenor between Westminster and Cardiff, Edinburgh too. A marked post-pandemic issue has been the reluctance of many to return to work. With such precarity in the jobs market, and such pressure in the jobs that there are, it is no surprise that people see acquisitive property portfolios as their safest bet. The meteoric rise of Airbnb and its kind has only hastened the process.

Wales and its borderland are ripe for all this, and always have been. Though the specific circumstances and cast of characters change, the core appeal mutates to fit each turbulent age in turn. And this is where it was born, two and a half centuries ago.

* * *

'The chief grace and ornament of my journey was the river Wye,' wrote poet Thomas Gray to a friend after being rowed down the river as part of a grand tour of Britain in the early summer of 1770. 'Its banks are a succession of nameless wonders.' A few weeks later, a Surrey priest made the same journey, sketching sights and jotting down notes along the way. William Gilpin circulated the journal of his trip among friends, including a printer who persuaded him to publish it. Finally coming out in 1783, *Observations on the River Wye and several parts of South Wales &c relative chiefly to Picturesque Beauty* demonstrated, in his own words, 'a new object of pursuit; that of examining the face of a country *by the rules of picturesque beauty*', defined as 'that kind of beauty which is agreeable in a picture'. To his publisher, he elaborated: 'If nature gets it wrong, I cannot help putting her right.'

Gilpin's rules were strict and intricate, but the aesthetic reward great, he assured his growing band of devotees. The picture needed a precise order of components: a background, a 'front-screen', 'side-screens' and 'ornaments', which came in a hierarchy of Picturesqueness, so that ruins and tumbledown cottages, for instance, were considered better than mansions or monuments. To help frame the scene, Gilpin recommended the use of a Claude Glass, a dark, convex mirror that the viewer held in front of them to capture the scene over their shoulder, so condensing and lightly decolorising it. 'They give the object of nature a soft, mellow tinge like the colouring of a Master,' he explained. His book changed everything, giving birth both to the commercial Wye Tour, the first incarnation of modern mass tourism, and to the Picturesque movement.

The two were a perfect match, at the perfect time. Rapid industrialisation and urbanisation had given us the first stirrings of pastoralism, as the taste for drama-in-landscape spilled over from the continent, just when access to it was suddenly cut off by the French Revolution. The Wye valley, from Ross all the way down to Chepstow, became an enthusiastic understudy for the wooded passes and mountainous scenery of the Alps and the Rhine, and like its European forebears, spawned notebooks, guides, sketches, paintings and poems.

The two-day tour, its itinerary as fixed as the stars, was the first big hit. Visitors joined their boats at the meadows below Ross early on the first morning, with a crew to row and guide them the 38 miles down to Chepstow. Brand-new sketchpads were soon cracked open as the boat rounded a bend, and gave the passengers their first glimpse of the grand red ruins of Goodrich Castle, high on a crag above the water. After a stop there, the scenery became rapidly more dramatic as the river ploughed in extravagant loops through wooded ravines and cliffs.

Lunch was taken below the Coldwell Rocks, a spring providing refreshment and a useful wine chiller, followed by an optional climb to the top of Symonds Yat rock, and a descent down the other side to rejoin those who'd stayed on the boat around the 4-mile Huntsham loop. If the river was sufficiently high, they then had the thrill of shooting the 'cascade' at the New Weir, before a beautifully tranquil section, the route of my walk to the Biblins, under cliffs, woods and dramatic limestone pinnacles all the way past the riverside church of Dixton and into Monmouth, their overnight stop. There were tea shops and taverns, the Vauxhall pleasure gardens for those who fancied something racier, or a little gentle sketching of the ancient gated bridge, the priory church, rustic cottagers or fisherman in the meadows.

Next morning, it was another early start as the boats headed down-stream towards the apogee of the entire tour, the gothic glory of Tintern Abbey. En route, some took a detour to St Briavels castle, once the political headquarters of the Forest of Dean, others happily sketched the wooded river banks, the intermittent stately houses or the mills and forges; in these early days of industrialisation, and far away from sulphurous cities, the landscape was still an object of fasci-nation for the genteel traveller. Even Gilpin, with all his pernickety rules about nature, admitted that a smidgeon of industry might enhance things, writing at Lydbrook that 'the contrast of all this busi-ness, the engines used in lading and unlading, together with the variety of the scene, produce all together a picturesque assemblage'.

For all that it was 'esteemed … the most beautiful and picturesque view on the river', Tintern aggrieved Gilpin in several ways. In common with many other visitors, he was disgruntled to find it 'encompassed … with shabby houses', though his main gripe was that the ruined twelfth-century Cistercian abbey did not sufficiently adhere to his strict compositional rules: 'Though the parts are beautiful, the whole is ill-shaped. No ruins of the tower are left, which might give form, and contrast to the walls, and buttresses, and other interior parts. Instead of this, a number of gable ends hurt the eye with their regularity; and disgust it by the vulgarity of their shape. A mallet judiciously used (but who durst use it?) might be of service in fracturing some of them.'

The last few miles to Chepstow were a very grand finale. The river was by now tidal, swelling and falling with theatrical grandeur, echoed by the wonders on its banks: designated viewing and sketching points, groves, ruins and *cottages ornés*. Just short of Chepstow was the Piercefield estate, in its day as much of a draw as Tintern. A series of paths led the visitor around ten or so viewpoints and 'stations', all garlanded with romantic names: Lover's Leap, a Druid's Temple, a Chinese Bridge, an Orangery, Cascade, Alcove and Grotto. The Giant's Cave had a huge stone figure carved above its entrance, holding a boulder over his head as if to drop it on incoming raiders, but frost damage did for him and by the beginning of the nineteenth century his arms had crumbled away. Predictably, more rarefied visitors found it all rather common, as had Gilpin. 'It is a pity that the ingenious embellisher of these scenes could not have been satisfied with the grand beauties of nature which he commanded,' he sniffed.

The final sight was Chepstow castle, already glimpsed from afar at some of the viewpoints, but suddenly hoving magnificently into view as the boats came round the final curve into town. Most tourists stayed the night, for there was plenty to see: the castle of course, a popular excursion by moonlight, the priory church, an Assembly Rooms, theatre and numerous inns, and various manifestations of the extraordinary tidal range, at the half-and-half Wye bridge (and its iron successor), in the town's 'hot and cold sea water Bathing Rooms …

replenished with water every tide', and behind a house on Castle Terrace, a well that filled and emptied in precise opposition to the tide.

Like a Claude Glass of carefully screened loveliness distilled into one bewitching image, Wales was always a tidy fit as the Picturesque, together with its more muscular cousin, the Sublime. The Wye Tour was a useful acclimatiser, an *amuse-bouche* for the full repast of the rude and mountainous interior. Between 1780 and 1815, when victory at Waterloo tentatively opened up the continent once more to young rakes for their Grand Tour, there were published dozens of books of gentry tours around Wales, as well as reams of romantic poetry by the likes of Shelley, Coleridge, Wordsworth and scores of others better forgotten. In visual art, pioneer Welsh landscapist Richard Wilson led the charge, followed most notably by J. M. W. Turner, who toured often and immersed himself in Welsh history and legend, or the more syrupy takes of Joshua Cristall, William Payne and David Cox.

At Symonds Yat and Tintern, where metal-bashing cohabited sometimes uneasily with tourism, the poverty was real, and the beggars inevitable. Gilpin found Tintern a 'scene of desolation' and devoted a large part of his account to being taken to see the monks' library by an old woman who could 'scarce crawl; shuffling along her palsied limbs'. The 'remnant of a shattered cloister' that she showed him turned out to be her own home, filthy, wet and freezing; 'I never saw so loathsome a human dwelling,' he writes, but also, a little guilt-ily: 'We did not expect to be interested as we were.'

Even grinding penury could be lightly Picturesqued after a fashion. The success of Gilpin's book made the haggard old woman a celebrity, something of a sight to be ticked off the list, though by 1791 one visitor noted that she had recently died in the workhouse. John Byng, the future Lord Torrington, let an old man begging at the Tintern quay accompany him around the abbey, for though he 'had forgotten everything … I kept him with me, as his venerable grey beard, and locks, added dignity to my thoughts; and I fancied him the hermit of the place'.

Most people wearied of William Gilpin's fussy edicts, but the essence of his take has endured, and continuously mutated. Nothing really changes. Eighteenth-century pearl-clutching over beggars and pickpockets is today's poverty porn television show or tabloid front page. The Claude Glass has been replaced by the iPhone, held in exactly the same position for the ubiquitous selfie. And Georgian gentlefolk tutting at Chepstow castle 'that the beauty of the ruin is deteriorated' (a Mr Webb in 1812) nod along with the lady who gives it one star on Tripadvisor, because 'It is a ruin, nothing to see other than grass, remains of castle and the river Wye.'

Stereotypes persist too from when the people of both sides of the border were meeting each other for the first time. Yorkshire Tory MP Sir Christopher Sykes was scathing when he visited Chepstow in 1796: 'a poor miserable town', with no bookshop and ignorant, heathen inhabitants. He scoffs at a local who tells him that the church 'was built about the time Julius Caesar came over', and inside was most displeased to find that 'the Church was ill attended both Morning and Evening'. He 'now judged that I was in Wales', and was not impressed.

Reading that, I was bumped back thirty years to an office in Covent Garden, the shiny new headquarters of the then-mighty Rough Guides. The impeccably liberal travel publishers were preparing for the first time books on the home countries: one on Scotland, and one on England, with Wales apportioned two chapters, north and south, at the back of that. I'd been arguing for months that Wales merited its own volume (England too, for that matter), but was getting nowhere. In a meeting, I pressed the case again, to the evident exasperation of one of the directors. Cutting dead my spiel about how if the Rough Guides prided themselves on cultural sensitivity they should commit themselves to three books for the three countries, he growled, 'but who the *fuck* is going to buy a book about *Wales*?'

I heard it everywhere. In 1990s Britain, flush on easy plastic and five-pound flights, Wales was grim memories of a childhood fortnight in a wet caravan, or a coach holiday for Nan. At best, it was a pleasant enough weekend, if a very poor second to a city break in Prague. When I mentioned that I was spending many months touring Wales and writing about it, people often asked if I was sorry not to have landed a better gig. September 11, the crash of 2007/8 and the deep-ening climate crisis changed the lens through which Wales and the borderland were viewed. Gilpin's Picturesque was born in an era of strife, of war and privation, and such times are never far away.

* * *

Close your eyes, and you might hear a cheer on the wind, perhaps the excitable chatter of children brought here to gaze at the future. That was me once. I insisted on it, begged and begged until my dad gave way and I was allowed half an hour at the Aust services, overlooking the Severn Bridge on the English bank. To a ten-year-old in the late 1970s, any motorway service station was a palace of thrills, but this one – a Motorport no less, whatever that meant – was the pinnacle. It housed Britain's biggest restaurant, its huge plate-glass windows look-ing out over the estuary, the bridge and the seductive curves of Wales beyond. I was allowed a quick peek, forbidden from touching anything or – god forbid – picking up any item of overpriced food, and then herded out to the free picnic area, where we belonged. At its apex was the shiny white memorial stone unveiled by the Queen on the day that the bridge had opened, three months before I was born.

The picnic area, the country's biggest restaurant and the gleaming optimism have all long gone. When the second bridge opened just shy of the millennium, the service station was shunted into the old truck-ers' rest stop two car parks away, and the main building sold. The royal memorial stone, stripped of its white paint, still holds court, but chiselled with graffiti, on a dais cracked with weeds and enclosed by walls chipped and broken. The view though, the view … look beyond the brambles and there it is still, as mesmerising as ever. Today, there's an extra excitement, one that would have made my ten-year-old self pop, as I'm walking from Chepstow to Aust, going by foot across the bridge for the very first time.

It's not the great lonesome trek I was anticipating. I have to share the bridge's walkway with work trucks, a motor bike, some joggers and cyclists, and there's more traffic than expected too. Since the new bridge took the main M4, this older one has been downgraded as the M48, an oxbow lake of the motorway system, but it's busy today. It is startling how near pedestrians are to speeding trucks, and how only four steel cables, less than two feet high, separate us. The noise is staggering, the vibrations immense, and so much worse when I stop. Keeping moving, even at walking pace, seems to fulfil the bridge's hunger for forward momentum, but on stopping, the kinetic gods are rudely resisted, and my innards instantly purée in protest.

Before long, I'm walking over the trim and tidy channel of the Wye. The tide is low, and as the sun comes briefly out, I'm dazzled by the shapes that the constantly rising and falling water have carved in the mudbanks, one English, one Welsh. The patterns mesmerise me: not just the rivulets through the mud, but the pavements of higher and drier marsh, baked and cracked into geometric shapes – a jigsaw perhaps, or a map of intricate borders.

For the past couple of years, this frontier has obsessed me, has entertained and haunted me, and this is our last encounter for now. The thought saddens me, for I have loved every moment of exploration in pursuit of this book. After thirty years on one side, and nearly twenty-five on the other, I thought that I knew the divide intimately, but no. These journeys have overturned so many of my assumptions, and have introduced me to places of such power and magic that I had previously passed by. Without question, their long existence on a live border is the key to so much of that magic.

Around 150 feet beneath me, the border runs along the mid channel of the Wye, and then deep down into the riverbed and rocks below. It slices the road behind me, the air above me, and cuts across the centuries both long past and yet to come. Even here, in this maelstrom of modernity, I can see in the distance the outcrop of Chapel Rock, where the waters of the Severn and Wye finally meet, and on it, the ruins of a tiny chapel founded in the fifth century by an anchorite from Gwynedd. In the chaotic aftermath of the Romans leaving Britain, she was brutally murdered by Saxon pirates pushing at the edges of their new world.

Is this an edge still? It is, though there are many who hope not, and work tirelessly to eradicate it. The political pressure for 'Greater Severnside', a hybrid of Cardiff and Bristol, with Newport and Chepstow squeezed inelegantly in between, is immense, and ripe with symbolism. Every few years, for instance, the idea of a new airport on an artificial island in the estuary crops up, gets discussed and then dropped. Some symbols are an easier sell. Almost no one objected to the dropping of the tolls on the Severn bridges, which by 2017 had climbed to over fifty times the price in 1966. That such a move was in the gift of the UK Treasury, rather than the Senedd in Cardiff, was milked dry by the Westminster government, who twinned their munificence with the announcement – and quarter of a million pounds worth of new signage – that the second crossing was henceforth to be known as the Prince of Wales Bridge. That was the new price.

The real stand-off between Westminster and Cardiff might yet happen where the twin motorways descend onto Welsh soil. An M4 relief road, going south of Newport across the wetland of the Gwent Levels, has been mooted for decades, and was only finally cancelled by the Welsh (Labour) government in 2019. The UK (Conservative) government continues to flirt with the idea of overriding the decision, a move that would be every bit as much to do with undermining devolution as tackling congestion.

Should the road get built, let alone the airport, then it might perhaps be all over, for the gravitational pull of the M4 corridor towards London would be too much to resist. That said, I may well be guilty of having been too long in Wales, of having supped too deep on its favourite nectar of imminent doom. When the Severn Bridge was planned in the 1950s and 60s, many warned that it would herald an overwhelming and probably fatal tsunami of anglicisation. Similar worries were voiced about the talkies, television and tourism, pop music and latterly the internet and smartphones, yet despite the globalising – and yes, anglicising – force of each, Wales endures, its old language, chippy distinctiveness and unique take on the world all rudely intact. It clearly has far greater resilience than some of its most ardent advocates seem to fear.

Between the Wye and the Severn estuary is a spit of land, the tadpole-shaped Beachley Head, 800 feet wide at its neck. Long of strategic significance, since the First World War the peninsula has been a military base of one sort or another, and as I cross over it I can see young riflemen yomping around a rugby pitch, massive kitbags on their backs, and another group doing burpee jumps on a thin patch of grass. They seem oblivious to us all up here, and gliding through, I feel oddly – and increasingly – insubstantial. It's not a wholly unpleasant sensation.

The sudden wind though is a shock. Above the old ferry slipway, barnacled and slathered in seaweed, I'm finally out over the wide open maw of the Severn, a surly brown sea chopped by the wind into yeasty peaks. It's tough, and not just physically. Since 1966, hundreds of people have ended their lives here, jumping into the underworld, and I wonder how many truly intended to. There is something so impersonal, almost existentially hopeless, on this walkway; the noise and vibrations play havoc with your head, while a gravitational pull tugs you to the edge. At the entrance to the bridge, I passed a dedicated Samaritans phone kiosk, but cloaked in plastic and tape, declared redundant in the age of the mobile. It was not a look to comfort the desperate. Instead, there are plaques at regular intervals along the walkway, advertising their twenty-four-hour freephone number. Halfway across the bridge, I see one in both languages – *y Samariaid*, which sounds so much more pleasingly Old Testament in Welsh. I reach for my phone to take a photograph, and it rages into life with news alerts.

Prime Minister Boris Johnson has just resigned.

The fire that was first ignited on the border, in the North Shropshire by-election seven months earlier, has finally immolated the tottering edifice of Johnson's premiership. After months of anger and anguish, of flagrant lies and bullshit denials, of increasingly tortuous rounds of recrimination and apology, words hand-stitched with the delicacy of lace to cover actions big, brutish and desperately ugly, it is over. The domino topple of ministers in the last few days has finally brought down the big one. All hell is breaking loose, and I'm standing in a stale summer wind, on a lonely gantry between two countries, with lorries rattling my bowels and a deep unease chewing at my heels.

Even as the traffic thunders past, I rush to social media. It's still quite early on a Thursday morning, but timelines are awash with popping champagne corks metaphorical and, in a few cases, literal. I'm in no mood to party, though, and that's not just down to the dislocation of the bridge. This dire regime was not some freak exception in the national story. It *is* that national story, the sum total of the delusions with which we constantly pamper ourselves. In every ounce of his gilded entitlement and faux humility, Boris Johnson was the United Kingdom incarnate, inevitable.

I look up to see the old Aust service station squatting like a toad on the rust-red cliffs ahead. It doesn't look like the future any more. Phone still gripped tight, I tap in an online search to find out what it is used for these days, and up comes the answer: the headquarters of an insurance company founded by Arron Banks, the self-declared

'Bad Boy of Brexit'. The millions made here propelled Johnson into Downing Street, Banks and Farage into Trump's golden elevator, and our collective discourse deep into the sewers. My mistake: perhaps the old service station *is* the future, the last of Little England perched all too literally on the edge of a cliff.

The need to get back to Wales seems suddenly so urgent, and I turn into the wind to begin the long trek home. Clouds are closing in, whipping in from the open ocean, damping down colour and making land, sea and sky hard to prise apart. The boundaries are blurring, but the waters remain so wide.

EPILOGUE

Thursday 8 September 2022

On the new Prime Minister's third day in office, she was on her feet in the Commons when one of her ministers snuck in, and handed her a note. A minute later, another note was passed to the leader of the opposition. I'm vaguely following the action on Twitter, where journalists are beginning to speculate. 'I think this might be it,' tweets one. 'Might be what?' I wonder. 'She's gone,' says another. 'Who?' I think, and then it all becomes clear as the tentative whispers swell into a roar.

* * *

For his first visit to Wales as king, Charles III crossed the border from above. The helicopter flight from his Gloucestershire estate to Cardiff took only twenty minutes, and a less seasoned operator might look at that, and the apparently indistinguishable patchwork of towns and fields that drifted by far below, as confirmation of how indissolubly samey the two countries are. Charles perhaps knew better. In more than sixty-four years as Prince of Wales, he'd learned a fair bit about his titular fiefdom: its history, geography and landscape, a few words of its language, and more than anything, its singular stubbornness. Perhaps he regarded the Welsh trip, the last of a breakneck tour of the four home nations in the week following his mother's death, as something of a homecoming.

Many in Wales felt the same way too. As his helicopter landed and a twenty-one-gun salute roared across Cardiff, thousands were waiting at his three scheduled stops: the city's cathedral at Llandaff, the Senedd down in the Bay, and in the city centre, the castle, a perfectly British confection of Roman walls, Norman keep and Victorian opium dream. Asked why they had come by television journalists, some well-wishers mentioned the late Queen or the new King, but most said that it was 'a bit of history' they wanted to see for themselves.

On his arrival at the castle, there was audible booing amid the cheers, and a sizeable silent protest. That the royal visit was taking place on Owain Glyndŵr day, the anniversary of the rebel prince's uprising, only exacerbated the opposition, especially as many of the planned Glyndŵr events had been forcibly cancelled by local authorities and Cadw, the Welsh heritage body. That evening, actor Michael Sheen posted a video online, expressing all condolences to the royal family, but saying too of the new King's visit that 'If it was done on purpose it seems insensitive to the point of insult. And if it wasn't done on purpose – if it was done accidentally without realising what that day was – then one does wonder what being Prince of Wales for so long actually meant if you were not aware of what that day means?'

His ire, shared by many, was sharpened to a blade by the swiftness with which Prince William had been declared the new Prince of Wales. Unlike the heir to the throne's hereditary Scottish titles and the Duchy of Cornwall, there is no constitutional imperative for the position, and all expectations were that nothing would happen immediately, that there might even be some debate as to what the title meant in the new, devolutionary age. His mother had been monarch for over six years before Charles himself was made Prince of Wales, but in his very first public broadcast twenty-four hours after her death he upgraded William immediately, and his wife too, making Kate the first Princess of Wales since Diana.

A whiff of political chicanery pervaded the pronouncement, buried deep in the rich layers of obsequy that instantly smothered everything on the death of the Queen. Throughout those twelve strange days of regulation mourning, all other news evaporated and voices offering anything other than the approved narrative were not so much outlawed, as simply ignored. Having proclaimed the new Prince of Wales on day two, by the time we were all once again allowed to breathe freely it was old news, a done deal.

Alongside the new king at the service in Llandaff cathedral was the new Prime Minister. The transfer of power from Boris Johnson to Liz Truss had been the Queen's final public act, two days before her death, and it's hard to imagine a greater baptism of fire for Truss, whose first brush with political fame had been as a young Liberal Democrat activist, stridently demanding an end to the monarchy. Enforced mourning trips with Charles to Edinburgh, Belfast and Cardiff were for her a crash course not just in royalty but in devolution too, another concept for which she'd shown scant enthusiasm. In the leadership campaign, she'd said that 'the best thing to do with [Scottish First Minister] Nicola Sturgeon is to ignore her', and she did. Throughout her entire forty-four-day premiership she made no contact with the First Ministers of either Scotland or Wales.

Her replacement, Rishi Sunak, very publicly phoned both on his first day in the job, not out of any great enthusiasm for them or for devolution, but more as a pointed rebuke to his predecessor, an easy way of showing that he was different. Quite how different remains to be seen. The fifth Conservative Prime Minister in six short years, since the political earthquake of Brexit had put a wreckers' cabal of English neoliberals in charge, he is a former investment banker and hedge fund manager, and as wedded as either of his predecessors to a vision of a stripped-back, deregulated Singapore-on-Thames. The Severn, the Dee and the Wye will need to fend for themselves.

The Queen's death pressed pause on the mounting fury and political chaos, and in that mummified hiatus the United Kingdom did a brief but passable impression of its name. 'No one does this as well as the British,' chuckled my dad on the phone, warm with reassurance and self-satisfaction. His was a sentiment purred constantly by black-tied correspondents on interminable television reports, and it is palpably true. We are magnificent at ostentation, world-beaters at old men in buckles, braid and the whitest of tights, boys in ruffles and ladies in hats, connoisseurs nonpareil of trumpets and flummery and golden carriages pulled by horses polished to a gloss. It is who we are and, we were repeatedly told, who we have always been.

Up to a point. A little over four hours after arriving in Cardiff, the royal helicopter took off once more. Charles was returning to London for that evening's Vigil of the Princes, when he and his siblings were to stand guard for ten minutes at their mother's coffin in Westminster Hall. Commentators again murmured about tradition that stretched back far into the mists, and how this was the first time in history that a monarch's daughter – Anne, the Princess Royal – had taken part in the ceremony. True enough, but the ceremony had happened only twice before, and was invented in 1936.

As they rose into the skies, Charles must have considered that it had been four hours very well spent in Wales. His personal approval ratings had soared since his mother's death, and although an online petition against the immediate elevation of William to the position of Prince of Wales had garnered tens of thousands of signatures, it had come to little. The media wasn't touching such topics right now, as that day's BBC Radio Wales was making abundantly clear. They were having a very busy Friday, covering not just the king's first Welsh trip, but also the shock at the sudden death of rugby icon Eddie Butler. Either side of the royal visit, they broadcast three and a half hours of tributes. Listeners heard the same cherished clips and anecdotes time and again, but never once mention of Butler's late conversion to the cause of Welsh independence, his work on its behalf and his barnstorming speech at the last Yes Cymru march before lockdown. Though a man of Monmouthshire, of English parents in the most tenuous border county of all, he saw it clear: 'for extreme ideologies, look now no further than Westminster,' he told the thousands at the rally. 'The United Kingdom that made my parents proud to call themselves British no longer exists.'

EPILOGUE

The king's helicopter banked higher, and headed towards the wide estuary of the Severn, dazzling bright in the afternoon sunshine. Like all foreshores, it is the property of the Crown; so too the countless Roman coins found in its muddy banks, tossed over the shoulders of men for luck as they crossed that infamously hairy tide. It was only on Thursday 8 September 1966 that the danger was finally overcome, when the Queen opened the bridge that consigned the ferries to history.

On another Thursday 8 September, fifty-six years later, Elizabeth II died, and with her went such an era. The original Severn Bridge was as much its symbol as any: elegant and confident, a grand statement of modernist ambition, but soon enough displaced. As they passed overhead, the new king surely looked down on the bridge and its young sibling striding across his royal domain, though from so far above and in such blinding golden light, it was impossible for him to tell whether that mighty tide was coming in, or fast flowing out.

ACKNOWLEDGEMENTS

The idea for this book first bubbled up in the summer of 2014, when I walked an extended version of the Mortimer Trail from the border at Old Radnor to Ludlow, three days away. It's a magnificent hike, weaving a stately and circuitous route that was clearly very carefully plotted to afford the walker a rolling feast of sights and viewpoints. Over a pint one evening, I enthused about the idea of writing about the border to my regular walking companions, Nicky Burgess and James Williams-Lucas. It was in fond memory – and I hope the adventurous spirit – of James, who died suddenly in 2021, that I conducted these later research trips.

On the ground, I met so many people who helped steer my thoughts and understanding. Thanks to them all, and especially to Kate Green, Bill Sample, Lisa Tulfer, Judith Dunkling, Mark Jickells, Andy Johnson, Su and Richard Wheeler, Graham Murphy, Jon Moses, Gee and David Williams, Nancy Durham and the lavender crew, Haydn Pugh (sharing such sweet memories of Lucy Powell of the Three Tuns, Hay), Michael Tavinor and Tim Bridges, Sue Parker, Andy Knight, Giuliana Beccui, Rob Burkitt, Alix Nathan, Miriam Ellison, John Geach, Marc Jones, Annie Garthwaite, Anna Dreda, Anne Rainsbury, Siân Whiteoak, Sarah Stanbridge, Andrew Fusek Peters, Ben Gwalchmai, Lowri Roberts, Charlotte Durie and her Merlina (this book's totem beast), Simon Scott, Morgan Davies, Sarah

Morris, Clare Grist Taylor, Myfanwy Alexander and Gill Powell. Apologies to anyone whose name has escaped me.

Further illumination came from Jon Gower, Peter Wakelin, David Rudkin, Charmian Savill and David Rabey, Gladys Mary Coles, Ian and Hilary Marchant, Myrddin ap Dafydd, Simon Moreton, Dr David Howlett, Rhys Mwyn, Matthew and Hannah Gidley, Jon Woolcott and Helen Baker, Seiriol Davies and Rich Thomas, Fern Smith, Phil Ralph, Alun Ephraim, Manni and Reuben Coe, Simon and Chris Savidge.

I am especially indebted to my dear friends and readers, Pamela Petro and Jay Griffiths, who gave me clear and invaluable thoughts on the book and its progress. Preds, as always, has been there with food and love, a well-mixed gin and an ever-perceptive eye on the whole project. He and Fflos have been the perfect companions on many borderland outings; the undoubted highlight a couple of nights 'champing' – church camping – in St Cuthbert's, Holme Lacy, near Hereford.

That the frontier is studded with superb little towns is clear from the fact so many of them have a brilliant independent bookshop. Thanks to the enthusiasm and support over the years of Stanton at Castle Bookshop, Ludlow; Tim and Carrie at Booka, Oswestry; Ros and team at Burway books, Church Stretton; Susan at Pengwern, Shrewsbury; Anna formerly of Wenlock Books; Sarah and Sheridan at Aardvark, Brampton Bryan; Barry and Richard at Eaves & Lord, Montgomery; Emma and co. at Book-ish, Crickhowell; Leigh and Nicky at The Hours, Brecon; Andy, Victoria, Rusty and co. at Rossister's in Ross-on-Wye and Monmouth (and now Leominster and Cheltenham too).

A little further afield, thanks too to Eirian and Sel at Palas Print, Caernarfon, Gwyn at Awen Meirion, Y Bala. In Machynlleth, we are so blessed to have the bookselling fraternity of Diane and Geoff at Pen'rallt, Liz at the Senedd-dŷ, Paul and Bethan at Coch-y-Bontddu, Neil at Dyfi Valley Books and Kees and co. at Literary Cat.

Thanks as ever to Julian Alexander, my agent, and Jonathan de Peyer and the team at HarperNorth. It's great to see one of the big publishers spin out into 'the provinces', for there is so much talent, wisdom and fire far, far beyond the M25.

I'm hugely indebted to the kindness and enthusiasm of so many people in the region's libraries and archives. Despite being cut to the bone in terms of both hours and stock, they have yet again provided untold help, far beyond the call of duty. Especial thanks to the staff at Newtown, Kington, Chester, Shrewsbury, Monmouth, Chepstow, Overton, Ludlow, Oswestry, Wrexham, Machynlleth, Hay and the Dean Heritage Centre at Soudley. Libraries are our communal reservoir of knowledge and history, and if we allow them to be drained dry, we will all die of thirst.

BIBLIOGRAPHY

Chimamanda Ngozi Adichie, *Half of a Yellow Sun*

Myrddin ap Dafydd, *The Welsh Marches from the West* (a translation by Susan Walton of *Y Gororau: Gwlad Rhwng y Gwledydd*)

Chris Barber, *In Search of Owain Glyndŵr*

Robert W. Barrett, Jr, *Against All England: Regional Identity and Cheshire Writing*

Elizabeth Beazley and Peter Howell, *The Companion Guide to North Wales*

Paul Binding, *After Brock*

Richard Booth, *My Kingdom of Books*

George Borrow, *Wild Wales*

Margaret Brentnall, *The Welsh Borders from Hereford to Chester*

W. T. Bryan, *The Roaring Bull of Bagbury*

Oliver Bullough, *Butler to the World*

Tom Bullough, *Addlands*

Tom Bullough, *The Claude Glass*

Helen Burnham, *A Guide to Ancient and Historic Wales: Clwyd and Powys*

'Cato' (Frank Owen, Michael Foot and Peter Howard), *Guilty Men*

Bruce Chatwin, *On the Black Hill*

Kate Clarke, *The Book of Hay*

Gladys Mary Coles, *The Echoing Green*

Gladys Mary Coles, *Mary Webb*

Peter J. Conradi, *At the Bright Hem of God: Radnorshire Pastoral*

John Davies, *A History of Wales*

John Davies, Nigel Jenkins, Menna Baines and Peredur L. Lynch, *The Welsh Academy Encyclopædia of Wales*

C. N. de Courcy Parry, *Here Lies My Story*

Hywel Dix (ed.), *After Raymond Williams: Cultural Materialism and the Break-Up of Britain*

Richard Dobson, *Border Crossings*

Richard Dobson, *In My Own Time*

J. R. Earp and B. A. Hains, *British Regional Geology: The Welsh Borderland*

Herbert L. Edlin (ed.), *Dean Forest and Wye Valley Forestry Commission Guide*

Islwyn Ffowc Elis, *Wythnos yng Nghymru Fydd*

Margiad Evans, *Country Dance*

Sheppard Frere, *Britannia: A History of Roman Britain*

Alan Garner, *The Voice that Thunders*

Geoffrey of Monmouth, *History of the Kings of Britain*

Gerald of Wales, *The Journey through Wales / The Description of Wales*

William Gibbs and Elizabeth Siberry, *Artistiaid Dyffryn Ewias*

William Gilpin, *Observations on the River Wye*

Julian Glover, *Man of Iron*

Geraint Goodwin, *The Heyday in the Blood*

Richard Perceval Graves, *A. E. Housman, the Scholar-Poet*

Charles Hadfield, *British Canals: An Illustrated History*

Michael Hall, *Francis Brett Young*

David Hart (ed.), *Border Country: Poems in Process*

Charles Henry Hartshorne, *Salopia Antiqua*

Cliff Hayes, *A Century of Chester*

Rosie Hayles, *Finding Hay: A Journey Up Broad Stre*et

Richard Hayman, *Severn*

Steve Haywood, *One Man and a Narrowboat*

John Heilpern, *John Osborne: A Patriot for Us*

BIBLIOGRAPHY

Geoffrey Hill, *Selected Poems*

John Hillaby, *Journey through Britain*

Richard Holland, *Supernatural Clwyd*

A. E. Housman, *A Shropshire Lad*

W. H. Howse, *Radnorshire*

Simon Jenkins, *England's Thousand Best Churches*

Martin Johnes, *Wales: England's Colony?*

Mervyn Jones, *Michael Foot*

Annette M. Kennett, *Chester and the River Dee*

Francis Kilvert, *Diaries*

Robert Lacey, *Aristocrats*

Quentin Letts, *50 People Who Buggered Up Britain*

Stuart Maconie, *Pies and Prejudice*

Jamie Medhurst, *A History of Independent Television in Wales*

Arthur Mee (ed.), *Cheshire: The Romantic North-West*

Arthur Mee (ed.), *Herefordshire: The Western Gate of Middle England*

Arthur Mee (ed.), *Monmouthshire: A Green and Smiling Land*

Arthur Mee (ed.), *Shropshire: County of the Western Hills*

Julian Mitchell, *The Wye Tour and its Artists*

Simon Moreton, *WHERE? Life and Death in the Shropshire Hills*

Chris Morris, *A Portrait of the Severn*

Mike Oldfield, *Changeling: The Autobiography*

George Orwell, *Coming Up for Air*

George Orwell, *Notes on Nationalism*

Peter Parker, *Housman Country*

C. A. Patrides (ed.), *The English Poems of George Herbert*

Susan Peterken, *Landscapes of the Wye Tour*

Andrew Fusek Peters, *Dip: Wild Swims from the Borderlands*

Andrew Fusek Peters, *Upland*

Pauline Phillips, *A View of Old Montgomeryshire*

Gavin Plumley, *A House for All Seasons*

Dennis Potter, *The Glittering Coffin*

Adam Price, *Wales: The First and Final Colony*

T. W. Pritchard, *A History of the Old Parish of Hawarden*

Sonia Purnell, *Just Boris*

Eleanor M. Rawling, *Ivor Gurney's Gloucestershire*

Mark Richards, *Through Welsh Border Country*

Dewi Roberts (ed.), *Both Sides of the Border: An Anthology of Writing on the Welsh Border Region*

Dewi Roberts (ed.), *A Powys Anthology*

Graham Robb, *The Debatable Land*

Byron Rogers, *The Man Who Went into the West*

L. T. C. Rolt, *Narrow Boat*

L. T. C. Rolt, *Railway Adventure*

L. T. C. Rolt, *Thomas Telford*

Trevor Rowley, *The English Landscape in the Twentieth Century*

Lorna Sage, *Bad Blood*

Sathnam Sanghera, *Empireland: How Imperialism Has Shaped Modern Britain*

Nicholas Shakespeare, *Bruce Chatwin*

Joan Shaw, *Borderline*

Owen Sheers, *Resistance*

John Shipley, *The Little Book of Shropshire*

Ron and Jennifer Shoesmith, *Alfred Watkins' Herefordshire*

Dai Smith, *Raymond Williams: A Warrior's Tale*

F. J. Snell, *The Celtic Borderland*

Anna Sproule, *The Lost Houses of Britain*

Michael Tavinor, *Saints and Sinners of the Marches*

R. S. Thomas, *Neb*

P. Thoresby Jones, *Welsh Border Country*

Malcolm Thurlby, *The Herefordshire School of Romanesque Sculpture*

David J. Vaughan, *The Little Book of Herefordshire*

John Wacher, *The Towns of Roman Britain*

Peter Wakelin, *Ffiniau*

Alfred Watkins, *The Old Straight Track*

Mary Webb, *Gone to Earth*

Mary Webb, *The House in Dormer Forest*

BIBLIOGRAPHY

Mary Webb, *Precious Bane*
Mary Webb, *Seven for a Secret*
Gee Williams, *Magic and Other Deceptions*
Gron Williams, *Firebrand: The Frank Owen Story*
Gruffydd Aled Williams, *The Last Days of Owain Glyndŵr*
Raymond Williams, *Border Country*
Raymond Williams, *The People of the Black Mountains*
Raymond Williams (ed. Daniel Williams), *Who Speaks for Wales?*

LIST OF PICTURES

All photos © Mike Parker

For more unmissable reads,
sign up to the HarperNorth newsletter at
www.harpernorth.co.uk

or find us on Twitter at
@HarperNorthUK

**Harper
North**